GOODWILL'S

DICTIONARY OF *SYNONYMS AND ANTONYMS*

GOODWILL PUBLISHING HOUSE®
B-3 RATTAN JYOTI, 18 RAJENDRA PLACE
NEW DELHI -110008 (INDIA)

Published by :
GOODWILL PUBLISHING HOUSE®
B-3, Rattan Jyoti, 18, Rajendra Place,
New Delhi-110008 (INDIA)
Ph. : 25750801, 25820556
Fax : 91-11-25764396
Web : goodwillpublishinghouse.com
E-mail : goodwillpub@vsnl.net

Laser Typeset at : Computer Corner, New Delhi

Printed at : Kumar Offset Printers, Delhi-92

PREFACE

Synonyms and Antonyms are an important part of the English language. They greatly help develop one's vocabulary and word power. They have the potential to equip the student with the ability to choose the right word for the right expression.

According to the Oxford Dictionary, "a **synonym** is a word identical and co-extensive in sense and usage with another. It is a word denoting the same thing (things) as another but suitable in a different context (as leap and slay compared to jump and kill) or containing different suggestion (as blind worm compared to low worm)". In short, a synonym is a word equivalent to another in one or the other sense (as ship compared to vessel).

An **antonym**, on the other hand, is a word of contrary or contrasted meaning of another word (as bad to good, high to low, short to long). Thus it is an anti-synonym, i.e., it is charged with the opposite meaning.

This dictionary is a discrete collection of synonyms and antonyms. It has all the essential words that a student would need to be able to write any type of composition—essay, article, letter, paragraph, story, anecdote, comprehension, precis or summary.

Vocabulary is the storage of words in a reader's brain. It plays a fundamental role in the learning of the language. It is the foundation on which a student's mastery of the language is based.

The present dictionary should suffice to lay the needed foundation of one's vocabulary. Having grasped the knowledge and meaning of the basic words, you should practice their use in your day-to-day needs of your writing and conversation.

By developing an open mind for new words, by reading through good books and conversing with good talkers, you can certainly obtain a good mastery of words.

Words may not have life as humans do, but they astonishingly cast their great influence. They move about. They have characters and personalities. They are 'honest, useful, obliging... or treacherous, vain, stubborn' depending on how we use them. As a famous linguist once said, "They shift as people do,with company. They are an endless study in which we are studying nature and ourselves at that meeting point where our minds are trying to give form to or take it from the world" .

The dictionary claims a very special place in the teaching of the English language as it not only gives the synonyms and antonyms of the basic words but also illustrates the true meaning of each word by providing its usage.

Each usage is so structured as to teach the student the art of using effectively and purposefully the vocabulary at his command.

It also empowers the reader to differentiate between different shades of meaning which different words denote. It should enable him to choose the exact word for any idea he wishes to express.

A frequent reference to this dictionary would help the student to reach at the exact word from amongst many choices to express his idea. The choice may, among other things, depend on the amount of emphasis you wish to lay on different aspects of the idea.

While the choice of words is somewhat easy on the writing table, it needs storage of thousands of words in your memory, as in a modern computer, so that they can be drawn upon for ready use in speech or conversation as and when necessary.

By devoting half an hour to this dictionary every day, you could expand your vocabulary by leaps and bounds and become a lovable personality. For words not only build your expression but also gift you new ideas, attitudes and so many other plus points. They give you breakthrough in imagination, literary inspiration, humour, will-power and confidence.

I hope the advent of this dictionary will open a new chapter in your academic or professional career (whatever it may be whether a student, teacher, businessman or social or physical scientist), this dictionary will push you forward on the track of optimum achievement. Also it will make you popular in your social circle by injecting speed and accuracy in your conversation, speech, debate and poetic expression or romantic exposition.

B.N. Ahuja

ABANDON

Synonyms : Relinquish, resign, forgo, discontinue, waive, abdicate, leave, quit, evacuate, desert, discard.

Antonyms : Pursue, chase, hunt, prosecute, follow, undertake.

Synonyms

- He *relinquished* charge of his post as manager on *resigning*.
- He may *forgo* some of his rights but he need not give up the right of doing something.
- It was decided to *discontinue* treatment after three months.
- The conditions of an agreement can be *waived* if both the parties agree to it.
- Rama *abdicated* his throne to fulfil the promise he had made to his father.
- Some children *leave* school when they are sixteen years old.
- If I don't get more money I'll *quit*.

- The seamen *evacuated* the ship as soon as they discovered it was sinking.
- Selfish people *desert* their friends in difficult times.
- He was *discarded* by his brothers because he wanted to become a poet while his brothers wanted him to take to the family business.

Antonyms

- I wish I could *pursue* my studies further.
- The lion *chased* the deer for some distance but gave up thereafter.
- In olden days humans had to *hunt* for food in the jungle.
- The government has *prosecuted* quite a number of officers for spying against the country.

ABASH

Synonyms : Humiliate, humble, shame, embarrass, disconcert, discontinuance.

Antonyms : Vanity, conceit, immodesty, self-esteem, self-love, smugness, self-praise, complacency.

Synonyms

- Napoleon was *humiliated* in the Battle of Waterloo by the *humble* British fleet under Lord Nelson.
- *Shame* on the traitors to their motherland.
- Immodesty is *embarrassing* for a woman.

- Red tapism is very *disconcerting* for any country.
- The aberrations in the original plan culminated in its *discontinuance.*

Antonyms

- *Vanity* is a common trait among beautiful women.
- A liar has a tendency to become a *conceit* in due course.
- In certain modern societies of the west, *immodesty* has become a part of civilisation.
- To judge your standing in society, you must develop *self-esteem.*
- *Self-love* and *self-praise* are new traits used in modern advertisements.
- His early success as a writer led to *complacency* and *smugness.*

ABATE

Synonyms : Decrease, lessen, moderate, diminish, subside, allay, slacken, subdue.

Antonyms : Increase, augment, extreme, magnify, enlarge, extend, dilate, sprout, expand, swell, grow, advance, develop, rise, ascend, enhance, deepen, heighten, intensify, aggravate, exaggerate, spread, disperse.

Synonyms

- The volume of a gas *decreases* as we increase the pressure on it.

- Antiseptics *lessen* the chances of infection.
- We agreed to *moderate* our demands.
- His influence has *diminished* with time.
- The tension generally *subsides* but intrasigence always expands.
- The police tactfully *allayed* the fears of the demonstrators.
- He had *slackened* in his duties, and was therefore, punished.
- The unabated rains *subdued* the spirits of the farmers.

Antonyms

- The volume of a gas *increases* as we decrease the pressure on it.
- Dirty food *augments* the chances of infection.
- *Extreme* temper is invariably destructive.
- It is the amplifier in a radio that *magnifies* the sound.
- Could you please *enlarge* these photographs.
- Plans are afoot to *extend* the house.

- Her eyes *dilated* with fear.
- The seeds will *sprout* in a few days.

ABBREVIATE

Synonyms : Abridge, condense, shorten, truncate, trim, contract, curtail.

Antonyms : Lengthen, extend, elongate, stretch, prolong, protract, draw out.

Synonyms

- The *abridged* edition of the book greatly curtailed its cost.
- The *condensed* ideas have not only reduced the size of the book, but also presented it in a better form.
- *Shorten* the length of the precis to its requirement.
- Mere *truncating* causes more loss than gain.
- I *trimmed* the hedge of my garden to give it a well-tended look.

Antonyms

- Daily exercise *lengthens* one's life.
- The government *extended* his service by three years due to good health.
- This looking glass gives an *elongated* view to one's face.
- The meeting *stretched* over two hours.

- ✦ The operation could *prolong* his life by two-three years.

ABDUCT

Synonyms : Kidnap, carry off, steal, spirit away.

Antonyms : Deliver, give away, surrender.

Synonyms

- ✦ The *kidnapped* child was restored to his distraught parents.
- ✦ He *carried off* most of the prizes.
- ✦ A thief is a person who *steals* things.
- ✦ The performers were *spirited away* before their fans could reach them.

Antonyms

- ✦ He *delivered* a beautiful speech at the meeting.
- ✦ The rich man *gave away* his property to the local orphanage.
- ✦ The thief *surrendered* to the police when his conscience pricked.

ABERRATION

Synonyms : Deviation, variation, distortion, disorientation, error.

Antonyms : Truth, sanity.

Synonyms

- ✦ We should not *deviate* from the path of morality.

✦ There was a conspicuous *variation* between the two figures.

✦ The culprit narrated a *distorted* version of the episode.

✦ The 19th century masses could not assimilate the *disorientations* of Galileo.

✦ Just one *error* cost him his job.

Antonyms

✦ Mahatma Gandhi propogated the spiritual value of *truth*.

✦ If *sanity* dawns on humanity, there will be no wars in the world.

ABET

Synonyms : Aid, assist, support, encourage, incite, instigate.

Antonyms : Hinderance, prevention, obstruction, interruption, interception, restriction, restraint, inhibition, prohibition, blockage, closure, difficulty.

Synonyms

✦ The generous *aid* by the society has *assisted* him to *support* his family through thick and thin.

✦ The glare of monetary *encouragement* culminates in *inciting* lethargy and *instigating* the people to resort to evil doings.

Antonyms

- ✦ Hot weather caused *hinderance* to his farming work.
- ✦ *Prevention* is always better than cure.
- ✦ The lack of capital causes *obstruction* in the growth of business.
- ✦ He worked for two hours without *interruption.*
- ✦ This device helps in the *interception* of enemy radio signals.

ABHOR

Synonyms : Hate, dislike, loathe, despise, abominate, excerate, detest.

Antonyms : Love, fondness, attachment, liking, inclination, desire, admiration, affection, yearning, passion, devotion, infatuation, advocation, idolatory.

Synonyms

- ✦ We should *hate* sin and not the sinner.
- ✦ His *dislike* for the type of work resulted in his very slow rise in position.
- ✦ The noble person *loathes crime.*
- ✦ The rich should not *despise* the poor.
- ✦ The conqueror should not *abominate* the defeated enemy.

Antonyms

- *Love* of humanity is the first condition of prayer to God.
- The father developed a *fondness* for his second daughter due to her caring nature.
- Ramesh has a deep *attachment* with his cousin sister but you can't call it love.

ABILITY

Synonyms : Power, competence, skill, efficiency, capability, aptitude, talent, capacity, faculty.

Antonyms : Unskilfulness, impotence.

Synonyms

- According to the latest instructions, he has the *power* to sign the agreement and we cannot doubt his *competence* in this regard.
- An artisan earns fame for his *skill* in the craft.
- *Efficiency* of a worker can be increased if he is given the required facilities.
- The *capability* of an individual is gauged by his background.

- ✦ He has every *aptitude* towards arts but his father compels him to study science.
- ✦ In India even *talented* people may remain unemployed.

Antonyms

- ✦ *Unskilfulness* is still a common phenomenon in the country, although facilities for general education are being increased.
- ✦ The governor of a state in India, though only a figurehead in the Constitution, is not to be considered entirely *impotent* as he is all-powerful during an emergency.

ABJECT

Synonyms : Degraded, contemptible, miserable, wretched, base.

Antonyms : Insolence, arrogance, haughtiness, presumption, pomposity, snobbery, domineering, defiance.

Synonyms

- ✦ By indulging in such an immoral act simply to earn the money, he has very much *degraded* himself.
- ✦ His *contemptible* rudeness to the guests cannot be forgiven.
- ✦ Poverty is the biggest bane; it makes the life of man quite *miserable.*

✦ He is a *wretched* fellow. He does not pay attention to the other's feelings.

✦ Greed, anger and lust are some of the *baser* instincts of man..

Antonyms

✦ The subordinate's *insolence* made him lose the job.

✦ *Arrogance* is the enemy of good education.

✦ *Haughtiness* and pride always lead to failure in any walk of life.

ABJURE

Synonyms : Forswear, recant, renounce.

Antonyms : Relinquish, abandon, renunciative, abrogate, expropriate, derelict, cease, surrender, abdicate, resign, withdraw, retire.

Synonyms

✦ The astronomer Galileo was forced to *forswear* his theory of the rotation of the earth.

✦ He has *recanted* the sinful ways after his release from the jail.

✦ It is not necessary to *renounce* the world for worshipping God.

Antonyms

✦ John voluntarily *relinquished* his right to the property of his father to benefit his sisters.

- ✦ If we can *abandon* our vices of anger, hatred and physical attachments, we are on the right path of progress.
- ✦ It is very difficult to *renunciate* worldly attachments.

ABNORMAL

Synonyms : Aberrant, eccentric, anomalous, insane, monstrous, irregular.

Antonyms : Sanity, conformity, soundness, reason, rationality, normality, sobriety, lucidity.

Synonyms

- ✦ He is too *aberrant* in taking the medicine and exercise, hence we cannot guarantee any great improvement in his health.
- ✦ He is not a fool, he is an *eccentric* and no one can predict his behaviour.
- ✦ His contradictory statement at different times have put him in an *anomalous* situation.
- ✦ The mental torture and agony have made him *insane*.
- ✦ Greed and lust take a *monstrous* form in due course.

Antonyms

- Only *sanity* at the highest political levels in superpower countries can save the world from destruction.
- *Conformity* to ideals of peace and development is needed to make the youth of our country use its power in the right direction.
- The financial *soundness* of a company should be ascertained before investing money.
- I tried to *reason* with him but he would not listen.

ABOLISH

Synonyms : Annul, cancel, nullify, exterminate, abrogate.

Antonyms : Approve, retain, continue, fabricate, build, erect, establish, achieve, complete.

Synonyms

- When two equal forces act on a point in opposite direction, they *annul* each other.
- His orders for transfer to Mumbai have been *cancelled*.
- It is generally believed that homeopathic medicines *nullify* the effect of allopathic medicines.
- Hitler wanted to *exterminate* the Jews from the world; that is why he killed them so ruthlessly.

Antonyms

- ✦ The non-aligned nations have unanimously *approved* the resolution on keeping the Indian Ocean zone arms-free.
- ✦ The principal decided to *retain* the old teacher for another 3 years.
- ✦ Are you going to *continue* with the project?
- ✦ She *fabricated* the story from start to finish.

ABRIDGEMENT

Synonyms : Abridged, Abbreviation, epitome, summary, digest, compendium, synopsis, analysis, outline, abstract.

Antonyms : Elaborate, expand, dissect elongate.

Synonyms

- ✦ This is an *abridged* form of the Webster Dictionary.
- ✦ In chemistry the use of *abbreviations* helps solve the chemical equations.
- ✦ We may have an *epitome* of religion but not its *abridgement.*
- ✦ A *summary* is the most condensed statement of results or conclusions.
- ✦ An *abstract* or *digest* is an independent statement of what the book contains.

- My uncle is very found of English literature; he always keeps a *compendium* of English poetry with him.
- In an essay one should first give the *synopsis* and then the description.
- Thorough *analysis* of data is important to reach a conclusion.

Antonyms

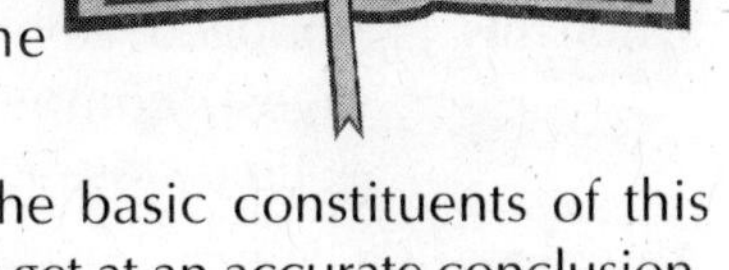

- This book beautifully *elaborates* the theory of business cycles.
- This is an *expanded* version of the Ramayana.
- Unless we *dissect* the basic constituents of this statement, we cannot get at an accurate conclusion.

ABSCOND

Synonyms : Hide, slip away, leave, decamp, depart, retreat, disappear, run away, flee, conceal oneself, steal away, retire, take oneself off, withdraw, run off.

Antonyms : Hold one's ground, reappear, present oneself, emerge, arrive, remain, be present, come into view, put in a reappearance.

Synonyms

- Don't try to *hide* behind a false identity.

- One may *slip away* from a company he does not wish to break up.
- He *leaves* his home for office in time but does not get a bus and is generally late.
- The traveller *decamped* in fear of lurking robbers.
- The traveller had some fears in mind when he *departed* on his journey.
- An army *retreats* from an untenable position or before a superior force.
- The police failed to catch the thief who *disappeared* in the crowd.

- A bonded labourer may *run away* from his master but the master generally succeeds in catching him again.
- The Jews had to *flee* from Germany when Hitler ordered their general massacre.

Antonyms

- The army *held its ground* against heavy firing from the enemy posts.

- The great leader *reappeared* after years of self-imposed exile.
- The witness *presented himself* in the court after repeated prompting.
- The recession is over and brighter prospects for the industry have now *emerged*.

ABSORB

Synonyms : Spend, waste, squander, destroy, exhaust, devour, assimilate.

Antonyms : Save, hoard, reserve, preserve, husband.

Synonyms

- We should *spend* money carefully.
- A wise man *spends* the money and a fool *wastes* it.
- The untimely cyclone *squandered* the crop away.
- The wounds of a stove burn *destroy* certain parts of the skin and hence take long to be healed up.

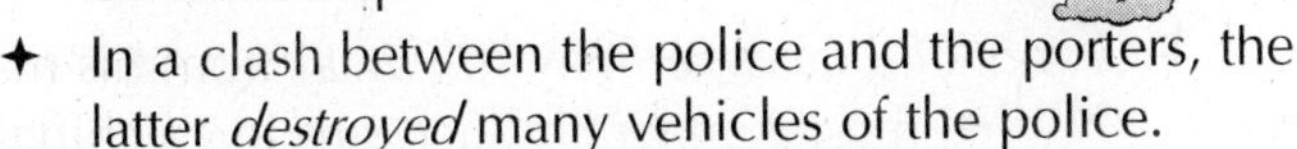

- In a clash between the police and the porters, the latter *destroyed* many vehicles of the police.
- Overwork will soon *exhaust* him.

Antonyms

- A wise man always *saves* something for a rainy day.
- The government has built storage facilities to *hoard* foodgrains for any emergency.

- We should *reserve* 25% of our income for emergencies.
- By adding these chemicals you can *preserve* the food.

ABSTAIN

Synonyms : Refrain, desist, withhold, forbear.

Antonyms : Pursue, adopt, persist, offer.

Synonyms

- We should *refrain* from reading cheap and sensational literature.
- Although already jailed once, he cannot *desist* from gambling.
- The government has the right to *withhold* his pension as a measure of penalty.

Antonyms

- Dr. Jain is *pursuing* his profession nicely.
- Rajneesh has *adopted* a definite progressive policy for his firm.
- If we *persist* on the path of success, we shall certainly achieve it in due course.

ABSOLUTE

Synonyms : Arbitrary, tyrannical, autocratic, dictatorial, overbearing, supreme, imperious, compulsory, haughty, arrogant, controlling, positive, imperative, authoritative, despotic, irresponsible, unconditional, commanding, domineering, unequivocal, compulsive, exacting, peremptory, unlimited.

Antonyms : Accountable, contingent, docile, lenient, mild, limited, responsible, compliant, lowly, submission, conditional, gentle, meek, yielding, constitutional, humble.

Synonyms

- Shah of Iran was an *absolute* monarch but the rule of Khoumeni and other religious leaders is *arbitrary, tyrannical, autocratic, dictatorial* and *over-bearing.*
- In India the President is the *supreme* commander of all the three wings - Army, Navy and Air Force.
- A person of an independent spirit is inclined to resent the *imperious* manner in anyone whose authority is not clearly felt and acknowledged.

- Knowledge of an Indian language has been made *compulsory* for the Indian Civil Services.

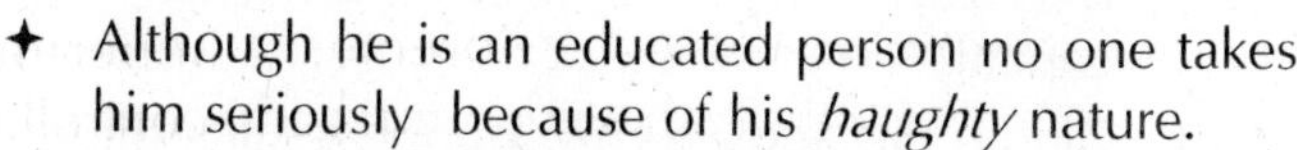

- Although he is an educated person no one takes him seriously because of his *haughty* nature.

- The politicians generally become *arrogant* after assuming power.
- There is imperative need to *control/check* the politicians from assuming unlimited power to themselves. They should be made to share it with the people at large.

Antonyms

- The prime minister is *accountable* to the parliament for the actions of his cabinet colleagues.
- Any further payments are *contingent* upon successful commissioning of project.
- It is good to be *lenient* in principles but bad to be *docile* in practice.
- The teacher is *lenient* to the small children.
- She would give only *mild* punishment to them.

ABSURD

Synonyms : Foolish, stupid, ridiculous, irrational senseless, silly.

Antonyms : Logical, sound, rational, sensible, consistent, reasonable.

Synonyms

- It is *foolish* to think of selfish interests in modern society.
- He was *stupid* enough to believe him.
- It is *ridiculous* to think of business without capital.
- Aladin did agree to his *irrational* suggestion.

- He felt it would be *senseless* to attack without proper force.

Antonyms

- The Congress party's victory in recent elections makes us reach the *logical* conclusion that people want a socialist system.
- This proposition is quite *sound* if worked out properly.
- Unless the modern youth develops a *rational* attitude, he cannot make due contribution to the country's progress.

ACCEPT

Synonyms : Believe, confirm, assent, agree, honour, admit, take.

Antonyms : Disbelieve, reject, refuse, disagree, non-consent.

Synonyms

- Most of the religions *believe* in the presence of some supernatural powers.
- His crime was *confirmed* by a number of eye witnesses.

- He was requested to give his *assent* in writing to be posted outstation or face dismissal for his misadventure.

- I will *agree* to his proposal if it does not harm anybody.
- He is a man of principles and will always *honour* his word.
- We should not feel guilty while *admitting* our fault.
- Smith was joking but his friend *took* it otherwise. Hence the misunderstanding between the two.

Antonyms

- There is no reason to *disbelieve* his personal observations in the matter.
- I already had such fears and had *rejected* the original statement.
- He *refused* to avail of my services.
- I have many reasons to *disagree* with your proposal.

ACCOMPANY

Synonyms : Escort, join, attend, chaperon, conduct, convoy, consort.

Antonyms : Discard, leave, abandon.

Synonyms

- The security guard acted as an *escort* to the political leader.
- I will *join* hands with you in this mission.
- Let us *attend* to this task with devotion.

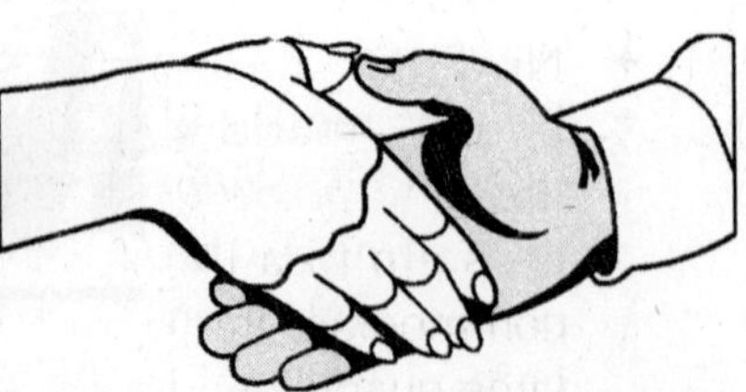

Antonyms

- ✦ It is high time you *discard* bad company if you wish to achieve something in life.
- ✦ It is good to *leave* bad habits in order to achieve something worthwhile in life.
- ✦ Let us *abandon* old traditions which stand in the way of our progress.

ACCUMULATE

Synonyms : Assemble, gather, congregate, hoard, store, rally, convene.

Antonyms : Disperse, scatter, broadcast, spread, dissipate, distribute.

Synonyms

- ✦ The members of the managing committee *assemble* every month to review the progress of the work and take necessary measures to step up construction of the houses.
- ✦ The *gathering* applauded the speakers.
- ✦ The strikers *congregated* at the gates of the factory.
- ✦ Now it has been made illegal to *hoard* essential commodities in large quantities.

- ✦ The medicines should be *stored* in a cool dry place.

Antonyms

- ✦ The police used tear gas to *disperse* the crowds.
- ✦ The people *scattered* in the nearby streets to save themselves from the lathi charge.
- ✦ The leaders *broadcast* the futility of the demonstrations taken out by the labourers.

ACCURATE

Synonyms : Correct, precise, exact, nice, right, true.

Antonyms : Incorrect, inaccurate, erroneous, inexact, wrong, false.

Synonyms

- ✦ Let us *correct* this exercise so that the students can understand it quickly.
- ✦ The prime minister tried to be as *precise* as possible in his statement on public policy.
- ✦ We should try to be *exact* in our calculations.

Antonyms

- ✦ This attitude on your part seems to be *incorrect.* You may annoy the public.
- ✦ The statistical statement seems to be *inaccurate* and *erroneous.* It needs to be done afresh for exact conclusion.

ACHIEVE

Synonyms : Attain, accomplish, do, win, effect, fulfil, gain, perform, finish, execute, acquire.

Antonyms : Fail, miss, miscarry.

Synonyms

- ✦ A yogi's only desire is to *attain* moksha.
- ✦ Rakesh Sharma, India's first cosmonaut, was able to *accomplish* the job successfully.
- ✦ Inspite of his best efforts he could not *effect* any change in the system because it was corrupt to the grass-roots.
- ✦ The gymnasts *performed* such feats that we could not help praising them. 
- ✦ His loan was cancelled because he did not *execute* the requisite agreement in time.

Antonyms

- ✦ The school doctor *failed* to save the life of the injured student.
- ✦ Ramesh *missed* the first division by a few marks.
- ✦ Babita took such risks that her baby in the womb could not help *miscarriage*.

ACKNOWLEDGE

Synonyms : Admit, own, profess, recognise, concede, confess, avow

Antonyms : Contradict, foreswear, disown, deny, disclaim.

Synonyms

- ✦ I *admit my* statement is not up to the mark but it does show the accurate position of the case.
- ✦ I can *own* all the blame for making a mess of this issue.
- ✦ I *profess* a religious attitude on material affairs of society to inspire social confidence.

Antonyms

- ✦ I cannot but *contradict* your stiff stand on this issue.
- ✦ I can *foreswear* the doom of this country, unless its citizens raise their national character in some ways.
- ✦ I *disown* responsibility for this severe action you propose on this small issue.

ACQUAINTANCE

Synonyms : Friendship, knowledge, information, familiarity.

Antonyms : Enmity, ignorance, hostility, lack of knowledge.

Synonyms

- ✦ His *friendship* with learned men greatly helped in increasing his *knowledge*.
- ✦ A senior retired officer was recently found passing secret *information* to the enemy.
- ✦ In modern society neighbours have little *familiarity* among themselves.

Antonyms

- ✦ Pakistan has never given up an attitude of *enmity* towards India.
- ✦ This attitude is partly based on his *ignorance* about the diplomatic manoeuvres.
- ✦ There is no *hostility* among the common people of the countries.

ACTUAL

Synonyms : Authentic, real, certain, demonstrable

Antonyms : Fabulous, virtual, possible.

Synonyms

- ✦ The statistics regarding foodgrains in the country is collected from *authentic* sources.
- ✦ The *real* cause of discontentment among the people in the country is all-round poverty.

- I am *certain* that poverty can be eradicated in the country only by changing the basic social-economic system.

Antonyms

- Do not make *fabulous* stories. I know the real facts.
- The *virtual* situation in this region smacks of acute localism.
- It is *possible* to change the circumstances by deliberate action.

ADMIRE

Synonyms : Applaud, extol, approve, praise.

Antonyms : Despise, blame, condemn, disapprove.

Synonyms

- The public *applauded* the sentimental speech made by the orator.
- The politician *extolled* the people to reform their character by giving up selfishness.
- The government has *approved* the proposal for the expansion of small-scale industries.
- Let us give *praise* where it is due.

Antonyms

- ✦ You are following the wrong path hence you *despise* my best advice.
- ✦ It is no use *blaming* others for the social ills; first we have to look within.
- ✦ Such attitude on the part of the administration needs to be *condemned.*

ADAPT

Synonyms : Fit, regulate, conform, suit.

Antonyms : Misfit, irregularise, differ, disagree.

Synonyms

- ✦ He may be *fit* for service but he is a *misfit* for business.
- ✦ Trade union leaders want adequate legislative measures being passed to *regulate* the working and service conditions of different classes of workers.
- ✦ A private company will accept the supply of goods only if they strictly *conform* to the specifications laid down by them in their order.
- ✦ The terms and conditions of this agreement do not *suit* me.

Antonyms

- ✦ He is a *misfit* for the work assigned to him.
- ✦ He indulges in *irregularities* which cause the failure of projects.
- ✦ He dares to *differ* with his colleagues over minor issues of business.

ADJUST

Synonyms : Set in order, arrange, set right, regulate, accommodate, settle, set, compose.

Antonyms : Displace, dislocate, disjoint, derange, disconnect, disarrange.

Synonyms

- ✦ One needs a lot of skill and courage to *set* the system in *order* in a corrupt department.
- ✦ It took him two hours to *arrange* the articles and *set* them *right*.
- ✦ A person has to *accommodate* himself to many upleasant things in life.
- ✦ We need not resort to war to *settle* our territorial disputes with the neighboring countries if we keep ourselves in good military strength.

Antonyms

- ✦ When he entered the room he found everything shattered and *displaced*.
- ✦ The life in war ridden Gulf countries stands *dislocated* and *disjointed*.
- ✦ His failure to effect a happy marriage left him gravely *deranged*.

ADMIT

Synonyms : Own, avow, grant, concede, give, yield.

Antonyms : Disown, deny, dispute, disavow, disclaim.

Synonyms

- ✦ We could locate no one to *own* the box found on the railway platform.
- ✦ He *avowed* to be not guilty in very strong terms but the judge remained unconvinced and sentenced him to imprisonment for five years.
- ✦ He has *conceded* to me a big loan for starting the construction of my house.
- ✦ You ought to *give* the porter a nice tip.
- ✦ Her parents *yielded* at last to let her marry with the boy of a low caste.

Antonyms

- ✦ We may *disown* responsibility for wrong doings of others.
- ✦ The guards *denied* him entry.
- ✦ Ram and Surbhi settled the *dispute* amicably.

ADVERSITY

Synonyms : Affliction, misery, poverty, misfortune.

Antonyms : Prosperity, luck, fortune, happiness.

Synonyms

- ✦ Although aware of the *affliction* of his son, the father did not lend him any help.
- ✦ Gambling was the root cause of the *misery* that befell the Pandavas.
- ✦ In Bihar, *poverty* is more widespread than that in the U.P.

✦ It-was his *misfortune* that despite all his training he could not find selection for the spaceflight.

Antonyms

✦ India cannot gain in *prosperity* until the village folk attain a better standard of living.

✦ I wish you good *luck* on your journey abroad.

✦ It is my good *fortune* to by your colleague.

✦ It gives me great *happiness* to release this book.

ADVISE

Synonyms : Warn, admonish, recommend, counsel, suggest, prompt.

Antonyms : Deter, dissuade, restrain, hinder, discourage, criticise.

Synonyms

✦ India has *warned* Pakistan that any accumulation of arms will go against its own interest.

✦ His officer *admonished* him for carelessness in handling the official work.

✦ The measures now *recommended* by the planning commission to improve the Indian economy are very practical.

✦ One has to repent if one goes against the *counsel* of the elders.

- ✦ He could not *suggest* even a single practicable solution of the problem.
- ✦ He was *prompted* by his father to embark upon such an ambitious plan.

Antonyms

- ✦ This warning need not *deter* the brave but rather prepare them to face the event more bravely.
- ✦ Mirchandani continues *dissuading* his son from going to the USA.
- ✦ I had to *restrain* my outburst on the arrival of the unwanted guest.

AFFECTING

Synonyms : Touching, melting, moving, pathetic, eloquent, impressive.

Antonyms : Amusing, ridiculous, funny, laughable, farcical, comic, absurd, droll.

Synonyms

- ✦ His acting was so *touching* that the audience could not help weeping.
- ✦ Wax solidifies again after *melting* and drying.
- ✦ Siddhartha's heart was *moved* on seeing the *pathetic* condition of the old lady.
- ✦ Swami Vivekananda's speech was so *eloquent* that the Amercians became his fans within no time.

- The data furnished by him was so *impressive* that none of the members of the society could oppose any of his suggestions.

Antonyms

- It is *amusing* to find him going up a tree.
- Your proposal to break this partnership is *ridiculous*.
- Don't act *funny*. Do as I say.
- This is a *laughable* situation.

AFRAID

Synonyms : Frightened, scared, panicky, anxious, fearful, faint-hearted.

Antonyms : Brave, bold, courageous, unafraid, daring, upright.

Synonyms

- The child was *frightened* to see a snake.

- Though he is very rich, he is always *scared* of the adversities of life.

- ✦ When it was announced that the ship was in danger, everybody aboard became *panicky.*
- ✦ He could not do well in his examination; but he is *anxious* to know the result now.
- ✦ When communalism erupts, even the neighbours are *fearful* of each other.
- ✦ He is posing as a brave man; but I know for certain he is *faint-hearted* when it comes to emergencies.

Antonyms

- ✦ Atul is a *brave* boy. He is bold and *courageous* when he faces emergent situation.
- ✦ He can take a daring decision on the spun of the moment. He is also *upright* on principles.

ALARMING

Synonyms : Frightful, terrible, ominous.

Antonyms : Hopeful, bright, auspicious

Synonyms

- ✦ The scene of the rail accident was *frightful.*
- ✦ War clouds always bring *terrible* circumstances.
- ✦ The present-day atmosphere round the world is charged with *ominous* fear of destruction.

Antonyms

- ✦ The new peaceful atmosphere in the country is *hopeful* of a brighter future.

- Recent US-USSR decision on disarmament gives a *bright* picture of the future world.
- The growth rate of 5% per annum for the tenth five year plan is considered *auspicious.*

ALLAY

Synonyms : Ease, lighten, abate, soothe, relieve, palliate, rid, assuage.

Antonyms : Aggravate, enhance, worsen, heighten.

Synonyms

- A person can *ease situations* by admitting his fault.
- You can *lighten* your heart by telling your difficulties to your friends.
- We should sincerely fight and *abate* the communal forces.
- This medicine has a *soothing* effect and is likely to *relieve* the patients of their pain immediately.
- His words sounded eloquent but could not *palliate* the sorrow of his friends.
- Ambitious young people try to get *rid* of the traditions.
- A stone-hearted person may repress his own feelings but he can not *assuage* the feelings of other.

Antonyms

- Timidity always *aggravates* a bad situation.
- It does not *enhance* resistance to dangers.
- It tends to *worsen* the overall circumstances.

✦ It *heightens* the fear-complex and dislocates high spirits and courageous action.

ALLURE

Synonyms : Charm, invite, entice, draw, fascinate, endear.

Antonyms : Deter, repulse, rebuff, reject, repel, check.

Synonyms

✦ Her exuberant beauty can *charm* even the stoics.

✦ There are occasions when the government *invites* opposition parties to discuss important subjects.

✦ Unscrupulous antisocial elements always try to *entice* the criminals for committing more crimes.

✦ The strickers resorted to hunger strike in order to *draw* the attention of the management to their problems.

✦ The thief was so much *fascinated* by the speech of the priest that he gave up thieving and became his disciple.

Antonyms

✦ The noisy atmosphere did not *deter* him from his studies.

✦ The very presence of the villain *repulsed* the good atmosphere of the scene.

- Ram *rebuffed* the satirical remark of the competitor about his product.
- Ram *rejected* the reconciliation offer of his supplier.
- Similar poles of a magnet *repel* each other.
- The opposition forces tried to *check* his advance but he was too determined to be held back.

ALLY

Synonyms : Friend, abettor, spies, colleague, partner, accomplice, accessory, companion, co-operator.

Antonyms : Enemy, opponent, rival, competitor, opposer, foe, antagonist.

Synonyms

- A *friend* in need is a friend indeed.
- The *abettor* is usually involved, either actively or passively, whenever there is a crime.
- Two *spies* were caught by the police in Ferozepore.
- Members of Congress from the same state are *colleagues,* though they may be political opponents.
- Their business flourished very much when they were *partners* but now both of them have become paupers.
- One of the pick-pockets was caught by the police but his *accomplice* managed to flee.

Antonyms

- The army defends the country against *enemy* attack.
- He had no chance against his formidable *opponent*.
- The two teams have always been sworn *rivals*.
- They were fierce *competitors* too.

AMAZING

Synonyms : Extraordinary, surprising, miraculous, marvellous, wondrous, stupendous, wonderful, astounding.

Antonyms : Ordinary, common, everyday, commonplace, average, habitual, usual, normal.

Synonyms

- One can attain *extraordinary* power through Yoga.
- The comet seemed to approach the earth at a *surprising* speed.

- The vehicle was totally smashed but the driver had a *miraculous* escape in the accident.
- Taj Mahal is a *marvellous* piece of architecture.
- The super powers spend *stupendous* amounts on nuclear weapons.

- When a villager comes to a city, everything looks *wonderful* to him.

Antonyms

- *Ordinary* citizens in India can spend a life of normal comfort.
- The *common* man in the country does enjoy *everyday* needs like food, clothes and shelter.
- Radio and TV have become *commonplace* items.
- An *average* individual has a reasonable scope for a minimum earning.

AMBITION

Synonyms : Purpose, wish, hope, intention, ambition, goal, end, desire.

Antonyms : Indifference, purposelessness, aimlessness.

Synonyms

- Selfish people develop friendship for one or the other *purpose*.
- I *wish* I were a king.
- *Hope* is the zest of life.
- His actions belied his *intentions*.
- His only *ambition* in life is to become a doctor, that is why he has taken up the study of Biology.
- Hinduism lays more emphasis on the *goal* of life.

- Revolutionaries and extremists hold the view that the means do not matter so long as the *end* is achieved.

Antonyms

- He is *indifferent* to the means; what matters to him is the objective.
- He keeps busy without a mission. His life is marked by *purposelessness.*
- *Aimlessness* causes wastage of time, money and effort.

AMPLE

Synonyms : Broad, full, unrestricted, sufficient, spacious, abundant, unlimited, extensive, large.

Antonyms : Scarce, short, restricted, limited, insufficient small, skimpy, narrow.

Synonyms

- For a man who has a smile, *broad* and liberal outlook, life is *full* of joy and happiness.
- If a man were given *unrestricted* liberties, he would tend to become a slave to greed and crime.
- It was a large house; there was *sufficient* room in it to accommodate the marriage party.
- Our college had *a spacious* building..
- In our office library we had collected *abundant* material for the study of public utility services.

Antonyms

- When a product becomes *scarce* in supply its price tends to rise.
- Kerosene is in *short* supply these days.
- We in India enjoy *restricted* yet abundant rights.
- In an incorporated company, the financial responsibility of the shareholders is *limited* to the value of shares held.
- The space at our disposal is *insufficient*; therefore, we cannot undertake additional activities.

AMUSE

Synonyms : Please, enliven, charm, cheer, entertain, gladden.

Antonyms : Bore, annoy, tire, fatigue, wax.

Synonyms

- No one can *please* everybody.
- A shrewd speaker *enlivens* the audience by quoting various jokes from daily life.
- The audience were *charmed* by the personality of Mrs. Gandhi and *cheered* her with great applause when she proceeded to the dais to deliver her speech.

- The artists were very *glad* to meet the soldiers and *entertain* them.

Antonyms

- ✦ The politician proved a *bore*. He was therefore hooted down by the audience.
- ✦ The subordinate happened to *annoy* his boss by his irresponsible behaviour.
- ✦ Ramesh got *tired* of the routine and employed a clerk to relieve him of routine duties.
- ✦ It is natural for an old man to feel the *fatigue* after a whole day's hard work.

ANNEXATION

Synonyms : Increase, expansion, supplement, augmentation, accession, extension, appendix.

Antonyms : Decrease, contraction, curtailment, subtraction, diminution, reduction, fall.

Synonyms

- ✦ The expenses of a man *increase* with income.
- ✦ There is much more *expansion* in gases than in liquids or solids.
- ✦ The scientists are now engaged in *supplementing* the efforts of agriculturists for *augmentation of* agricultural produce.
- ✦ The *accession* of the king was celebrated with pomp and show.
- ✦ In view of unabated local disturbance, *extension* of curfew by another 24 hours was announced.

✦ The note should be brief and precise; the details may be added as an *appendix* if necessary.

Antonyms

✦ India's annual death rate has greatly *decreased* since independence owing to better medical and health facilities made available to the common people.

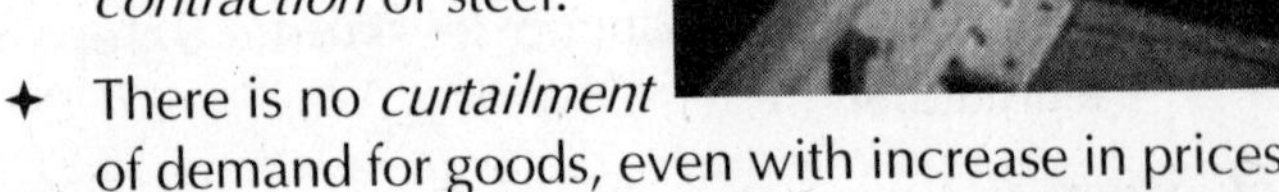

✦ A gap is left between rails to provide for expansion and *contraction* of steel.

✦ There is no *curtailment* of demand for goods, even with increase in prices.

ANNIHILATE

Synonyms : Destroy, cancel, annul, suppress, extinguish, supersede, repeal.

Antonyms : Establish, confirm, support, encourage, promote, forward, produce, testify.

Synonyms

✦ The enemy kept bombing the city until all the buildings were *destroyed.*

✦ The prime minister *cancelled* his tour of North-eastern states to preside over the non-aligned meet in New Delhi.

- The policies adopted by the new mayor *annulled* the good results of the schemes initiated by his predecessor.
- The fireman struggled hard for the whole night to *extinguish* fire.
- Two of his junior officers *superseded* him because of a vigilance case pending against him.

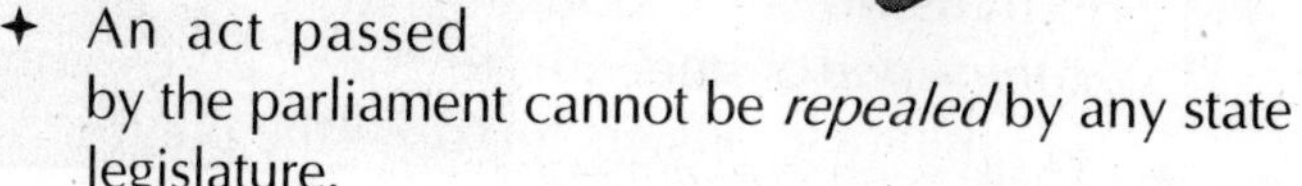

- An act passed by the parliament cannot be *repealed* by any state legislature.

Antonyms

- The Non-aligned meet in New Delhi agreed to *establish* an independent news agency for covering reports on the activities of the movement round the world.
- The Geneva Conference of the super powers on disarmament *confirmed* the need to have a nuclear-free outer space.
- India and other non-aligned countries have *supported* the move for a nuclear-free outer space.

ANNOY

Synonyms : Worry, trouble, irritate, disturb, harass, tease, bother, vex, torment.

Antonyms : Please, charm, oblige, delight, gratify, gladden.

Synonyms

- ✦ A man who believes in luck does not *worry* about his future.
- ✦ The opposition parties always try to *trouble* and vex the government by politicising the national issues.
- ✦ A sportsman should not feel *irritated* if he is defeated by his opponent.
- ✦ His habit to flout his subordinates *disturbs* the whole business.
- ✦ This drastic and unfair law gives ample opportunity to officers to *harass* the public.
- ✦ In colleges the students are nowadays prone to *teasing* the teachers.

Antonyms

- ✦ She has a *pleasing* personality.
- ✦ Her *charm* leaves the onlookers spellbound.
- ✦ You can *oblige* me by helping in solving my little financial problem.
- ✦ It will *delight* me if you pay an early visit.

ANSWER

Synonyms : Reply, retort, repartee, rejoinder, response, solution.

Antonyms : Query, question, defiance, interrogation.

Synonyms

- It is always advisable to *reply* business letters the same day.
- I *retorted* to his charges in a rejoinder.
- George Bernard Shaw always had a witty *repartee* to match every situation.
- The caretaker had to serve a *rejoinder.*
- We all waited anxiously for their *response*..

Antonyms

- Nowadays business *queries* have to be answered the same day.
- In day-to-day affairs of business there are many *questions* to be tackled and answered.
- Over-expectation usually brings *defiance.*

ANXIETY

Synonyms : Restlessness, apprehension, foreboding, worry, concern, misgiving, uneasiness, disquiet, dread.

Antonyms : Assurance, calmness, composure, confidence, ease, security, quietude, equanimity.

Synonyms

- Every election brings *restlessness* among the people by raising their expectations.
- People's *apprehensions* get highlighted by political trickery.
- Unlucky events always cast their *foreboding* before happening.

- You just have to appear in the examination, do not *worry* about the result.
- It was a matter of great *concern* for the entire nation.

Antonyms

- The prime minister gave an *assurance* to the people that he would try his best to improve the economy of the country. 
- Problems of the country can be solved with *calmness* rather than with worry.
- Mahatma Gandhi solved every problem with *confidence*.

APPARENT

Synonyms : Clear, visible, obvious, evident, manifest, distinct, patient.

Antonyms : Hidden, behind, obscure, veiled, secret, covert, latent, marked.

Synonyms

- In winter, the nights are generally *clear* and the stars are *visible* to the naked eye.
- His intentions became *obvious* when he started criticising his friend.
- Deep fears were *evident* from the face of the criminal when he was sentenced to life imprisonment.
- The character of a man is *manifest* from his activities.
- Leonardo da Vinci had the *distinct* qualities of a great scientist.

Antonyms

- There is a *hidden* hand of God in every human activity.
- He worked sincerely and from *behind* the scene.
- He wanted to remain *obscure* due to his over-modesty.
- He expressed his feelings to his beloved in a *veiled* manner.

APPEARANCE

Synonyms : Sight, view, outlook, scenery, landscape, show, scene, tableau, setting, picture.

Antonyms : Formless, distorted, skeleton, insulting.

Synonyms

- Rhinoceroes is deadly to *sight.*
- What a beautiful *view* of the sea from this window?

- Your *outlook* on life seems quite positive.
- The *scenery* of Kashmir attracts our poetic admiration.
- The *landscape* of Ooty is comparable to the one in Kashmir.
- It was a memorable *show.*

Antonyms

- ✦ The area surrounding this coal mine is the least interesting. It is almost *formless.*
- ✦ The scene in Teheran today gives a grim *distorted* picture of the war-torn great city.
- ✦ Children got scared seeing a *skeleton* hanging in the middle of the room.

APPRECIATION

Synonyms : Love, regard, respect, praise, approval.

Antonyms : Hate, disrespect, disregard, condemnation, disapproval.

Synonyms

- ✦ *Love* for humanity is the greatest service to God.
- ✦ The rich should pay due *regard* to the poor.
- ✦ *Respect* for religion and community makes a complete man.
- ✦ A just *praise* is a gift and unjust praise flattery.
- ✦ The committee granted the bill its *approval.*

Antonyms

- ✦ The greatest *disrespect* one shows to God is by *hating* a human being.
- ✦ All religions unanimously *disapprove* the use of violence in human relations.

APPROPRIATE

Synonyms : Confiscate, take, allot, seize, correct.

Antonyms : Release, loosen, open, incorrect.

Synonyms

- This act will empower the government to *confiscate* the property of smugglers.
- He *took* my advice on all important issues.
- He was *allotted* a piece of land in Anand Vihar.
- The documents *seized* by the police prove that he was guilty. 
- This action on the part of the government is *correct* for the solution of the problem.

Antonyms

- The principal *released* the plot of land which had been inappropriately occupied by the institution.
- The government has *loosened* its hold on the private sector by announcing its new industrial policy.
- The new policy has *opened* the scope for new ventures in industry and trade.

ASCENT

Synonyms : Further, go forward, progress, proceed.

Antonyms : Bend, go backward, regress, recede.

Synonyms

- Gandhiji sacrificed his life to *further* the cause of the humanity.

- He went *forward* with his technique of non-violence in spite of severe criticism from many quarters.
- Hard work and firm determination are the two planks to *progress.*
- He is a clever man. He takes necessary precautions before *proceeding* further.

Antonyms

- Gandhiji made British government *bend* at last.
- Some people are criticising the Chinese government for its *going backwards* from the socialist system.
- The stiff attitude of President Bush of the United States on the issue of nuclear disarmament means a *regress* in international relations.

ASSOCIATE

Synonyms : Connect, ally, band, combine, unite, fraternise, join, relate, link.

Antonyms : Disconnect, separate, break apart, defy, dissociate, desert.

Synonyms

- This road *connects* Connaught Place with many important suburbs.
- An *ally* and close friend of Rajat betrayed him.
- It is necessary to keep admiring the *band* of martyrs for the sake of keeping patriotic spirit among the youth.

- ✦ The *combination* of these two ideas may resolve the problem.
- ✦ In India, opposition parties *unite* during elections only.

Antonyms

- ✦ The electrician *disconnected* the electricity supply at the mains to test the safety of wires.
- ✦ We cannot reach the right conclusion without *separating* the discussion of the two issues involved.
- ✦ The opposition political parties *broke apart* as they could not fit their irrespective ideologies in one frame.

ASSURE

Synonyms : Ensure, guarantee, certify, uphold, encourage, promise, inform.

Antonyms : Imperil, unsettle, discourage, mislead, warn, jeopardise.

Synonyms

- ✦ We have to *ensure* necessary circumstances before taking up the proposed measures.
- ✦ It is very difficult to *guarantee* the right to work to every body in a newly independent country.
- ✦ The documents have to be *certified* by a competent authority.
- ✦ The constitution of India *upholds* the six fundamental rights to the citizens in the country.
- ✦ They *encourage* the citizens to take part in the progress of the country.

Antonyms

- It is very difficult to undertake this project without *imperilling* the economy of the firm.
- The personal misuse of the company's funds by directors tended to *unsettle* its very continuance.
- Lack of law and order *discourages* the propensity to save.

ASTONISH

Synonyms : Surprise, amaze, astound, startle, confound.

Antonyms : Forewarn, caution, warn.

Synonyms

- The final reversal in election fortunes *surprised* the masses.
- People stood *amazed* at the feat of the juggler.
- Victory of the Indian team over West Indies in the 1985 World Cup Cricket *astounded* the whole word.
- The deviation in the Pyramids of Egypt has *startled* the intellectuals.

Antonyms

- The doctor *forewarned* the parents of the sick child against optimism about quick recovery.
- The government *cautioned* the police against complacence.

✦ Let me *warn* you about your health, so that you may care to improve your diet.

ATTENTION

Synonyms : Care, study, heed, regard, notice.

Antonyms : Absence, distraction, remission.

Synonyms

✦ God will *care* for us if we care for humanity.

✦ We should *study* all the aspects of a problem before finding a solution.

✦ We must *heed* the feelings of others before passing sweeping comments.

✦ Let us pay due *regard* to the views of others before passing any judgement.

✦ Roop Singh *noticed* some discrepencies in the script.

Antonyms

✦ Your *absence* was greatly felt at the party.

✦ The presence of ladies in the meeting caused unwanted *distraction.*

✦ The poor student applied to the Principal for *remission* of tuition fees.

AUSPICIOUS

Synonyms : Successful, hopeful, fortunate, happy, lucky, reasonable.

Antonyms : Despairing, hopeless, unhappy, unfortunate, unlucky, luckless, ill-fated.

Synonyms

- ✦ India has been *successful* in sending its own satellites to space.
- ✦ He has fared well in the examination and is *hopeful* of getting first division.
- ✦ He is *fortunate* that he could avoid the accident by turning his car suddenly.
- ✦ A man who considers himself *lucky* is always *happy*.
- ✦ None of the demands made by the agitators was *reasonable*.

Antonyms

- ✦ With possibilities of star wars occurring in outer space, the world is going through a *despairing* period.
- ✦ The situation seems quite *hopeless* unless the super power negotiations at Geneva can take a more constructive turn.
- ✦ The people of the world are so *unhappy* over the dim prospects.

AUTHORITY

Synonyms : Power, right, jurisdiction, influence, prestige, title, control, command, sway, rule.

Antonyms : Submission, obedience, subjection, thraldom, slavery.

Synonyms

- *Power* corrupts a man and absolute power corrupts absolutely.
- Freedom is my birth *right* and I shall have it.
- The *jurisdiction* of each state is clearly defined in the constitution.
- He was under the *influence* of liquor when he met with an accident.
- She is orthodox and so makes even a small thing involving her an issue of *prestige*.
- He cannot sell the house to you because the *title* to that property vests in the president.

- In modern times, the government not only rules the masses but also *controls* their economic and social activities.
- Only a field marshal can take *command* of all the three forces upon the advice of the president.
- At the last moment, his speech *swayed* the voters and he won the election.

Antonyms

- The papers are at present under *submission* to the President for orders.
- The state is authorised to exact *obedience* of the citizens.
- The bonded labour is put to *subjection* by the village landlords in some places even in this last quarter of the 20th century.

AVOIDANCE

Synonyms : Retract, abstinence, evasion, truant, escape, regression, the brush-off, the go-by.

Antonyms : Continuation, firmness, status quo, pursuit, discipline.

Synonyms

- The army was so heavily shelled that it had to leave the post and *retract*.
- His *abstinence* (voluntary absence) from the meetings of the committee has helped the secretary to take arbitrary decisions.

- ✦ The statement made by him was utilised by the authorities to substantiate the charges of *evasion* levelled against him.
- ✦ It is an experience in itself to enjoy playing *truant* during school times.
- ✦ The leader had a narrow *escape* in his counter with the enormous elephant.
- ✦ His *regression* from public life resulted in his total defeat in the elections.

Antonyms

- ✦ This process involves *continuation* of the old technique.
- ✦ Only *firmness* on the fact of officers can restore honesty in administration.
- ✦ So long as *status quo* prevails. the pursuit of the new mission is out of question.

AWKWARD

Synonyms : Unskilful, uncouth, rough, bungling, maladroit, ponderous, heavy handed.

Antonyms : Skilful, dexterous, clever.

Synonyms

- ✦ His *unskilful* handling of the situation led to violence and arson by the mob.
- ✦ His letter was drafted in *uncouth* language, so his friend did not care to reply him.
- ✦ I have a *rough* idea of the location of his house but I don't know the exact address.

- He was sentenced to one year's rigorous imprisonment for *bungling* in the accounts.
- The drama presented by the society was *maladroit* and boring.

Antonyms

- Ramesh brought success to the project by his *skilful* handling.
- The new manager introduced *dexterous* techniques in administration of the company to pull it out of morass.
- A *clever* gun, he made friends with the bosses, as well as subordinates.

BACKWARD

Synonyms : Unwilling, behind, dull, sluggish, late, tardy, reluctant.

Antonyms : Willing, ahead, anterior, quick, alert, early, advancing, forward, prompt, eager.

Synonyms

- ✦ An introvert is *unwilling* to work in the company of other people.
- ✦ Some countries are much *behind* India so far as technological development is concerned.
- ✦ When India was not free, Indians were considered *dull* and *sluggish* by the Britishers.
- ✦ Some people are habitual *late* comers to office. They present a very *tardy* picture of government offices.
- ✦ In the beginning he was *reluctant* to accept the help offered by me but later on accepted it.

Antonyms

- ✦ A smart person is generally more *willing* to cooperate with people.

✦ Ramesh is far *ahead* of Mahesh in mathematics.

✦ The student gave a *prompt* reply to the question asked by the teacher.

BALANCE

Synonyms : Equalise, adjust, poise, pit, weight

Antonyms : Over-balance, tilt, upset

Synonyms

✦ The new finance act provides for *equalisation* of wages of men and women in the public sector.

✦ Let us *adjust* our differences, before they become public.

✦ The *poise* that Mahatma Gandhi carried in his personality remains unmatched.

✦ The authority *pit* the brothers against each other.

✦ His statemarts carried *weight*.

Antonyms

✦ With no strong opposition party in India, the Congress *over-balances* political power.

✦ Because of a democratic constitution, the power is *tilted* in favour of the masses.

✦ Gas tragedy in Bhopal *upset* the life of the city.

BANKRUPT

Synonyms : Penniless, Insolvent, ruined, indigent, destitute.

Antonyms : Solvent, credit-worthy, well-off, prosperous, rich.

Synonyms

✦ He became *penniless* in a single transaction because his speculations proved entirely wrong in the share market.

✦ He was declared *insolvent* and his property auctioned.

✦ His greed for money *ruined* him completely.

✦ In spite of his *indigent* circumstances, he is always ready to help others.

✦ The hermit believes that man is a *destitute* soul destined to die one day.

Antonyms

✦ This firm is strong and *solvent.* We may buy its shares with benefit.

✦ The firm has enough *credit-worthiness.* People are prepared to supply it raw material on credit.

✦ Its director are all *well-off* people, *prosperous* and *rich.*

BARGAIN

Synonyms : Deal, inexpensive, transaction, agreement.

Antonyms : Account, closed, payment, expensiveness, quittance.

Synonyms

✦ Dishonest officers sometimes try to strike a *deal* with the income tax assessees.

✦ Because of its comparative *inexpensiveness,* the new design of the furniture became popular.

✦ A clever businessman believes in cash *transactions* only.

✦ In legal terminology, marriage is regarded as an *agreement.*

Antonyms

✦ The use of local parts in this equipment *accounts* for its economical price.

✦ China, which was a *closed* country until now, has been reopened to the visitors from other countries under ordinary international law regulations.

✦ The balancing of sales and purchases of a firm means that the firm is sound for making all *payments* on liabilities in time.

BASE

Synonyms : Corrupt, shameful, mean, sordid, low, dishonourable, vile.

Antonyms : Above-board, pure, honoured, esteemed, noble, exalted, lofty.

Synonyms

- *Corrupt* practices among government officials are being investigated by a special commission appointed for the purpose.
- It is *shameful* that even 60 years after independence, poverty has not been eradicated in the country.
- How *mean* for selfish landlords in villages to exploit the poor Harijans as bonded labour even today!
- The woman narrated her *sordid* tale.
- The morale of the forces was very *low*.

Antonyms

- Most of the officers today are *above-board* but a few corrupt ones spoil the *purity* of administration.
- *Honoured* are those that do self-less service to their countrymen.
- The Hindustan Times is one of the *esteemed* dailies in northern India.

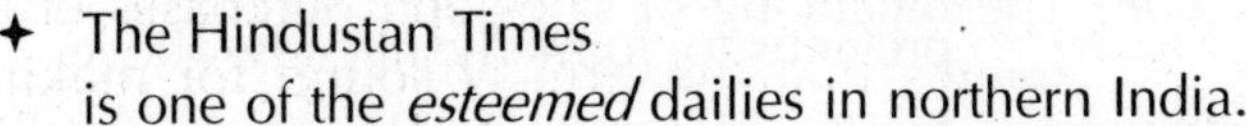

BEND

Synonyms : Bow, submit, stoop, yield, condescend, lean, tend, incline.

Antonyms : Break, stiffen, stand, straighten, advance, rise.

Synonyms

- ✦ Mohan *bowed* before his grandmother.
- ✦ The company *submitted* its accounts to the Income Tax officer.
- ✦ The corrupt officer *stooped* to accept the bribe.
- ✦ She could not do anything but to *yield* to her husband's cruelty.
- ✦ The bride's father *condescended* at last to raise a loan for the dowry of his daughter.

Antonyms

- ✦ Atul has *broken* new ground in the field of Hindi poetry.
- ✦ The demand for dowry in such an open way *stiffened* the bride's father.
- ✦ Rama's father took a brave *stand* on the issue of dowry.
- ✦ Let's *straighten* this controversy in the General meeting of the company.

BEFORE

Synonyms : Preceding, ahead, prior to, in front of, previous to, formerly, already, above.

Antonyms : Succeeding, after, behind, later, following, subsequently, afterwards.

Synonyms

- ✦ In an essay, each paragraph should be connected by sequence with the *preceding* one.
- ✦ Will you go *ahead* with this project?

- The picture must be painted *prior* to its fitting in the frame.
- They have built a factory *in front of* my house; it will always be a source of noise and nuisance.
- He had already visited Canada *previous* to his present tour of Moscow.
- *Formerly* he was an ambassador, now he has been appointed governor.
- The hare was surprised to see that the tortoise had *already* reached the destination.

- The passage quoted *above* has been taken from Hamlet, the famous play of Shakespeare.

Antonyms

- We have added a few notes on the subject in the *succeeding* chapter.
- The minister also addressed the meeting *after* the secretary had finished his introductory remarks.
- *Later* the local leaders spoke one by one.
- The audience was keenly *following* the script of the drama.

BELIEF

Synonyms : Trust, credit, faith, opinion, view, mind, idea.

Antonyms : Distrust, whim, misgiving, discredit, suspicion, doubt, disbelief.

Synonyms

- We should not *trust* those politicians who make lofty promises at the time of elections.
- Some businessmen sell their goods on *credit* but they charge higher rate of interest.
- People had unflinching *faith* in the leadership of Mr. Rajiv Gandhi.
- Students generally hesitate to express their *opinion* frankly about the teacher.
- They have been selected with a *view* to illustrate both the thought and action of the writer's life.
- Das will not *mind* spending more money provided he is convinced that this venture will fetch him large profits.

Antonyms

- *Distrust* once let loose gains more momentum in the public mind than the trust which takes more time to grow.
- The officers who are *whimsical* can not be depended upon to perform their duty efficaciously.
- Ram has of late development some *misgivings* about Shyam.

BENEATH

Synonyms : Below, underneath, under, down.

Antonyms : Up, overhead, above, high.

Synonyms

- The footnote given *below* from the text of the speech must be read to know the mind of the speaker correctly.
- The archaeologist excavated the earth *underneath* the arches to trace its origin.
- Everyone was curious to know about the treasures hidden *under* the tree.
- Mani walked *down* the aisles selling popcorn and balloons.

Antonyms

- *Up* and up goes the balloon!
- There is an aeroplane flying *overhead*.

- The *above* sentence is related to the air flight of our pilots.
- Our pilots can fly very *high*.

BENEFIT

Synonyms : Profit, gain, favour, advantage, avail, service, boon.

Antonyms : Harm, loss, damage, disadvantage, injury, calamity.

Synonyms

- ✦ The whole district will stand to *profit* from this industrial estate.
- ✦ Each day that Fortune gives you, be it what it may, is set down for *gain.*
- ✦ The government selected electronics as an industry for special *favour* in the seventh plan.
- ✦ They took *advantage* of her simple nature.
- ✦ He could not *avail* the opportunity due to his exams.

Antonyms

- ✦ Laziness does more *harm* to studies that gossiping.
- ✦ This factory is now running under a *loss* of Rs. 50,000 per month.
- ✦ The new budget is rather *damaging* to this industry.

BENEVOLENCE

Synonyms : God's grace, selflessness, charity, good nature, humanity, fellow feeling, brotherly love, good offices, kindness, kindliness, mercy, pity, bounty, public service.

Antonyms : Ill-nature, spite, cruelty, inhumanity, evil eye, evil intent, enmity, hate, malice, venom, churlishness, outrage.

Synonyms

- ✦ With *God's grace,* he survived the accident.
- ✦ Swami Ramakrishna Paramhansa was a living example of *selflessness, kindness* and *kindliness.*

- He believes in the maxim *'Charity* begins at home'.
- Doris has a benign personality; she has a *good nature* and feels *pity* for others.
- Unesco has done a tremendous work for the cause of *humanity*.
- Mechanical life makes a man lose *fellow feeling* and *brotherly love* for others.
- Officers of industrial relations machinery are supposed to use their *good offices* to bring harmony between the employers and the employees.

Antonyms

- His *ill-nature* is responsible for his unpopularity.
- He has developed *spite* against many friends due to his basic churlishness.
- He does not hesitate to indulge in *cruelty* against his enemies.

BEWILDER

Synonyms : Problem, poser, mystery, enigma.

Antonyms : Enlighten, teach, illuminate, inform, edify, instruct.

Synonyms

- For every *problem* there is a solution but one needs determination to solve it.
- Existence of God was a great *poser* for the priest to prove.
- Even the experts have failed to unveil the *mystery* of this plane crash.

✦ His behaviour has become an *enigma* for the psychiatrists which the latter are trying to analyse for the last two months.

Antonyms

✦ Only an *enlightened* approach can solve the common problems of humanity.

✦ Buddha's *teachings* had a great impact on the rulers of ancient India and China.

✦ The Prime Minister's national broadcast from the Red Fort *illuminated* the country's problems in all their perspectives.

✦ His approach was *informative, edifying,* and *instructive.*

BEYOND

Synonyms : Across, farther, yonder, over.

Antonyms : Adjacent, beside, along, near, close.

Synonyms

✦ The dissident leaders have been requested by one and all to sit *across* the table with the government and solve all differences or difficulties through healthy discussions.

✦ We watched the car gradually going *farther* away.

✦ He noticed the vehicle *yonder.*

✦ The driver carried *over* the bike.

✦ He can walk *over* a rope as easily as on the road.

Antonyms

✦ The *adjacent* building is owned by K.K. Birla.

✦ The multi-storeyed building *beside* this structure is merely an annexe.

✦ We can motor *along* the whole locality in five minutes if you so like.

✦ Once you go *near* him, he will look after you for ever.

BINDING

Synonyms : Obligatory, contracting, holding, restraining, stringent, valid.

Antonyms : Optional, voluntary, elective, discretional.

Synonyms

✦ It is *obligatory* for a doctor to go to see a patient even at midnight if he gets an emergent call.

✦ Contrary to our expectations he came forward *contracting* himself to complete the project within three months.

✦ The commandos had to fire upon the hijackers who kept *holding* the passengers even after their demands had been met.

- Her domestic engagements have *restrained* her from going to the arts college.
- The new principal has taken *stringent* measures to maintain discipline in the college.
- Your ignorance about animals is astonishing. Your information regarding the hippopotamus is also not *valid.*

Antonyms

- The second language becomes an *optional* subject after the 12th class.
- Military service is not left to the *voluntary* discretion of young men in western countries during external emergencies.
- Language is an *elective* subject in the graduate course in this university.

BIRTH

Synonyms : Origin, delivery, beginning, creation, genesis.

Antonyms : End, finish, close, death, conclusion.

Synonyms

- Archaeologists may sometimes find it impossible to trace the *origin* of the monuments.
- The doctor had to resort to caesarean operation in this complicated *delivery* case.

- ✦ His testimony was pure fiction, mendacious from *beginning* to end.
- ✦ Meghdoot is one of the best *creations* of Kalidas.
- ✦ The *genesis* of any communal violence can be traced to fanatic religious leaders.

Antonyms

- ✦ Every life on this planet must one day come to an *end*.
- ✦ We can *finish* this task in a month's time.
- ✦ The completion of this project will mean the *closing* of one chapter of our technological history and the beginning of the new.

BITTER

Synonyms : Sad, acrid, intense, harsh, sour, severe

Antonyms : Mild, sweet, pleasant, genial, light.

Synonyms

- ✦ The news of failure in the examination made him very *sad*.
- ✦ As our bus passed by the nullah, we felt a severe *acrid* smell.
- ✦ With the passage of time, heat is becoming more *intense*.
- ✦ His treatment of the employees was very *harsh*.

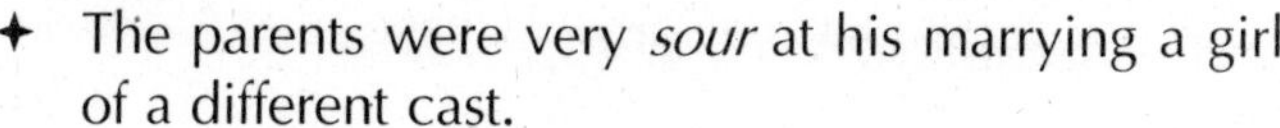

- ✦ The parents were very *sour* at his marrying a girl of a different cast.

Antonyms

- I prefer *mild* drinks.
- Spending a few minutes with the poetess was a *sweet* experience.
- Her company was very *pleasant* and *genial.*

BLAME

Synonyms : Criticism, reproach, censure, rebuke, guilt.

Antonyms : Praise, appreciation, applaud, approval, exhort, extol.

Synonyms

- Politicians may do their best but they cannot avoid *criticism* by their opponents.
- He has done the job so honestly that he cannot be *reproached.*
- The teacher *censured* the boy for trying to cheat his class fellows.
- He was *rebuked* by his father for securing such a low percentage of marks.
- Some reformers forget their own *guilt* and try to teach others. What a farce?

Antonyms

- We should *praise* our military personnel for the great amount of risk and sacrifice they take during an emergency.
- They deserve our *appreciation* if they succeed in defending the country.

✦ We should *applaud* their valour.

BLESSING

Synonyms : Good wishes, prayer, praise, thanks, consecration.

Antonyms : Bad wishes, curse, evil thought.

Synonyms

✦ He is a very popular leader and receives *good wishes* from people all over the world on his birthday every year.

✦ His philosophy was no doubt profound but his method of *prayer* was impractical for the masses.

✦ The secretary of the co-operative society deserves all *praise* for the work he has done for the society and we must all *thank* him.

✦ *Consecration* of the male child is a very important religious ceremony of the Muslims.

Antonyms

✦ He is so popular, even his enemies can not dare to have *bad wishes* for him.

✦ There is hardly a soul that *curses* him.

✦ There is no place for *evil thought* in his mind for any human being.

BLISS

Synonyms : Joy, pleasure, happiness, rapture.

Antonyms : Sorrow, sadness, pain, dejection.

Synonyms

- A thing of beauty is a *joy* for ever.
- Children get *pleasure* out of playing truants.
- *Happiness* lies in selfless service of others.
- A Yogi believes that he could live in a state of *rapture* after attaining Moksha.

Antonyms

- Every life has its share of *sorrows.*
- *Sadness* and happiness are two sides of the life of every individual.
- *Pain* and pleasure flow side by side in human life.
- It is *dejection* that shatters our personality sometimes.

BLUNT

Synonyms : Direct, insensitive, dull, undiplomatic.

Antonyms : Diplomatic, sensitive, sharp, sophisticated.

Synonyms

- The politicians, being practical and realistic men, avoid *direct* confrontation with their opponents.
- This salesman is *insensitive* to the complaints of the customers.
- The debate in the council over the budget was rather *dull* and boring.

- The dilemma he faced was the result of his *undiplomatic* handling of the affairs in the beginning.

Antonyms

- If we handle our affairs *diplomatically* there is no need for frustration later.
- He is too *sensitive* to remain in poise during controversies.
- His reaction is too *sharp* to allow for healthy discussion on any controversial subject.
- His *sophisticated* manners win him applause everywhere.

BOOST

Synonyms : Encouragement, lift, aid, help, recommendation, hoist.

Antonyms : Rebuke, discouragement, hindrance, obstacle, rebuff.

Synonyms

- At the time of frustration and disappointment, my teacher is a great source of *encouragement*.
- He is called modern Bheem as he can *lift* as much weight as four persons together.
- The terrorists were getting a lot of *aid* from CIA and other foreign agencies.

- We should always be ready to *help* our neighbours.
- It was on the *recommendation* of an architect that we opted for this design of the furniture for our new house.
- The prime minister will *hoist* the flag at the Red Fort on Independence Day.

Antonyms

- Only encouragement can better reform a modern young man than *rebuke*.
- Inequality is the biggest *hindrance* in the way of social and economic progress.
- Lack of close liaison between the public and private sectors is the biggest *obstacle* to the speedy expansion of small-scale industries.

BOLDER

Synonyms : Edge, limit, margin, boundary, brim, rim, brink.

Antonyms : Centre, midst, point, middle, axis.

Synonyms

- After stitching the pages, the binder cuts the book from its *edges* to give it a final shape.
- He is a very short-tempered man. He ignores the *limits* of decency while talking to others.
- The clerk was instructed by his officer to leave wide *margins* on the left while writing a draft.

- He has erected a wall along the *boundary* of his plot so as to stop its trespassing.
- The magician filled the glass with water up to its *brim* and tilted it but the water did not fall out.
- He loaded the trunk beyond the prescribed limit. The result was the breakdown of the *rim* of its rear wheel.

Antonyms

- Draw a circle in the *centre* of this line.
- The thief was spotted in the *midst* of the crowd.
- A circle has a *point* in its centre.
- The tailor cut the cloth at its *middle*.
- The earth revolves round the sun at an *axis* of 66½°.

BORE

Synonyms : Troublesome, talker, nuisance, talkative, pest.

Antonyms : Thinker, genial, entertainer, amusing, listener.

Synonyms

- Surely they will not tolerate such a *troublesome* member in their society.
- He is just a shallow *talker* and cannot inspire confidence in his friends.

- Their spoiled child has become a great *nuisance* in the family.
- Women are presumed to be *talkative* by nature, but it is not always true.

Antonyms

- Marx and Engels were great *thinkers* and philosophers of their time.
- John has a *genial* temperament. He has therefore made a circle of good friends.
- P.C. Roy was not only a great magician but also a great *entertainer*.
- His manners are so *amusing* that many of his obvious lies go unnoticed.

BORROW

Synonyms : Receive, appropriate, take, adapt, steal, imitate, copy, pilfer, pirate, adopt.

Antonyms : Lend, advance, give, invent, improve, make, credit.

Synonyms

- You can determine your net loss on investment for the year only if you know the exact amount you *received* and spent during the year.
- Delhi Administration has *appropriated* all the vacant land in Delhi.

- We shall have to *take* the children away from their parents during such a ceremony.
- You will have to *adapt* your food habits to items that improve health.
- The child was so hungry that he could not help *stealing* some bread from the shop.
- Some actors can *imitate* the politicians very well.
- He has *copied* the style of his writing from the essays of Bacon.
- In the army also there may be traitors who would *pilfer* away the secret information to the enemy.
- The law of high seas allows every state to punish a *pirate* irrespective of his nationality.

Antonyms

- Could you *lend* me Rs. 50/- for a week?
- I will need an *advance* of 50% of the contracted amount to start the project.
- I have *given* a word of honour to my friend to keep the information confidential.
- Edison *invented* a number of devices.

BRACE

Synonyms : Support, refresh, invigorate, prop, strengthen.

Antonyms : Weaken, degenerate, raze, knock, enfeeble.

Synonyms

- The kind rich man *supported* many poor students.
- Sleep *refreshes* us when we feel tired.

- ✦ A catalyst is a substance which *invigorates* chemical reaction.
- ✦ As the only son he should *prop* up his old parents.
- ✦ Exercise *strengthens* our body and mind.

Antonyms

- ✦ Lethargic habits *weaken* our body and mind.
- ✦ Too much materialism has *degenerated* our youth.
- ✦ The earthquake *razed* many buildings to the ground.
- ✦ Mohan *knocked* at every door during his financial bankruptcy to save his firm from collapse.

BRAVE

Synonyms : Bold, courageous, dauntless, gallant, heroic, intrepid, plucky, undaunted, valiant, valorous.

Antonyms : Afraid, cowardly, timid, daunted, intimidated, unheroic.

Synonyms

- ✦ Atul is a *bold* and *courageous* young man.
- ✦ Jawaharlal Nehru was a *dauntless* and gallant freedom fighter.
- ✦ Bhim was a very *gallant* man.
- ✦ *Heroic* adventures of the characters in Jonathan's stories have always inspired the children round the world.

Antonyms

- Mahatma Gandhi was never *afraid* of the consequences of his non-violent satyagraha.
- The *cowardly* attitude of the leaders caused failure in their mission.

- The cat is a *timid* animal as it runs to safety on the slightest noise of any other animal.

BREAK

Synonyms : Interlude, intermission, interval, respite, let-up, lull, pause, recess, spell.

Antonyms : Continuation, connection.

Synonyms

- Most of the feature films have *interludes* of jokes to break the seriousness of the story.
- Feature films also have an *intermission* around the middle part of their duration.
- We used to take our lunch during the *interval*.
- The five-minute *respite* in the heavy rain gave us the chance to slip away to our destination.

- ✦ Seeing her boy friend Rima's anger was *let-up*.

Antonyms

- ✦ This serial is a *continuation* of the earlier series.
- ✦ There is a great *connection* between the budgetary policy and the industrial development of a country.

BREED

Synonyms : Produce, raise, beget, conceive, train, hatch, incubate.

Antonyms : Destroy, slay, murder, annihilate, kill.

Synonyms

- ✦ Our gardener *produces* many nice vegetables in our new farm.
- ✦ The farmer sells his *produce* at the market. 
- ✦ Nowadays the army is *raising* a special fund for the assistance of the ex-soldiers.
- ✦ Love *begets* love and even a spoilt child can be reformed through love.
- ✦ Only a genius like him can *conceive* of such a utopian situation.
- ✦ My cousin is being *trained* as a hospital nurse. Her training is near completion.
- ✦ The old hen has *hatched* eight chicks.

✦ She first *incubated* them for a period of four weeks.

Antonyms

✦ The grasshoppers badly *destroyed* his crop.

✦ The villain *slayed* the very hoodlum who had helped him to hide the stolen treasure.

✦ The wicked man has after all been arrested for a *murder*, rape by the police.

✦ Atomic warfare can *annihilate* the whole of mankind in no time.

✦ We went to the coffee house to *kill* time.

BREEZE

Synonyms : Storm, gust, hurricane, wind, blast, gale, typhoon.

Antonyms : Lull, placidity, doldrums, Calm.

Synonyms

✦ The weather office has predicted a *storm* in the coastal areas within the next 48 hours.

✦ It was only the courage and ability of the captain that the ship has survived the *hurricanes* of the Bay of Bengal.

✦ Due to a stormy *wind* the leaves were blown off the trees.

✦ The *blast* of the explosion shook the building.

✦ Don't go out into the *gale*.

Antonyms

- There is often a *lull* before the storm.
- His *placidity* has won him the title "man of peace".

- The failure of his son in the examination has put him in the *doldrums*.
- After five days of storm, we have *calm* weather today.

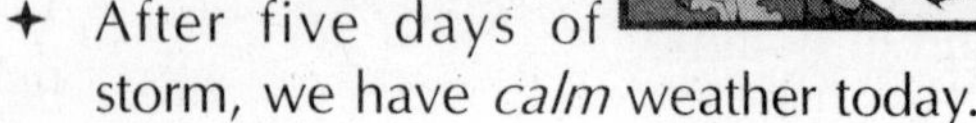

BREVITY

Synonyms : Concise, short, succinct, brief.

Antonyms : Confused, addleheaded, loquacious.

Synonyms

- In precis writing, the matter remaining *concise* is of the utmost importance.
- The duration of the training was so *short* that all the participants felt sorry for its being *brief*.
- Essays of Bacon are admired for their *brevity*.
- His comments were detailed yet *succinct*.

Antonyms

- His ideas are good but his style is so *loquacious* that his writings get *confused*.
- His habit of non-stop speech during his waking hours has made him *addleheaded*.

BRIGHT

Synonyms : Shining, quick-witted, intelligent, luminous, resplendent, sparkling.

Antonyms : Dull, dim, dull-witted, foolish, dark, ignorant, faint.

Synonyms

- The sun was *shining* brightly when clouds appeared suddenly and the rain started.
- Birbal was a very *quick-witted* minister of Akbar.. Nobody in the court of Akbar could defeat him in wit and humour.
- Einstein was not considered an *intelligent* child at his school.
- My wrist watch has a *luminous* dial.
- The light of the chandelier made her modest necklace look *resplendent*.
- Her diamond *sparkled* like fire.

Antonyms

- Long speeches are always *dull*.
- Sheela keeps a *dim* light in her bed room.
- Although the son of a great politician, Johny is a *dull-witted* personality
- Very often he makes *foolish* comments on the people.
- It was *dark* when we reached our destination.

BRISK

Synonyms : Quick, alert, industrious, busy, lively, prompt, energetic.

Antonyms : Slow, lethargic, dull, lazy, indolent, inactive.

Synonyms

- We should make a *quick* decision about our route when driving, otherwise we may meet an accident.
- The engine driver was *alert* enough to save the train from collision with the oncoming train.
- You should be as *industrious* as an ant.
- Are you *busy* this evening?
- The hikers kept up a *brisk* pace.
- We had a *lively* game of musical chairs last evening.
- You must take *prompt* action to control this situation, otherwise it will go out of your control.
- Smith was *energetic* in the performance of his duty.

Antonyms

- *Slow* and steady wins the race.
- His *lethargic* habits will one day greatly depress him.
- His very presence makes the atmosphere *dull* and *drab*.

✦ Ever since his last sickness, he has become *indolent* and *inactive*.

BRUSQUE

Synonyms : Discourteous, gruff, curt, abrupt.

Antonyms : Courteous, smooth, polite, polished.

Synonyms

✦ Though he is an educated person, he is often *discourteous* to his elders.

✦ The sergeant always gave a *gruff* answer to the soldier's questions.

✦ The programme came to an *abrupt* end when the lights went off.

✦ I was surprised at his *curt* reply.

Antonyms

✦ Romy was highly *courteous* to us when we visited him.

✦ He was *smooth* and soft whenever we went to seek his favour for a party not so well known to him.

✦ His *polite* behaviour in fact greatly surprised us.

✦ His behaviour proved that he is a man of *polished* manners.

BRUTAL

Synonyms : Inhuman, merciless, savage, pitiless, barbarous, cruel.

Antonyms : Humane, merciful, sympathetic, kind, compassionate, tender.

Synonyms

- ✦ He treated his servant in an *inhuman* way.
- ✦ The prince of the castle of Toranto was *merciless* to his attendants.
- ✦ He behaves like a *savage* when he is angry.
- ✦ He is so *pitiless* that nobody likes to talk to him and share feelings with him.
- ✦ In ancient times there were many *barbarous* kings who killed people for the sake of maintaining an atmosphere of terror.

Antonyms

- ✦ Mahatma Gandhi measured the quality of life by the element of *humanity* ingrained in it.
- ✦ God is *merciful* to those who are merficul to humans.
- ✦ Jawaharlal Nehru was *sympathetic* to the interests of the poor.
- ✦ Atul is *kind* to the animals.

- ✦ Mrs. Indira Gandhi was highly *compassionate* to the bonded labourers and got passed adequate legislation to free them from the clutches of the zamindars.

BUILD

Synonyms : Construct, erect, fabricate, make.

Antonyms : Destroy, devastate, raze, unmake.

Synonyms

- ✦ This canal was *constructed* during the first five year plan.
- ✦ This pole is not perfectly *erect*. It can cause an accident.
- ✦ Indian cotton cloth is *fabricated* into garments and exported on a large scale.
- ✦ You have to *make* it perfect.

Antonyms

- ✦ This building is so old it needs to be *destroyed* and re-built.
- ✦ The Second World War caused a lot of *devastation* of men and materials.
- ✦ During its recent raids, Israel has *razed* many Lebanese buildings to ground.

BUSTLE

Synonyms : Rustle, flutter, stir, fluster, ado.

Antonyms : Inertness, laziness, fatigue, dormancy, lull, rest, unemployment, passivity, dullness, delay, inaction.

Synonyms

- Whenever I go to the park I enjoy listening to the *rustle* of the leaves.
- I enjoy watching a sparrow *fluttering* its wings.

- Nobody *stirred* when the dacoit came into the house.
- I have never been so much *flustered* as when the boss came two days earlier than his schedule.
- He is in the habit of making much *ado* about nothing.

Antonyms

- He lay *inert* with half-closed eyes
- *Laziness* is the root cause of all illness.
- Don't work so hard that you feel so *fatigued.*
- His brilliance lies *dormant* under the veil of passivity.

BUSY

Synonyms : Active, occupied, diligent, industrious, enervated, engrossed.

Antonyms : Indolent, idle, passive, relaxed, inactive, lazy, unoccupied, inert.

Synonyms

- Dr. Abdul Rehman is a very *active* teacher of medicine.
- Studies keep the youth *occupied* during the examinations.
- Atul is a *diligent* student and takes serious interest in all subjects.
- He is very *industrious* at work.

Antonyms

- Since his visit to the hill station, he has become rather *indolent* and *idle* in temperament.
- This child is inert and *passive* but can be toned up with the help of better diet.

- You must *relax* after a hard day's work to regain strength for the next day.

CAJOLE

Synonyms : Inveigle, beguile, coax, flatter, blandish, wheedle.

Antonyms : Cool, dampen, flout, dam, dissuade.

Synonyms

- He *inveigled* himself into her affections.
- The innocent girl was *beguiled* into thinking she could become a famous actress.
- Smith *coaxed* his father to let him use his new car.
- The servant *flattered* his master by telling him he was a good writer.
- Even her *blandishments* could not win him over.
- Mother tried to *wheedle* Father into going to the party.

Antonyms

- Jane was in a temper. It took me some time to *cool* her down.

- I was in very high spirits. Maria has *dampened* these by asking for a loan.
- The subordinate *flouted* the order of the manager.
- The water of the river has been well *dammed* by this barrage project.
- You should *dissuade* him from undertaking this risky project.

CALAMITY

Synonyms : Misery, distress, misfortune, trouble, catastrophe, affliction, disaster.

Antonyms : Prosperity, fortune, peace, joy, tranquillity, happiness.

Synonyms

- The minister was moved to see the *misery* of the *distressed* child labour employed in the weaving industry.
- The loss of her job was a big *misfortune*.
- Sometimes the members of the opposition party create lot of *trouble* in the parliament and obstruct the proceedings of the house.
- The land reforms may have benefitted the poor but did not prove to be a *catastrophe* for the rich land-owners.
- Our country is *afflicted* with twin disasters of food shortages and an exploding population.

Antonyms

- Recent agricultural research has made the farmers quite *prosperous.*
- Land reforms have also brought *fortune* for the small farmer.
- *Peace* is essential for the economic development of Punjab.
- It gives me immense *joy* to inaugurate this library in the village.

CALCULATE

Synonyms : Reckon, count, assess, estimate, number, compute.

Antonyms : Imagine, conjecture, surmise, suppose.

Synonyms

- Corruption is a problem the government must *reckon* with more seriously.
- Some children are intelligent and learn to *count* very fast.
- The achievements of scientific research cannot be *assessed* in monetary terms.
- The engraver could not *estimate* the cost of enlarging the emblem without first calculating the price of the metal to be used.
- The *number* of vehicles passing through the Janpath crossing is not less than 5000 a day.
- Although the rules have been amended, his pension has been *computed* at old rates.

Antonyms

- *Imagine* the beauty of nature in this season on a hill station.
- Do not *conjecture* the price of this present. It is invaluable.
- My calculation of the cost of this project is based on mere *surmise*.
- It is no use *supposing* negative things without rhyme or reason.

CALL

Synonyms : Bid, recall, invite, summon, convene, muster, invoke.

Antonyms : Remove, dismiss, discharge, exile, banish.

Synonyms

- Tears rolled down his cheeks when he *bade* farewell to his mother.
- The ambassador of India to China has been *recalled* by the government for the time being.
- I have been *invited* to participate in local committee meetings.
- He was *summoned* to court for giving evidence a in case.

- A meeting of the general body was *convened* by the secretary of the society to discuss some urgent matters.

- He could barely *muster* the courage to raise his head from the pillow.
- Once it was believed that witches could *invoke* the evil powers and harm anybody.

Antonyms

- The general body of the company in a meeting *removed* Mr. Murarka from chairmanship.
- The officer *dismissed* the corrupt subordinate.
- The railway employee, who had caused an accident through negligence, was *discharged* from service.
- The extremist leader, who was responsible for creating disturbances in the capital, was *exiled* from the country.

CALM

Synonyms : Pacify, hush, quiet, solace, mitigate, palliate, lull, compose.

Antonyms : Agitate, excite, perturb, crisis, disturb, fluster.

Synonyms

- ✦ At last he was able to *pacify* the processionists.
- ✦ He was caught red-handed accepting the *hush* money.
- ✦ Ram is a *quiet* little man who does his work unobtrusively but well.
- ✦ The assurances given by him could give no *solace* to the mourners.
- ✦ This new medicine is designed to *mitigate* the after-effects of heat strokes and heart attacks.
- ✦ This medicine has a *palliative* effect but cannot cure the disease.
- ✦ Before every storm there is a *lull* for some time.

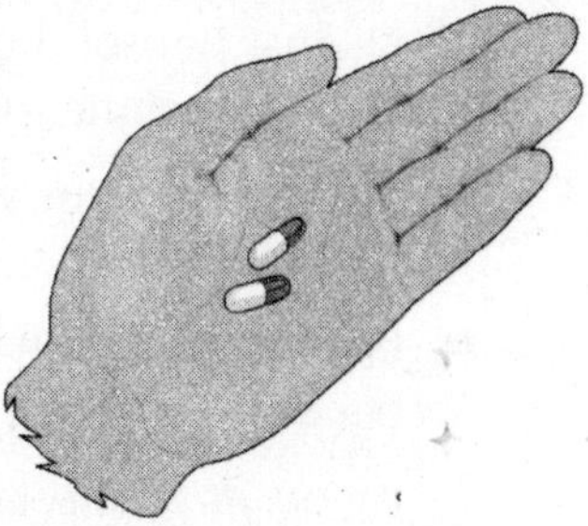

Antonyms

- ✦ The labourers are *agitating* for higher wages.
- ✦ Modern civilisation *excites* our nerve at every step.
- ✦ The clouds of war are presently *perturbing* the whole mankind.

- ✦ Ramesh does not seem to have a solution for this *crisis.*
- ✦ It is a *disturbing* sign.

CANCEL

Synonyms : Destroy, abolish, obliterate, nullify, invalidate, erase, blot out, efface.

Antonyms : Establish, ratify, corroborate, substantiate, endorse, confirm.

Synonyms

- ✦ An atom bomb can *destroy* the whole city within a few minutes.
- ✦ The post of Junior Investigator has been *abolished* in our office with effect from 1.4.2006.
- ✦ The murderer tried to *obliterate* all the evidences against himself but the handkerchief found in his pocket became the needed evidence.
- ✦ This act of yours will *nullify* all the good you have done to him.
- ✦ His nomination for election was *invalidated* because he is not a citizen of India.
- ✦ If you *erase* the last paragraph of the story, it will lose all its literary charm.

Antonyms

- ✦ Let us *establish* new rules and regulations for our society.

- Any amendment passed by the US Congress has to be *ratified* by at least 2/3rd number of states to go on the statute.
- This fact is so well-known it needs no *corroboration.*
- There is no evidence to *substantiate* your theory.
- I *endorse* your views on the present political situation in the country.

CAPACITY

Synonyms : Capability, ability, competence, aptitude, faculty, wit, skill, power, talent.

Antonyms : Incapability, inability, incompetence, inaptitude.

Synonyms

- It is beyond his *capability* to tackle such a complex problem.
- We cannot challenge his *ability* to handle this newly developed machine.
- His termination orders were set aside by the Court because these were not within the *competence* of the Director who issued them.
- He has an *aptitude* for science but his parents are compelling him to study commerce.
- His *faculties* are not sharp enough to understand the complexities of the new technique.
- A shrewd salesman possesses *wit,* humour and *skill* to convince the customer to buy his articles.
- Knowledge is *power.*

Antonyms

- Don't exhibit your *incapability* to handle this computerised machine.
- Ramesh has expressed his *inability* to help us in this project, not because he is *incompetent* but because he is going abroad.

CAPTURE

Synonyms : Arrest, seize, snatch, catch, apprehend.

Antonyms : Liberate, release, acquit, free, disengage.

Synonyms

- At last the police was able to *arrest* the thief.
- The army has *seized* three checkposts of the enemy.
- The incidents of chain *snatching* are on the increase in the capital these days.
- Although he ran fast, he could not *catch* the bus.
- The police has *apprehended* a number of terrorists during the last two days.

Antonyms

- The United Nations is now seriously trying to *liberate* Namibia from South Africa's white government rule.

- The government has *released* a number of political prisoners recently.
- The judge has *acquitted* one of the accused in the bank robbery base.
- My examinations are over. I am a *free* bird now.
- Unless you *disengage* yourself from political activities, we cannot offer you this whole-time job.

CARE

Synonyms : Prudence, thrift, wariness, custody.

Antonyms : Remissness, temerity, neglect.

Synonyms

- Your good *prudence* alone can save your family from break-up.
- Only *thrift* and hardwork can pull this factory through the present crisis.
- The present circumstances need some *wariness* in financial dealings.
- Telgi was taken into judicial *custody*.

Antonyms

- Any *remissness* on your part can land you in trouble.
- Now when the product is lying unsold, he has the *temerity* to blame the sales department for inefficiency.
- A little *neglect* today causes great loss tomorrow.

CAREFUL

Synonyms : Meticulous, conscientious, scrupulous, punctilious.

Antonyms : Negligent, heedless, sloppy, slipshod.

Synonyms

- ✦ Anil's *meticulous* manners won him a highly paid job at a young age.
- ✦ Gandhi was too *conscientious* and *scrupulous* to compromise with other leaders on the basic principle of non-violence as a technique of fighting against the British rule.
- ✦ He proposes to celebrate his marriage *punctiliously*.

Antonyms

- ✦ If you become *negligent* of your duty, you will not rise much in life.
- ✦ He became *heedless* in the civil case and in the end lost it.
- ✦ His writing is *sloppy* and slipshod.

CARRY

Synonyms : Bear, bring, haul, convey, take, transport.

Antonyms : Leave, abandon, drop.

Synonyms

- ✦ He *bears* all the features of his father.

- *Bring* all the luggage here and store it on the top floor.
- The police *hauled* all the smuggled goods.
- Moin *conveyed* the message responsibly.
- Both of them were *taken* to the court.

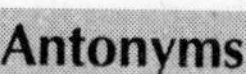

Antonyms

- I *left* the luggage at the railway station.
- I *abandoned* the idea of going abroad.
- I have *dropped* the proposal of marriage with a rich girl.

CASUALTY

Synonyms : Mishap, incident, chance, calamity, misadventure.

Antonyms : Design, purpose, intent, meaning, adventure.

Synonyms

- You can never foresee a *mishap.*
- Further inquiries show that he had visited the place of *incident* a few days ago.
- The teacher gave him another *chance* to mend himself.
- His family was shocked to know of the *calamity* that befell him.
- His attempt to scale the Himalayas without proper equipments proved a *misadventure.*

Antonyms

- The architectural *design* of this building was prepared with great care.
- The *purpose* of my visit is to apprise you of the present circumstances.
- He is *intent* on buying this plot of land.
- There is a definite *meaning* to his frequent visits.
- I am out for *adventure* in the hilly terrain this summer.

CATCHING

Synonyms : Charming, attractive, enchanting, captivating, appealing, fascinating, winning.

Antonyms : Unpleasant, ugly, unattractive, revolting, loathsome, repellant, odious, disagreeable.

Synonyms

- Her *charming* face, shining like moon, stultified every body present on the occasion.
- The reformer was preaching sermons in an *attractive* and appealing manner. The people listened to him in pin drop silence.
- The *enchanting* personality of the teacher made the students attentive in the classroom.
- His resistance entirely gave way to her *captivating* figure and moonlit eyes.
- Her strong appeal for help *won* his heart. He sacrificed himself to save her.

- He found himself caught up by the *fascinating* and sensuous movements of her body.

Antonyms

- The weather has become *unpleasant* with the onset of the summer season.
- Rhinoceros is an *ugly* creature to look at.
- She is very intelligent but her appearance is rather *unattractive*.
- The brigade was ready for *revolting* against the regime.

CAUSE

Synonyms : Produce, bring about, originate, effect, create, evoke.

Antonyms : Destroy, demolish, kill, devastate, ruin, desolate.

Synonyms

- Hybrid varieties of seed have helped the Indian farmer to *produce* more foodgrains.
- In spite of his best efforts he could not *bring about* any tangible change in her attitude.
- This idea has *originated* from the contract theories of state propounded by mid-age writers like Hobbes and Rousseau.
- The pilot *effected* a take-off despite the bomb packed runway.
- He is a great novelist. He can *create* a unique view of life by using every-day language.

- The hostages tried to *evoke* the noble passions of the terrorists but the latter showed no mercy.

Antonyms

- An atomic bomb can *destroy* the whole universe in no time.
- This house is now too old. It should be *demolished* and built anew.
- This phenyl is enough to *kill* all the little germs in the house.
- His new thinking has *devasted* the logic of all old theories of management.
- Let's not *ruin* the present happy atmosphere by talking of unpleasant history.

CEASE

Synonyms : End, discontinue, halt, pause, stop.

Antonyms : Start, continue, begin, carry on, pursue.

Synonyms

- The proceedings of the committee came to an abrupt *end*.
- After the death of his father, he had to *discontinue* his studies.
- Some miscreants pulled the chain and the train came to a *halt* suddenly.

- As the duke *paused* on his way downstairs, he was at ease and looked like an eagle standing at the edge of a cliff.
- As the bus *stopped* far from its stand, the passengers had to run fast to catch it.

Antonyms

- Now don't *start* crying over spilt milk.
- Let us *continue* our best efforts to achieve the goal leaving the result to god.
- Marry *began* his studies with renewed vigour after his initial failure in the examination.
- Let's *carry on* the work, come what may.
- Pritam Singh has *pursued* the new profession with greater zeal.

CELEBRATED

Synonyms : Notable, distinguished, eminent, illustrious, noted.

Antonyms : Unnoticed, undistinguished, unknown, unnoted, nameless.

Synonyms

- Towards the end of the session, the Prime Minister made a *notable* speech. The press correspondents rushed to him for interview thereafter.

- His son was blessed by the *distinguished* guests after the birthday ceremony.
- Bertrand Russell is an *eminent* prose writer of the modern times.
- Soni has been awarded Ashok Chakra for his *illustrious* services.

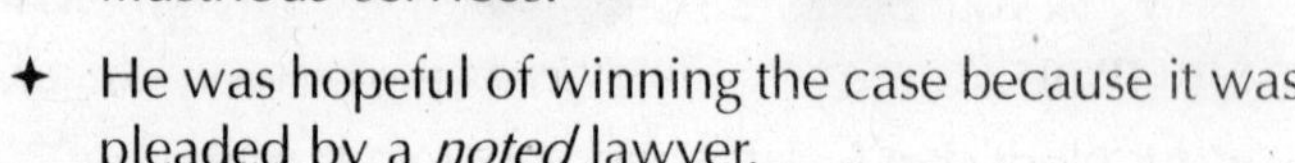

- He was hopeful of winning the case because it was pleaded by a *noted* lawyer.

Antonyms

- His brilliant performance at the meeting went *unnoticed* because the press had a prejudiced view of him.
- He has many literary works to his credit, yet he remains in the category of *undistinguished* writers.
- Most of his literary pieces are still rather *unknown.*
- Hence the press still regards him an *unnoted* literary critic.

CELIBACY

Synonyms : Single, singleness, bachelorhood, virginity, blessed, chastity, maidenhood.

Antonyms : Engagement, wedlock, married state, matrimony, union, nuptial tie.

Synonyms

- He has decided to remain *single* as he feels matrimony will distract him distract him from his work.
- He had decided to get married because now he feels that his *singleness* is too boring.
- Hinduism lays great emphasis on *bachelorhood* of man and *virginity* of woman.
- A yogi believes that he will live in a perpetual state of *blessedness* after his communion with God.
- India has lodged a strong protest against the *chastity* tests of Indian women carried out by the British government at Heathrow Airport before allowing them entry into Britain.

Antonyms

- The *engagement* of Jim with Jane is now almost certain.
- In due course the two will enter into *wedlock*.
- They will be called as being in a *married state*.
- Their *matrimony* is attributed to a chance meeting in a tea party at a common relation's place.

- Their *union* is likely to be very happy as their temperaments match very well.

CENSORSHIP

Synonyms : Disapproval, criticism, blame.

Antonyms : Approval, commendation, appreciation, approbation.

Synonyms

- ✦ The government's *disapproval* of his request for import of machinery has caused him great loss.
- ✦ In a democratic state, *criticism* of the government by opposition parties is allowed to check its arbitrary functioning.
- ✦ He has put all the *blame* for his failure on his predecessors.

Antonyms

- ✦ She knew that the industrial policy of the government will lead to the *approval* of her application for import of the desired machinery.
- ✦ The management has issued a *commendation* note praising the services rendered by the retiring executive.
- ✦ In this way the retiring executive has won the *appreciation* of the management.

CENTRAL

Synonyms : Convenient, accessible, mediate.

Antonyms : Remote, inaccessible, inconvenient.

Synonyms

- ✦ My residence is situated at a *convenient* place.
- ✦ It is *accessible* from all sides of the road.
- ✦ Let us *mediate* a common goal for all of us.

Antonyms

- ✦ I did not have even a *remote* idea that the exhibition of our products will bring such response.
- ✦ Mount Everest is *inaccessible* to most of us even in these days of scientifically aided mountaineering techniques.
- ✦ I am afraid it will be quite *inconvenient* to hold the marriage in our small premises.

CERTAIN

Synonyms : Positive, definite, indisputable, sure, actual, unequivocal, incontestable.

Antonyms : Doubtful, indefinite, disputable, uncertain, ambiguous, equivocal, contestable.

Synonyms

- ✦ His blood report indicates *positive* signs of Malaria.
- ✦ Although he has undergone several body examinations, the doctors have not yet reached a *definite* conclusion about his disease.
- ✦ This piece of land is a part of his *indisputable* property.

- ✦ The minister was *sure* that the proposed legislation will stop the exploitation of the emigrants completely.
- ✦ We have to take into account the *actual* figures only.
- ✦ Deployment of missiles in Europe by America was criticised by India in *unequivocal* terms.
- ✦ Hindu law gives an *incontestable* right to the daughters over the property of their parents.

Antonyms

- ✦ I am *doubtful* about the prospects of any early settlement of dispute between Iran and Iraq.
- ✦ Mahatma Gandhi went on an *indefinite* fast to persuade the people of Noakhali to maintain communal harmony.
- ✦ The wisdom of your complacent attitude on this issue is *disputable*.
- ✦ It is no use undertaking new business projects in the present *uncertain* circumstances.
- ✦ His speech was quite effective but some of his assessments were rather *ambiguous*.

CHANGE

Synonyms : Veer, alter, shift, diversity, modify, convert, transfigure, transform, transmute.

Antonyms : Hold fast, clinch, maintain, fix, sustain, stabilise, stand.

Synonyms

- ✦ He *veered* round to my point of view when I gave him complete facts of the case.

- ✦ I gave my old coat to the tailor to *alter* its inner lining.
- ✦ We will have to *shift* our stand on policy matters if we want to augment the state resources.
- ✦ All the big industrialist have a trend to *diversify* their business.
- ✦ You have to *modify* the sculpture before putting it in the exhibition.

Antonyms

- ✦ I still *hold fast* to my old belief that only non-violent methods can solve our national problems.
- ✦ The two leaders decided to *clinch* the issue by yielding on disputed points.
- ✦ To *maintain* the first position you have to work very hard.

CHAOS

Synonyms : Disorder, confusion, jumble, abyssmal, void.

Antonyms : Order, organisation, government.

Synonyms

- ✦ An accident on the road put the traffic to *disorder.*
- ✦ When you are in a hurry, you make *confusion* worse confounded.
- ✦ He is very quick in making words from *jumbled* letters.
- ✦ He tried to conceal his *abyssmal* ignorance of the subject by side-tracking the issue.

- Negotiators made *void* the disputed clause in the contract, thereby invalidating its provisions.

Antonyms

- Our prime Mminister has the capability to create *order* out of chaos.
- What we need is an efficient *organisation* to look after our economic interests.
- Democracy is defined as a *government* of the people, by the people and for the people.

CHARITY

Synonyms : Kindness, generosity, philanthropy, alms-giving, liberty, benevolence, beneficence, benignity.

Antonyms : Meanness, illiberality, greediness, selfishness.

Synonyms

- The *kindness* and *generosity* of the priest kindled new light in the heart of the culprit.
- The institutions engaged in *philanthropic* activities have been exempted from the new taxes.
- Religious-minded people consider *alms-giving* a sacred act.
- Hinduism gives full *liberty* to worship God in any manner one likes.
- You can witness his *benevolence* when a poor man approaches him for help.
- St. John's attitude as a good teacher is one of *beneficence* to the students.

✦ Malignancy and *benignity* can be tested through response of a person in marginal cases of abnormal growth.

Antonyms

✦ To criticise the activities of a dead person is nothing but *meanness*.

✦ The lukewarm response of the US President to Russian gestures on disarmament is characteristic of his *illiberality*.

✦ Most of the ills in the world are caused by inherent *greediness* of the *selfish* people.

CHASE

Synonyms : Follow, hunt, pursue, track.

Antonyms : Forgo, renounce, withdraw, leave, abandon, forsake (foresake).

Synonyms

✦ All religions teach us to *follow* the principles of non-violence and morality.

✦ He was warned not to *hunt* in the reserved forests or face prosecution.

✦ Inspite of his domestic problems, he has decided to *pursue* his studies.

✦ The criminal ran into the jungles but the police was able to *track* him.

Antonyms

✦ Nita was advised to return to India or *forgo* the property rights for ever.

- The UN advised the warring nations to *renounce* violence and sit round the negotiating table for settlement of their disputes.
- Mohan *withdrew* his resignation upon satisfactory settlement of the pending dues.
- Sohan applied for five years' *leave* to be able to go abroad and try to settle there.
- He *abandoned* the idea of staying in India for ever.

CHEAP

Synonyms : Worthless, inferior, mean, inexpensive, common, paltry.

Antonyms : Worthy, noble, lofty, honourable, eminent, expensive, dear, costly, superior.

Synonyms

- His parents considered salesmanship as a *worthless* career but Atul changed their attitude by showing remarkable success in sales.
- The job of a cobbler is by no means *inferior* to that of a priest.
- He was poor but not *mean*, he had no complexes.
- He always wears *inexpensive* yet sober clothes.

- ✦ She captures in her writings the turbulence of the *common* man.
- ✦ He will never agree to work for such a *paltry* sum.

Antonyms

- ✦ This work is not *worthy* of your qualifications; you have a more superior talent than the one demanded for this job.
- ✦ Sudhir is a *noble* soul, always serene and inspired.
- ✦ He has *lofty* ideals in life.
- ✦ We have to address the members of the jury with the prefix "*Honourable*".
- ✦ B.C. Roy was an *eminent* freedom fighter and politician.

CHEAT

Synonyms : Deceive, swindle, defraud, fleece, hoodwink, hoax, dupe, delude, bilk, gull.

Antonyms : Fair, true, above-board, just.

Synonyms

- ✦ His heart was filled with rancour when he found that his dearest friend had *deceived* him.
- ✦ He is the chief of the famous stock-market racket that *swindled* investors with forged share certificates.
- ✦ Beware of the door-to-door salesmen who *defraud* the housewives by taking advances for the articles which they never deliver.
- ✦ An art collector was *fleeced* of a million rupees by a cheat who sold him counterfeit paintings.

- ✦ The barrister tried to *hoodwink* the jury by confusing the main issue.
- ✦ The television play *hoaxed* viewers into believing an invasion was imminent.
- ✦ The innocent villagers are often *duped* by crooks when they come to the cities.
- ✦ This news is designed to *delude* the public about the true extent of casualties in the army action.

Antonyms

- ✦ This, in a nutshell, is a *fair* assessment of the present situation.
- ✦ I shall be grateful if you give us a *true* picture of the problem.
- ✦ In that case I will offer you my *above-board* opinion.
- ✦ The government tries to be *just* while settling industry labour disputes.

CHECK

Synonyms : Stop, impede, hinder, control, curb, subdue, repress.

Antonyms : Speed, hurry, expedite, accelerate, quicken, hasten, precipitate.

Synonyms

- ✦ They put up all the resistance but could not *stop* the enemy forces from advancing.

- The crowd at the scene of accident *impeded* the arrival of the police.
- Bad weather *hindered* the military operation.
- He was able to *control* his momentary impulse to tell his boss what he thought of him.
- The movement became so overwhelming and unwieldy that the police force could not *curb* it.
- It has become difficult for him to *subdue* his spoiled child.

- The situation has exploded. The government cannot now *repress* the rebellion.

Antonyms

- In large cities, the government fixes a maximum limit on the *speed* of vehicles.
- *Hurry* up! Buy, before the stocks are exhausted.
- You should *expedite* the completion of this book.

- ✦ The driver *accelerated* the speed of the car to catch up with the on-going traffic.

CHEER

Synonyms : Comfort, solace, gladden, exhilarate, enliven, applaud, praise, clap.

Antonyms : Deject, depress, dishearten, sadden, discourage, damp, decry, deprecate, disparage, villify, condemn, condole.

Synonyms

- ✦ Some politicians are more worried about their own *comfort* than about the welfare of the public.
- ✦ The captain did his best to bring *solace* to the wounded and dying soldiers during the battle.
- ✦ He was *gladdened* by the news of his success in the examination.
- ✦ He felt listless until the sea breeze *exhilarated* him and steadied his nerves.
- ✦ The outspoken couple can always be counted on to *enliven* a dull party.
- ✦ The audience rose as one to *applaud* the captain on his victory.
- ✦ He *praised* his friend as being one of the finest human beings he had ever met.
- ✦ The audience *clapped* for five minutes when the film stars appeared on the stage.

Antonyms

- I felt *dejected* on hearing the news of my brother's failure in the examination.
- This *depressed* him for a number of days. I told him not to feel disheartened but work hard from now on.
- The parents *condoled* and wept over the loss of their child.

CHEERFUL

Synonyms : Joyous, blithe, sunny, happy, bright, gay, lively.

Antonyms : Sullen, gloomy, miserable, downcast, sad, woebegone.

Synonyms

- The child felt *joyous* on his success in the examination.
- The *blithe* colours of the painting made the viewers so happy.
- It is always advisable to look at the *sunny* side of life in this era of clouded intentions of jealous nations.
- The children were very *happy*.
- It was a *bright* day.
- Everything looked *gay* and *lively*.

Antonyms

- The father became *sullen* on going through the poor progress report of his only son.

✦ He said to his son: "Instead of looking *gloomy* get ready to work harder next year".

✦ The mother felt *miserable* on her child's indifferent attitude to studies.

CHIEF

Synonyms : Premier, main, leading, supreme, principal, cardinal.

Antonyms : Petty, lesser, minor, inconsiderable, inferior, subsidiary, subordinate, junior.

Synonyms

✦ The *premier's* conduct was exemplary in the handling of a very difficult situation.

✦ Delhi Public School is a *premier* educational institution in Delhi.

✦ Poor attendance at the chapel was his *main* concern.

✦ One of our *leading* atomic scientists was killed in an air crash.

✦ It is an event in which she reigns *supreme*.

✦ A minister can appoint anybody as his *principal* secretary.

✦ Carelessness is the *principal* cause of highway accidents.

✦ The *cardinal* point of our foreign policy is not to join either of the super power blocs.

Antonyms

✦ He is a *petty* officer in a public sector firm.

- ✦ He has *lesser* influence than his brother who is a boss in the same company.
- ✦ Rita is still a *minor*. She cannot open an independent account in the bank.
- ✦ The number of scenes exhibiting him as a dancer was *inconsiderable*.
- ✦ He holds an *inferior* position in the school than a junior teacher.
- ✦ Tooth brush is a *subsidiary* product of Palmolive Ltd.

CHIEF

Synonyms : Leader, head, captain, chieftain, ruler, commander.

Antonyms : Follower, servant, dependent, parasite, minion.

Synonyms

- ✦ The opposition parties have failed to elect a common *leader*.
- ✦ The Indian delegation to Gulf countries was *headed* by the foreign secretary.
- ✦ The *captain* of our Hockey team was injured during the last Olympics.
- ✦ For the tribals, the word of their *chieftain* is as good as law.
- ✦ After the French Revolution, most of the European *rulers* had to honour the wishes of the masses.
- ✦ The *commander* loved to narrate the story of his adventurous life to the soldiers.

Antonyms

- I was a staunch *follower* of Jawaharlal Nehru.
- Our boss has started treating some of us as his domestic *servants.*
- He thinks we are *dependent* on him for our livelihood.
- Jack behaves as if he were a *parasite* of the boss.

CHILL

Synonyms : Coldness, chilliness, shivering, frost, shake.

Antonyms : Warmth, fire, flame, glow, bonfire, fervour.

Synonyms

- Mountain climbers should make due preparations to stand the *coldness* of the peaks they wish to scale.
- *Chilliness* is the first symptom of malaria.
- The poor boy was wearing only a shirt in the *shivering* cold and chilly winds.
- It is amusing to see the windows turning *frosty* at hill stations.
- I will like to have a milk *shake,* please.

Antonyms

- The *warmth* of his welcome pleased me.
- Light a *fire* in the centre of the room to make its cold tolerable.

- The new gas cooker has a strong blue *flame.*
- Her colour *glows* red in the morning sunshine.
- We made a *bonfire* of the waste material.
- Rajiv Gandhi displayed a strong patriotic *fervour* like Jawaharlal Nehru.

CHOICE

Synonyms : Selection, option, alternative, preference, adoption.

Antonyms : Refusal, denial, rejection, cancellation.

Synonyms

- His *selection* of the art pieces is marvellous.
- He has given his *option* for his pension being calculated under new rules.
- He had no *alternative* to accepting the invitation.
- He has become so materialistic that he gives *preference* to money over his friends.
- *Adoption* of an orphan child by him was greatly resented by his relatives.

Antonyms

- His *refusal* to accept knighthood from the British government made him world famous.
- The thief's *denial* of the theft in the court greatly upset the public prosecutor.
- *Rejection* by the party high command of his candidature for membership of the Parliament made him defect to the other party.

✦ The *cancellation* of his tour programme abroad depressed him.

CHOKE

Synonyms : Strangle, suffocate, smother, stifle, throttle.

Antonyms : Oxygenate, freshen, ventilate, air.

Synonyms

✦ She was *strangled* to death by the dacoits.

✦ The atmosphere of the room was so *suffocating* that I could not stay there for over a minute.

✦ The caravan was *smothered* in dust while passing through Rajasthan.

✦ The heat in Kolkata was *stifling.*

✦ The angry woman *throttled* her daughter-in-law to death.

Antonyms

✦ The patient was first *oxygenated,* then put on glucose.

✦ Campa Cola is an effective *freshener.*

✦ This house is OK, except for its *ventilation.*

✦ We need fresh *air* to keep healthy.

CHOOSE

Synonyms : Select, prefer, pick, elect, cull.

Antonyms : Reject, discard, renounce, spurn, disapprove.

Synonyms

- She was so confused to see the large variety of sarees that she could not *select* one for herself.
- Chandrashekher Azad *preferred* death to yielding to the Britishers.
- The beginning of the trial had to be delayed owing to difficulty in *picking* the right kind of jurors.
- The high school hockey team *elected* John as the captain.
- A sheep breeder *culls* the weak animals from his flock.
- A housewife in a supermarket, confronted by several tins of tomato of identical size and quality, often *picks* the one nearest to her.

Antonyms

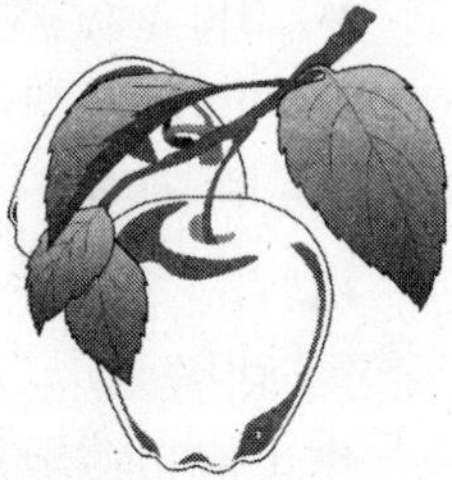

- I *rejected* the over-ripe apples but bought the rest.
- I have *discarded* the old furniture, so I need a new set.
- The old bachelor has *renounced* this world and gone to the Himalayas for meditation.
- I am a democrat but *spurn* the overcrowded and underfed poor.
- He has *disapproved* the purchase of this building.

CIRCULATE

Synonyms : Propagate, spread, advertise, publish, diffuse, disseminate.

Antonyms : Quieten, silence, hush, repress.

Synonyms

- ✦ Some politicians even today *propagate* the concept of racial superiority for their dubious ends.
- ✦ Ideas *spread* more rapidly in the present age of instant communications.
- ✦ Only big companies can afford to *advertise* their products through the television.
- ✦ The editors have formed a guild to *publish* a new magazine.
- ✦ The *diffused* light of the candles on every table lent a pleasant intimate air to the restaurant.
- ✦ In recent times, it was Gandhi who *disseminated* the gospel of truth and non-violence.

Antonyms

- ✦ Calmpose tablets will *quieten* the patient and let him sleep.

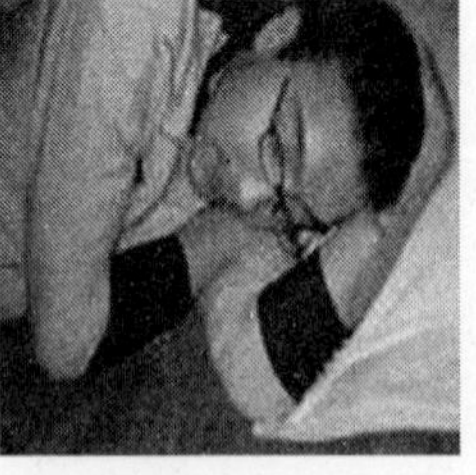

- ✦ There was complete *silence* in the room after Satish left the meeting abruptly.
- ✦ The police have *hushed* the murder case to avoid damage to their reputation.

- ✦ Any control on news media will only *repress* the anti-government circles.

CLAIM

Synonyms : Maintain, require, assume, challenge, demand.

Antonyms : Waive, drop, forgo, yield, renounce.

Synonyms

- ✦ I will need more vacation to *maintain* the lodge any longer.
- ✦ The law *requires* him to pay heavier taxes.
- ✦ Bureaucrats have, of late, *assumed* greater importance in the governance of the country.
- ✦ For its smooth functioning, the society *demands* your sincere compliance of all norms.

Antonyms

- ✦ The umpire *waived* the rule to help the weaker side to maintain its resistance.
- ✦ The crane *drops* the cargo on the truck after picking it up from the seaplane.
- ✦ We can *forgo* many small privileges in order to enjoy the main ones.
- ✦ At long last, the American forces *yielded* to Vietnamese pressure and withdrew.

CLASS

Synonyms : Group, rank, distribute, dispose, classify, arrange.

Antonyms : Disarrange, display, upset, disorder, confuse, derange.

Synonyms

- ✦ The soldiers were *grouped* according to their rank and ordered to march.
- ✦ He *ranked* first in the University examination.
- ✦ The teacher *distributed* the copies of notes among the students and asked them to work hard for the ensuing examinations.
- ✦ He is the sole owner of his property and can *dispose* it off in any manner he likes.
- ✦ He sorted out the books and *classified* them as per the international system.
- ✦ He was busy *arranging* his vast library subject-wise and authorwise.

Antonyms

- ✦ The children *disarranged* his books in heaps when he was away.
- ✦ We found the books *displayed* haphazardly at the counter.

- ✦ We had to *upset* our drawing room to accommodate more guests.
- ✦ The furniture is now lying in *disorder*.

- Let us not *confuse* the main issue by sidetracking the discussion on minor issues.
- The divorce has led to *derangement* of his mental make-up.

CLEAN

Synonyms : Purify, clarify, cleanse.

Antonyms : Corrupt, infect, defile, soil, pollute, taint.

Synonyms

- Hindus believe that fasting *purifies* the heart.
- The lawyer tried to *clarify* the issue further but the judge refused to listen to him any more.
- The doctor *cleansed* the wound of the injured patient and dressed it.

Antonyms

- Marx felt that religion always *corrupted* society by its fundamental belief in fate and God.
- The dog's bite has *infected* the body of the boy. Hence he should be immediately vaccinated.
- The western movies of crime, horror, sex and violence *defile* the character of the youth.
- He has *soiled* the image of his family by acting this way.

CLEAR

Synonyms : Definite, distinct, unmistakable, explicit.

Antonyms : Blurred, confused, doubtful, foggy, vague, unintelligible.

Synonyms

- Your stay in the hostel seems to have brought a *definite* change for the better.
- There is a *distinct* improvement in your manners and all-round demeanour.
- There is an *unmistakable* boost in your personality.
- Will you make this explanation of your theory more *explicit* ?

Antonyms

- The politician could give only *blurred* impressions of his visit to Algeria.
- We should not make a final decision on this important subject in the present *confused* situation in the trade.
- You are yourself *doubtful* whether to make this decision today or defer it to a future date.
- The weather is quite *foggy* today. We should avoid driving the scooter.
- The doctor's diagnosis is rather *vague*. Further examination by a more qualified doctor is necessary.

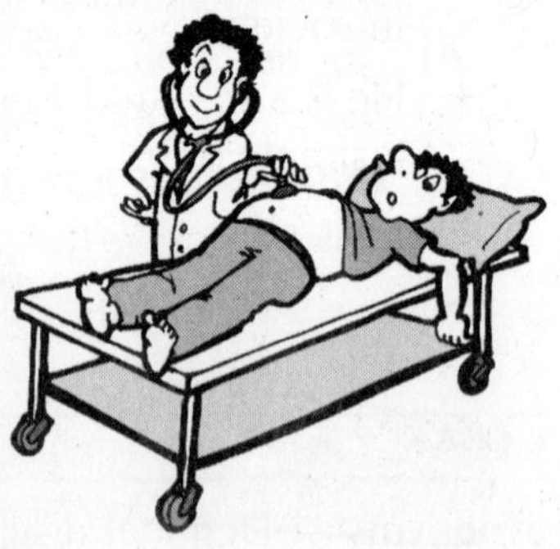

CLEVER

Synonyms : Talented, gifted, capable, smart, dexterous, natural, Sharp.

Antonyms : Foolish, dull, doltish, incapable, insensate, stupid.

Synonyms

- ✦ He is a very *talented* actor, he can even stage and direct plays.
- ✦ God has *gifted* him with a sharp sense, poet's sensibility and verbal acumen.
- ✦ The company pays him so well because he is *capable* of doing many odd jobs.
- ✦ Sportsmen are always active and *smart.*
- ✦ A surgeon should be manually *dexterous.*
- ✦ I cannot help praising his *natural* awareness of social niceties.

Antonyms

- ✦ His *foolish* activities have brought him disrepute in society.
- ✦ He is a *dull* student and takes a long time to grasp a simple point.

- He is too *doltish* to grasp wit and humour.
- He is *incapable* of performing intricate jobs.
- He is thick-skinned and *insensate*.
- Call him *stupid* if you like.

CLING

Synonyms : Attach, adhere, stick, cleave, together, embrace, hold, hug.

Antonyms : Surrender, give up, forgo, relinquish, resign, cede.

Synonyms

- A door is *attached* to the doorpost by hinges.
- He always *adheres* to his principles.
- This tape won't *adhere* to a slick surface.
- He *sticks* doggedly at his physics homework until midnight.
- A Hindu considers it his duty to *cleave* to his marriage partner through thick and thin.
- Religion has a force which can *hold* the masses *together* for long.
- They turned to *hug* each other as soon as they were in a secluded corner of the park.
- This thesis *embraces* the major ideas you suggested.
- You seem to *hug* at all the facts, old and new.

Antonyms

- ✦ After long discussion I *surrendered* to his way of thinking.
- ✦ I *gave up* the hope of winning her over.
- ✦ I cannot *forgo* my respect for matrimony.
- ✦ I *relinquished* the charge of my old post the other day.
- ✦ I *resigned* from the old post last month.
- ✦ Israel has *ceded* west bank of the canal to the Palestinians.

CLOUDY

Synonyms : Gloomy, dark, dim, murky, foggy, overcast.

Antonyms : Sunny, undimmed, unclouded, clear, bright, cloudless.

Synonyms

- ✦ His *gloomy* comments on the trouble they would face in customs clearance upset me very much.
- ✦ *Dark* shadows loomed out of the steam and acrid fumes.
- ✦ The room was veiled with *dim* light of the candles.
- ✦ The body was fished out of the *murky* water of the pond.
- ✦ I haven't the *foggiest* notion of what you are talking.
- ✦ The sky was *overcast* with clouds when the bomb blasted.

Antonyms

- *Sunny* weather is welcome after so many days of dark clouds.
- The *undimmed* rays of the sun fall on the eastern wing of our house every morning.
- The hearty discussion between us has *unclouded* the controversial points.
- We have already *cleared* the problematic issues.
- The sun is too *bright* to be welcome in this hot summer.
- The weather is *cloudless* after many days of heavy rains.

CLUTCH

Synonyms : Grip, seize, catch, grab, grasp.

Antonyms : Release, liberate, emancipate.

Synonyms

- A strong administration is one that can have a *grip* of the circumstances and tackle each problem on merit.
- The wise *seize* the opportunity of accomplishment at the right moment.
- The fieldsman *caught* the ball in both hands after the batsman hit it upwards.
- A wiseman will always *grab* the opportunity.
- You have keep your *grasp* tight so that it does not slip from your hands.

Antonyms

- The government *released* all the political prisoners on Independence Day.
- The government has ordered all agricultural landlords to *liberate* the bonded labour from compulsory work.
- This has led to the *emancipation* of the bonded labour who now have wider opportunities of work of their choice.

COARSE

Synonyms : Unpolished, harsh, unrefined, rude, gross, indelicate.

Antonyms : Polished, polite, elegant, refined, civilised, genteel.

Synonyms

- *Unpolished* surfaces do not reflect light.
- He is very *harsh* in dealing with his subordinates.
- His popularity among his friends has reduced because of his *unrefined* manners.
- The teacher has condoned the student for his *rude* behaviour.
- We were shocked at his *gross* ignorance of the subject under discussion.

Antonyms

- His *polished* manners win him new friends.
- His *polite* behaviour is responsible for his success with subordinates.

✦ He looks *elegant* in his new suit.

✦ She is well *civilised*, has *refined* tastes and *genteel* outlook.

CLOD

Synonyms : Chilled, chilly, cool, frigid, frosty, icy.

Antonyms : Hot, passionate, balmy, warm.

Synonyms

✦ *Chilled* Campa Cola gives great refreshment in the summer.

✦ With the onset of winter the weather has become somewhat *chilly*.

✦ Let us discuss this subject in a *cooler* atmosphere.

✦ He is a *frigid* person.

Antonyms

✦ It is very *hot* today. The day's temperature has touched 40^0C.

✦ The boss has taken a *passionate* attitude towards the young girl.

✦ The couple went out for a walk in the *balmy* weather.

COMBAT

Synonyms : War, battle, action, contest, conflict, broil.

Antonyms : Harmony, peace, concord, amity, agreement, quiet.

Synonyms

- Everything is fair in love and *war.*
- Many historical *battles* have been fought at Panipat.
- The army *action* in Bangladesh was praised by all.
- It is little use *contesting* the election as an independent condidate.
- The policies they are following will surely bring them in *conflict* with each other.
- The travellers were *broiling* in the sun as they crossed the desert.

Antonyms

- Communal *harmony* is the first condition to keep India strong and united.
- It is also a must for *peace* within.
- India and Pakistan must reach a *concord* to avoid disturbances in the Indian subcontinent.
- They should develop *amity* among the people of the two countries.
- They have to work out an *agreement* on disputes of various types.

COMFORT

Synonyms : Comfort, ease, rest, leisure, relaxation, repose, relief.

Antonyms : Unrest, restlessness, agitation, nervousness.

Synonyms

- The electrification of the village gave great *comfort* to the villagers.

- The rules of the game were *eased* out for the children.
- The old patient needs complete *rest*.
- Modern life leaves little scope for *leisure*.
- All were in a mood of *relaxation*.

Antonyms

- There is *unrest* in most of the underdeveloped countries. 
- *Restlessness* is a regular feature of the modern youth in all big cities.
- National trade unions have ordered an *agitation* in all coal mines until settlement of new wage rates in the UK.
- *Nervousness* is a common disease among the unemployed youth.

COMFORTABLE

Synonyms : Agreeable, cosy, pleasing, convenient, pleasant.

Antonyms : Irritating, disagreeable, displeasing, aggravating, distressed, disturbed.

Synonyms

- All the saints *agree* that the goal of life prescribed by different religions is the same although the paths to achieve it may differ.

- This restaurant has a very *cosy* atmosphere because of its comfortable furniture, mild air-conditioning, delicious food and soothing music 
- The salesman had a *pleasing* personality which could convince the customers easily.
- Kindly make it *convenient* to attend the meeting.
- The diffused light of the candles lent a *pleasant* aura to the rooms.

Antonyms

- The atmosphere in this factory is rather *irritating* because of bad smell, smoke, noise and dirt.
- All this gives a *disagreeable* nausea to my senses.
- The speech of the general manager about the conditions of the factory workers was *displeasing* to the managing committee.
- Presently *aggravating* tension on nuclear disarmament can be checked only by an understanding among the super powers.

COMMAND

Synonyms : Commandment, order, directive, mandate, rule, behest, decree, direct.

Antonyms : Comply, submit, obey.

Synonyms

✦ Every Muslim considers it his sacred duty to follow the *commandments* of the Holy Quran.

✦ The boss *orders* and the subordinate obeys.

✦ In view of the new *directive* issued by the government, our co-operative society will have to amend its bye-laws.

✦ The *mandate* given by the masses through 'Vote' is the main characteristic of democracy.

✦ He did not present himself before the court, therefore, the court has passed ex-parte *decree* against him.

✦ The Supreme Court is empowered to *direct* the High Courts on any substantive matter of law.

Antonyms

✦ The teacher asked the students to *comply* with the regulations pertaining to the examination.

✦ I have *submitted* my income-tax returns for the current year.

- ✦ As sportsmen we should strictly *obey* the rules of the game.

COMMON

Synonyms : Usual, frequent, ordinary, familiar, vulgar, mean, trite, hackneyed, low.

Antonyms : Unusual, infrequent, extraordinary, exceptional, unfamiliar, choice, refined, cultured, polished, genteel.

Synonyms

- ✦ Father has gone out for his *usual* evening walk.
- ✦ The patient was *frequented* by malaria every year.
- ✦ We travelled in an *ordinary* compartment.
- ✦ It is nice to be back in the old *familiar* room.
- ✦ His *vulgar* table manners shocked all the guests.
- ✦ He is so *mean* that he never helps the poor.
- ✦ This is a story written beautifully but concerned with the *trite* theme of adolescent loneliness.
- ✦ I don't like the *hackneyed* jargon of movie-romance magazines.
- ✦ His *low* position in the society was exploited by his neighbour.

Antonyms

- ✦ It is *unusual* of the director to visit the factory without prior notice.

- The director's visits to our establishment are *infrequent.*
- The *extraordinary* meeting of the Non-aligned members was held in New York to press for an early freedom of Namibia.
- There are many topics in our syllabus which need *exceptional* treatment.
- These premises are *unfamiliar* to our pet dog.
- Zimbabwe was the unanimous *choice* of the Non-aligned members for the summit in 1986.
- Nescafe is one of the *refined* brands of Indian coffee.

COMPANION

Synonyms : Friend, colleague, pal, shadow, accomplice, associate, comrade.

Antonyms : Enemy, rival, partisan, unsportsmanlike.

Synonyms

- Jonathan, a close *friend* of mine, stands by me in thick and thin.
- One of my *colleagues* is very kind-hearted and helps everyone.
- I have made many pen-*pals* through the Science Master Monthly.
- In Hindu religion the wife is considered to be a *shadow* of her husband.

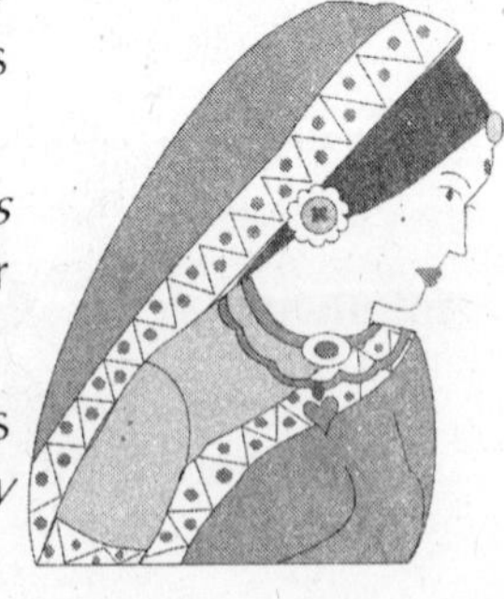

- ✦ The elder man planned the crime, the younger one acted as his *accomplice.*
- ✦ These two men are business *associates.*

Antonyms

- ✦ Jill and Sam are staunch *enemies* of each other.
- ✦ They are *rivals* in studies and sports.
- ✦ They always carry *partisan* attitude against each other.
- ✦ Hence, they are considered to be *unsportsmanlike* by the students and teachers.

COMPANY

Synonyms : Troupe, collection, crowd, assemblage, group, gathering, firm, assembly, gang, conclave, house.

Antonyms : Individual, isolated, alone, single.

Synonyms

- ✦ This dance *troupe* is setting out on a world tour very shortly.

- Have you seen my stamp *collection*?
- Rotary Club is a *collection* of educated and kind hearted persons who occasionally organise charitable programmes for the poor.
- The angry *crowd* raised slogans against the leader because he did not keep his word of honour on an important issue.
- There was an *assemblage* of workers at Boat Club who were on strike.
- The *group* leaders elected by the students have given a representation to the vice chancellor.
- There was a large *gathering* of villagers at the cattle show.
- A large number of stores were purchased by a new *firm.*
- All the ministers gathered in the *Assembly* Hall after the question hour.
- A *gang* of dacoits looted the whole village.
- The *conclave* of opposition leaders will meet at Bangalore next month.

Antonyms

- The Indian constitution provides numerous freedoms to the *individual.*
- These freedoms are part of the fundamental rights but not *isolated* from the directive principles.
- The freedoms are not *alone*; they are accompanied by fundamental duties of citizens.
- My uncle is *single,* i.e., he is not married.

COMPARISON

Synonyms : Similitude, illustration, simile.

Antonyms : Difference, contrariety, contrast.

Synonyms

- ✦ His poetry is full of *similitudes* and makes very interesting reading.
- ✦ He threw in two humorous anecdotes as *illustrations* of his main point.
- ✦ He was so brave that in his biography the writers refer to the lion as a *simile* to describe his bravery.

Antonyms

- ✦ There is a world of *difference* between this printing machine and the one fitted at Okhla.
- ✦ The two machines are opposite in their costs and functioning and are characterised by *contrariety* in many ways.

✦ One is letter press. It prints composed matter. The other is an offset press. It prints off prints of sheets already made-up. They are thus *contrast* to each other.

COMPASSION

Synonyms : Kindness, tenderness, mercy, sympathy, condolence.

Antonyms : Cruelty, malignity, barbarity, savagery.

Synonyms

✦ Impressed by the *kindness* of the priest, the thief became his follower.

✦ She was nursed back to health with *tenderness* and loving care.

✦ He shows no *mercy* towards his horse and flays it with baton continually.

✦ The boss had no *sympathy* for his subordinates and always illtreated them.

✦ The boss expressed his sorrow but pointed out his inability to attend the *condolence* gathering.

Antonyms

✦ Highly prosperous himself, his attitude to the poor shows his basic selfishness and *cruelty*.

✦ The great boss shows *malignity* towards those subordinates who come late to office.

✦ Although known for his civilised manners in his high circle, he often shows acute *barbarity* to his low-paid workers.

✦ The beginning of the Industrial Revolution in England showed an attitude of *savagery* of the barons to the working classes.

COMPEL

Synonyms : Bind, coerce, drive, oblige, force, constrain, necessitate.

Antonyms : Acquit, induce, allure.

Synonyms

✦ Our government has done well to amend the constitution to *bind* citizens to fundamental duties while they enjoy fundamental rights.

✦ There is found an element of *coercion* in establishing state authority in every country.

✦ Let me *drive* home in your mind that the time and date scheduled for the meeting of the shareholders on Friday cannot be altered.

✦ They *obliged* us with a gift each.

✦ The team was driven by a *force* unseen.

Antonyms

✦ The court *acquitted* the accused of all charges after examining the evidence.

✦ Instead of compelling the people to family planning it is desirable to *induce* them to it through proper media like the radio and TV.

- ✦ Family planning can be presented in such a way that the couples at large are *allured* by it in their own interests.

COMPOSE

Synonyms : Write, pacify, form, calm, allay.

Antonyms : Excite, irritate, criticise, dissect.

Synonyms

- ✦ The poet *wrote* most of his poems sitting in a garden.
- ✦ His poetry was meant to *pacify* the aggrieved lovers.
- ✦ He *formed* images of love and romance better amidst the natural surroundings than in the air-conditioned room of his villa.

Antonyms

- ✦ Marx's writings greatly *excited* the workers to revolt against the capitalists.
- ✦ Don't *irritate* me by repeating your heresay.
- ✦ Let us *criticise* the government in a constructive way, i.e., by making suggestions.

COMPRESS

Synonyms : Abridge, contract, crowd, compact, condense.

Antonyms : Diffuse, dilate, expand.

Synonyms

- ✦ The edition is highly *abridged*.
- ✦ Better *compress* your ideas in a page or two and leave them with me for consideration.

- We *contract* many diseases from the foul environment of the industrialised cities.
- *Crowded* cities are a menace to nature.

Antonyms

- We can *diffuse* the negative aspects of elections by educating the voters with more constructive campaigning.
- Her eyes *dilated* with fear.
- Let us *expand* this paragraph into an essay.

CONCEAL

Synonyms : Suppress, screen, disguise, hide.

Antonyms : Expose, confess, avow, manifest.

Synonyms

- Every individual has good and bad points. The one who can *suppress* the bad points and bring out the good ones becomes great.
- Dark glasses *screened* his eyes from the sun.
- The actor has to *disguise* himself to live the character he plays.
- He had to *hide* behind the tree.

Antonyms

- It is always better to avoid *exposing* one's bad thoughts in public.
- Let us *confess* our faults before God.
- He *avowed* his responsibility for the failure of the project.

CONCORD

Synonyms : Unity, peace, amity, accord.

Antonyms : Animosity, variance, discord, disagreement.

Synonyms

- ✦ People showed an immense sense of *unity* at the meeting.
- ✦ There was an implied atmosphere of *peace* at the inter religious conference held in Allahabad.
- ✦ Indo-USSR *amity* has become a world known fact.

Antonyms

- ✦ He felt no *animosity* towards his critics.
- ✦ There was *variance* of views on some issues at the India-Lanka meet in New Delhi.
- ✦ US-USSR *discord* on disarmament proposals can lead to serious consequences for the whole world.

CONCRETE

Synonyms : Consolidated, compact, firm.

Antonyms : Loose, shifting, sloppy, boggy.

Synonyms

- ✦ There is immense need for *consolidating* all races into one human race irrespective of colour, creed or religious affiliation.
- ✦ The Indian nation is a *compact* of numerous races, religions, regions and tribes.
- ✦ Ashoka had *firm* ideas on the goodness of soul and non violence in human affairs.

Antonyms

- The Janata Party is a *loose* combination of politicians with divergent views.
- Lok Sabha has passed the Anti-defection law to stop *shifting* loyalties of politicians.
- His *sloppy* members surprise me.

CONFESS

Synonyms : Acknowledge, reveal, own, aver.

Antonyms : Deny, suppress, disavow.

Synonyms

- It is good to *acknowledge* one's weaknesses before indulging in self-praise.
- The working of the economy has *revealed* many weaknesses in the basic economic policies of the country.
- There is nothing wrong in *owning* one's faults. Self-analysis is good for self-development.

Antonyms

- One who *denies* his imperfections is telling a lie; suppress your evil-self, if you want to develop good-self.
- They were guilty of *supressing* the facts.
- Nobody can *disavow* responsibility for the consequences of bad actions.

CONFINE

Synonyms : Bind, narrow, impute, immune, bound, limit.

Antonyms : Extend, expand, loosen, widen, dilate.

Synonyms

- I am *bound* by the limits of my little knowledge.
- *Narrow* thinking never makes a great man.
- Let us not *impute* bad intentions to others and good ones to self.
- We mortals cannot be *immune* to disease and death.

Antonyms

- It is wise to *extend* the frontiers of knowledge as far as possible.
- Metals *expand* on heating.
- This knot needs to be *loosened* with a pin.
- *Widen* the mind's horizon if you want to be a poet.

CONFIRM

Synonyms : Fix, prove, strengthen, settle.

Antonyms : Cancel, upset, refute, repeal, shake.

Synonyms

- The firm has yet to calculate its cost to *fix* the price of this product.
- Proper evidence is called for to *prove* the authenticity of this statement.
- This will *strengthen* our stand.
- One can *settle* the accuracy of this remark without any fuss.

Antonyms

- Our arguments certainly *cancel* the logic propounded in this historical theory.
- I am *upset* due to my son's behaviour.
- The law relating to the Privy purses was *repealed* long back.
- The disturbances in some states in India have *shaken* my faith in the concept of the 'open state'.

CONQUEST

Synonyms : Overthrow, victory, triumph.

Antonyms : Forfeiture, surrender, retreat, defeat.

Synonyms

- In recent decades, monarchies have been *over thrown* in many countries.
- Socialist democracies have won *victories* in many states.
- Democracy has *triumphed* over political dictatorship in most countries, although military dictatorships persist in some states.

Antonyms

- In communist countries, there has followed the *forfeiture* of private properties by the state.
- Many imperialist regimes have *surrendered* to the popular movements of independent countries.
- Military occupation of foreign powers has been compelled to *retreat*.

CONSCIENTIOUS

Synonyms : Uncorrupt, principled, faithful, straightforward, honourable.

Antonyms : Corrupt, profligate, wicked, vile.

Synonyms

- It is difficult to find an *uncorrupt* politician in any country where there is no limit on the owning of private property.
- Money cannot deter a *principled* man from his path.
- The students must be *faithful* to their teacher.
- He is quite *straightforward* and calls a spade without fear or favour.
- The prizes were distributed by the *honourable* chief minister at our school function.

Antonyms

- A number of *corrupt* officials have been dismissed from our Ministry recently.
- They were charged of *profligate* activities connected with selling confidential information to foreigners.

- The *wicked* persons could not conceal their evil designs for long.

✦ Their *vile* habits gave way to the security of their service.

CONSIDERABLE

Synonyms : Thoughtful, attentive, heedful, circumspect, kind.

Antonyms : Thoughtless, inattentive, heedless, negligent, unconcerned.

Synonyms

✦ She is *thoughtful* of her friends.

✦ The teacher asked him to be *attentive* in the class.

✦ The driver was *heedful* but the brakes of his vehicle failed and he met with an accident.

✦ The *circumspect* investor put his money in blue-chip stocks.

✦ The rich should be *kind* to the poor.

Antonyms

✦ For a moment he became *thoughtless* of the consequences.

✦ Ramesh is never *inattentive* in his class. No wonder he secures good marks in his examination.

✦ On the other hand, Satish is *heedless* of lessons taught and is rather low in results.

- Ahmed is equally *negligent* in his studies and hence he keeps failing in the exam.
- Their teacher is *unconcerned* with the individual progress of his students. He cares only for those who work hard.

CONSIDERATE

Synonyms : Attentive, careful, reflective, tactful, helpful, thoughtful, unselfish.

Antonyms : Rude, heedless, negligent.

Synonyms

- The students listened to the speech of the Principal *attentively.*
- The Principal advised the students to be *careful* against mixing of politics with education.
- Mita's objection made him *reflective.*
- He advised the teacher to be *tactful* in guiding the students in this matter.

Antonyms

- The manner of his conversation with the boss was rather *rude,* which led to the rejection of his demand for promotion.
- When an institution is *heedless* to the genuine demands of its staff, its standard of teaching is bound to dwindle.
- The teachers became *negligent* of their duties and concentrated on the agitation for better salaries.

CONSTANT

Synonyms : Steady, firm, unswerving, steadfast.

Antonyms : Unsteady, flexible, variable, inconsonant, unreliable, unstable, fickle.

Synonyms

- Slow and *steady* wins the race is a well known maxim.
- India takes a *firm* stand on international issues.
- The crew had *unswerving* faith in the captain.
- The *steadfast* attitude of Muslims has made the Muslim law static.

Antonyms

- He is so *unsteady* in his career. He keeps changing jobs every six months.
- He is *flexible*. He draws deep every influence that comes his way.
- His is a *variable* temperament. He therefore keeps changing his attitude with the environment.
- He is so *inconstant* in his objectives, he has to change his policy frequently.

CONTEMPTIBLE

Synonyms : Despicable, vile, pitiful, detestable, execrable, paltry.

Antonyms : Respectable, admirable, excellent, weighty, grave, important.

Synonyms

- The attitude of some high-caste members towards the scheduled castes is still *despicable* and should be condemned by all sane people.
- The *vile* attitude of some rich snobs is still responsible for class divisions in society.
- The snobs in society look down at the poor with *pitiful* attitude.

Antonyms

- India has earned a *respectable* position among comity of nations after independence by her support to freedom movements in Asia and Africa.
- The role played by Jawaharlal Nehru and his daughter, Mrs. Indira Gandhi in this behalf is *admirable*.
- The Indian team played *excellent* cricket in the last international match.

CONSUMPTION

Synonyms : Extinction, decline, waste, destruction, expenditure, dissipation.

Antonyms : Preservation, increase, gain, income, accumulation, addition.

Synonyms

- The government has taken several steps to protect the species of animals facing *extinction*.

- The number of lions in India is on the *decline* these years.
- The enemy laid *waste* a number of villages before they retreated.
- The typhoon caused great *destruction* in Manila last year.
- Although his income has increased considerably, his *expenditure* still exceeds his income.
- He *dissipates* his energies in productive works. That is why he remains short of funds.

Antonyms

- *Preservation* is the first law of a healthy life.
- There has been a tremendous *increase* in the production of food grains during the last decade.
- There is a phenomenal *gain* in the national produce this year.
- My *income* has increased more than my expenditure in recent years.
- Hence I have *accumulated* some savings.

CONTENTED

Synonyms : Satisfied, gratified, pleased, content.

Antonyms : Discontent, frustrated, miserable, malcontent.

Synonyms

- John is *satisfied* with the progress of his son.

- ✦ Mr. Samson was *gratified* to know that his son had secured a top position in the higher secondary examination.
- ✦ I was *pleased* with the sincere attitude of my employee and gave him an increment.
- ✦ Rohit is a *content* person.

Antonyms

- ✦ There is general *discontent* among salaried classes owing to galloping inflation in the economy.
- ✦ Deepak felt *frustrated* with his routine work and resigned to take up a more creative job.
- ✦ I feel *miserable* when I look at the way slum-dwellers live.

CONVEY

Synonyms : Transmit, transport, carry, bear, take, transfer.

Antonyms : Stow, house, drop, fetch.

Synonyms

- ✦ Radio and TV organisations *transmit* lot of entertainment programmes round the world.
- ✦ Modern *transport* comprises of motor cars, buses, aeroplanes and jets.
- ✦ Modern transport and communications enable cables and letters to be *carried* instantly to distant places round the world.
- ✦ He had to *bear* the expenses.
- ✦ There was no one to *take* the responsibility.

Antonyms

- The exporters nowadays *stow* their products to ensure accurate delivery to importers.
- Nowadays there are big ware *houses* where food grains are kept safe and sound.
- The aeroplanes are used to *drop* food and medicine to people in flooded areas.

CONVICT

Synonyms : Condemn, sentence.

Antonyms : Discharge, acquit.

Synonyms

- The spy was *condemned* to long imprisonment by the court.
- The thief was *sentenced* to one year's rigorous imprisonment.

Antonyms

- The corrupt official was *discharged* from service.
- The accused was *acquitted* by the judge as the prosecution failed to produce adequate evidence against him.

CONTROVERSY

Synonyms : Dispute, argument, contention, bickering, debate.

Antonyms : Agreement, compromise, accord, unanimity.

Synonyms

- The judge advised the parties to settle their *dispute* mutually.

- ✦ He tried to win the case by furnishing ingenious *arguments.*
- ✦ The lawyer failed to produce any witness to prove his *contention.*
- ✦ He is a miser and starts *bickering* if he has to spend even a meagre amount on an avoidable item.
- ✦ He was awarded the first prize in the college *debate* competition.

Antonyms

- ✦ India and Yugoslavia have signed a new bilateral *agreement* to expand their trade.
- ✦ The disputing parties came to a *compromise* owing to the mediation of a well-wisher.
- ✦ Opposition parties have reached an *accord* on the nomination of candidates for membership of the legislative assembly.
- ✦ There was *unanimity* of opinion on the basic issues among the participants.

CONVENIENT

Synonyms : Suitable, comfortable, adapted, handy, advantageous.

Antonyms : Untoward, inconvenient, cumbersome.

Synonyms

- He was not considered *suitable* for the job of an engineer.
- The journey by air is fast as well as *comfortable.*
- He has *adapted* himself to the environment of his new job.
- The students must always keep a dictionary *handy* with them.
- Being on the hill top, our soldiers were in an *advantageous* position as compared to the enemy.

Antonyms

- His *untoward* remark caused an uproar.
- This house is too *inconvenient* for my living.
- The procedure adopted by the committee for distribution of essential commodities is still *cumbersome.*

COOPERATE

Synonyms : Work together, abet, concur.

Antonyms : Oppose, counteract, rival, thwart, feel jealous.

Synonyms

- Mohan and Sohan *work together,* both in studies and sports.

- ✦ They *abet* each other to perform better in both class tests and sports events.
- ✦ Their methods of work are identical and they *concur* on most of the ideas and proposals of work.

Antonyms

- ✦ Rahul and Atul are classmates in the college but they are *opposed* to each other on most of the important issues.
- ✦ They behave as *rivals* in and outside the class.
- ✦ They are always bent upon *thwarting* each other's progress.

CORDIAL

Synonyms : Hearty, sincere, warm, earnest.

Antonyms : Formal, distant, ceremonious, cold.

Synonyms

- ✦ Ramesh and Sumesh are classmates and close friends. They are both *hearty* and *sincere* to each other.
- ✦ Their friendship is quite *warm;* they help each other in and outside the class.

- ✦ They are *earnest* in their endeavour to perform better and better.

Antonyms

- ✦ Anil and Atul are also classmates. But they are *formal* in their attitude to each other.
- ✦ Their friendship is rather *cold* and *distant.*
- ✦ Their personal relations are *ceremonious.*

CORRUPT

Synonyms : Pollute, impair, spoil, infected, putrefy, defile, decayed, vitiated.

Antonyms : Cleanse, purify, repair, mend, pure, undefiled, uncorrupt, uninfected.

Synonyms

- ✦ Insincere friends *pollute* the word 'friendship'.
- ✦ Their relationship is *impaired* and *spoiled* at one stage or the other. They tell lies to each other and thus *putrefy* their minds. It may *defile* their character.
- ✦ Ganguly's inclusion *spoiled* the game.
- ✦ Do not use *infected* needles while injecting a patient.

Antonyms

- ✦ It is high time the prime minister should *cleanse* the administration of corruption of all type.
- ✦ Factors polluting the atmosphere should be addressed to *purify* day-to-day life of the people.

COVER

Synonyms : Hide, screen, veil, shield, protect, mask.

Antonyms : Expose, unveil, uncover, exhibit.

Synonyms

- ✦ The ravines of Chambal area provide a very good *hide* to dacoits.
- ✦ The police *screened* the whole village but could not trace the thief.
- ✦ People would vanish under a *veil* of secrecy if they excited the vengeance of the old tyrant.
- ✦ The mother *shielded* the son when the father was beating him.
- ✦ It is the responsibility of the police to *protect* the life and property of the people.
- ✦ The dacoits had covered their faces with *masks* when they attacked the village.

Antonyms

- ✦ His interview with a foreign correspondent has *exposed* his hypocrisy on the sensitive issue of dowry.
- ✦ The vice president *unveiled the* portrait of Mahatma Gandhi to celebrate his 100th birth anniversary.
- ✦ The newspapers have *uncovered* the mystery of a bride's recent death in Chandigarh.

COURAGE

Synonyms : Bravery, boldness, heroism, intrepidity, valour, mettle.

Antonyms : Cowardice, timidity, diffidence, pusillanimity.

Synonyms

- The constable was awarded gold medal for his *bravery* and promoted.
- They taught their students *boldness* and *bravery*.
- The *heroism* of Bhagat Singh has no parallel in history.
- He was praised for his *intrepidity* in climbing a peak that no one else had dared to climb.
- The fireman *exhibited* his valour when he saved several persons trapped in a burning building.
- If you want him to do his best put somebody on his *mettle*.

Antonyms

- To throw down arms at this stage will be sheer *cowardice*.
- The labour leader advised the workers to shed off *timidity* in their bargaining with the management.
- The speech delivered by the chairman of the company showed his *diffidence* on the issue of labour welfare.

CREED

Synonyms : Belief, articles, faith, confession, catechism, dogma, doctrine, tenet.

Antonyms : Disbelief, recantation, protest, obduration.

Synonyms

- ✦ It is our *belief* in the principle of human dignity which makes us work for the welfare of the poor.
- ✦ Our constitution comprises of about 400 *articles*.
- ✦ I thank you for the *faith* you have placed in me by re-electing me as the chairman of the company.
- ✦ The robber made a *confession* of his guilt when handled by the police.

Antonyms

- ✦ *Disbelief* in God implies hundred per cent control of nature by man — an impossible idea in theory or practice.
- ✦ Many a disbeliever *recants* when he finds human power never superseding natural power or destiny.
- ✦ The workers held a *protest* demonstration against the management's stiff attitude on wages.

CRIME

Synonyms : Sin, evil, wrong-doing, offence, felony, outrage, guilt.

Antonyms : Modesty, incorruption, guiltlessness, blamelessness, artlessness.

Synonyms

- Untouchability is a *sin* against humanity.
- His *evil* habits have estranged him from his kith and kin.
- The Hindus believe that everyone is punished by God for his *wrong-doing* to others.
- The motorist was fined for the *offence* of illegal parking.
- He was punished for the *felony* of raping a girl.
- Six persons were killed in the *outrage* committed by the mob.
- He confessed his *guilt* before the priest and prayed for his guidance.

Antonyms

- *Modesty* is the first virtue of a successful individual.
- *Incorruption* is the first virtue of a successfui socialist democracy.
- Very seldom can one enjoy the bliss of *guiltlessness* as humans may commit one guilt or the other, consciously or unconsciously.

CRIPPLE

Synonyms : Disable, curtail, cramp, impair, weaken.

Antonyms : Free, ease, renovate, augment.

Synonyms

- ✦ The accident *disabled* him from attending the meetings of the board.
- ✦ It also *curtailed* his other day-to-day activities of business.
- ✦ The new law has *cramped* the powers of the government to curb individual liberties.
- ✦ His eye sight was *impaired.*
- ✦ This move will *weaken* the opposition.

Antonyms

- ✦ You are now *free* to go anywhere you like.
- ✦ I *eased* myself into a comfortable seat before undertaking the bus journey.

- ✦ Let us *renovate* the shop before the next Deepavali.

CRUEL

Synonyms : Inhuman, merciless, inexorable, callous, pitiless.

Antonyms : Merciful, humane, kind, compassionate, sympathetic, tender.

Synonyms

- Orphans are brought up in *inhuman* conditions in this so called orphanage.
- The dacoits were *merciless* upon the villagers and killed a few of them to terrorise the others.
- His *inexorable* propaganda against his opponents brought him temporary victory but ultimate defeat.
- Don't be *callous* to the sufferings of others.
- His work is generally compared with the *pitiless* efficiency of a machine.

Antonyms

- O God! Take *mercy* on the *humans*. Save them from mutual warfare and destruction.
- Although a rich man, Ramesh has always exhibited sympathy and *kindness* to the poor.
- The Principal remitted the tuition fee of the poor child on *compassionate* grounds.

CURRENT

Synonyms : Popular, present, ordinary, prevalent.

Antonyms : Rejected, private, confined, secret.

Synonyms

- Loren has become the most *popular* student in the college by his sweet manners and innate intelligence.

- The *present* position of the company is rather bad. The value of its shares has fallen by 25%.
- He is rich in wealth but *ordinary* in intellect.
- These clothes are very much *prevalent.*

Antonyms

- Rakesh passed the examination but was *rejected* in the final interview.
- John D'Souza has been admitted in the *private* ward of the medical college hospital.
- The thief was *confined* to custody until the decision in his case.
- It is very difficult to hold on to a *secret.*

DANGER

Synonyms : Risk, peril hazard, menace, threat, jeopardy.

Antonyms : Protection, safeguard, defence, safety, security.

Synonyms

- The element of *risk* justifies some margin of profit in all business.
- All great achievements, like conquest of Mount Everest, can be made with great *peril* to life.
- The journey to Shillong proved to be rather *hazardous.*
- We have to deal with this *menace.*
- Dengue has become a *threat* to life in the metros.

Antonyms

- Modern aircraft provide complete *protection* to the passengers.

- The aeroplanes are equipped with numerous mechanical *safeguards*.
- India is well-equipped militarily for *defence* against any foreign attack.

DEADLY

Synonyms : Fatal, baleful, mortal, noxious

Antonyms : Vital, healthful, life-giving, nutritious.

Synonyms

- Alfred met with a *fatal* accident. He was run over by a fast-moving truck.
- His activities against the state are rather *baleful*. He was caught red-handed passing on strategic confidential information to the foreign powers.
- Each man is *mortal* but mankind as a species is immortal.

Antonyms

- This is one of the *vital* medicines for human beings. Hence its production and supply is controlled by the state.
- Carrot and peas are *healthful* vegetables.

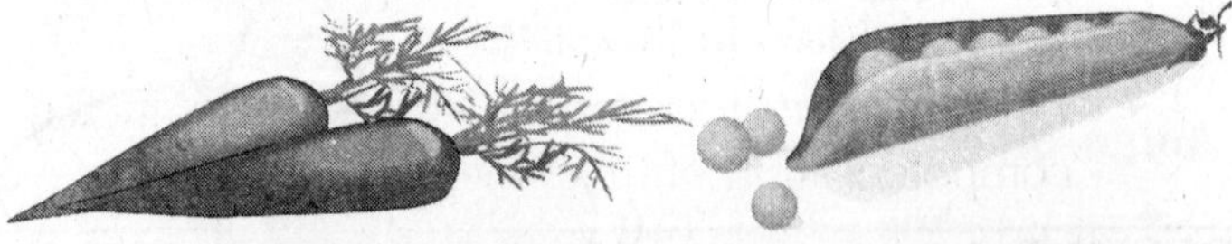

- Modern biotics is trying to invent *lifegiving* enzymes.

DECAY

Synonyms : Deterioration, sinking, decline, wearing, degeneracy.

Antonyms : Improvement, progress, expansion, development.

Synonyms

- ✦ Some *deterioration* in the quality of workmanship of this jewellery had set in from this year.
- ✦ As the saying goes — Rats are the first to desert a *sinking* ship.
- ✦ Cheap and sensational literature sets in a *decline* in the moral standard of the children.
- ✦ The water flowing underneath is *wearing* out the stone gradually.
- ✦ Drug addiction is the main cause of *degeneracy* among teenagers.

Antonyms

- ✦ There is great scope for *improvement* in the quality of workmanship in this piece of jewellery.
- ✦ India has greatly *progressed* since independence.
- ✦ There is great *expansion* in the enrolment of school-going children in this state.
- ✦ *Development* programme of the company includes computerisation of machines.

DECEIVE

Synonyms : Betray, dupe, entrap, cheat, trick.

Antonyms : Enlighten, guide, deliver, advise.

Synonyms

- ✦ Smugglers of foreign goods try to make big money by *betraying* national interests.
- ✦ They *dupe* the customers and officials in one way or the other.
- ✦ Sometimes the officials are able to *entrap* them but often are cheated badly.
- ✦ If he doesn't win he will *cheat.*
- ✦ The smugglers have many *tricks* up their sleeves.

Antonyms

- ✦ Unless the masses are *enlightened* about their individual, social and national interests, they cannot be expected to enjoy their right of vote wisely.
- ✦ It is for the educational and mass communication system to *guide* them.
- ✦ The transport company *delivered* the goods at the destination in time.

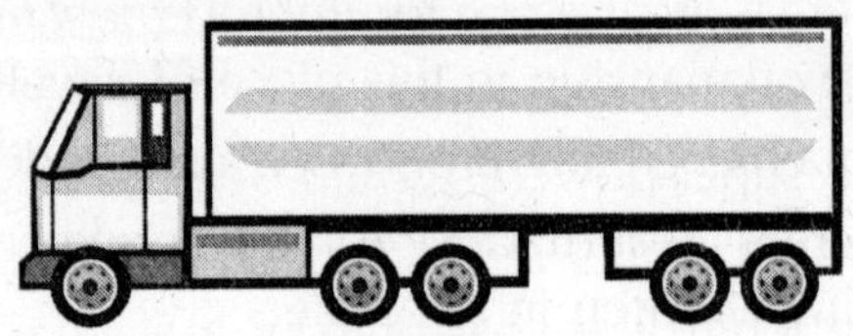

DECEPTION

Synonyms : Fraud, deceit, trickery, chicanery, equivocation.

Antonyms : Sincerity, veracity, honesty, candour, frankness.

Synonyms

- The supplier has played a *fraud* upon me by delivering substandard products.
- It is an open case of *deceit* against which I can move in the court.
- Buying votes is the worst kind of *trickery* against democracy.

Antonyms

- It requires all the *sincerity* at your command to prove a successful administrator.
- Mrs. Indira Gandhi inherited the desired *veracity* from her father.
- It is only through *honesty* to your principles that you can become a great man.

DECIDE

Synonyms : Settle, fix, determine, resolve.

Antonyms : Hesitate, doubt, fluctuate, waver, waive.

Synonyms

- The super-powers should *settle* their differences over the disarmament issue amicably.
- The tenth five year plan of India has *fixed* high targets of production in every field.
- An evaluation process needs to be formulated before we can *determine* the viability of a project.
- In the end the matter was *resolved.*

Antonyms

- Do not *hesitate* if you consider this action as righteous.
- If you have any *doubt* in your mind, I will be happy to clear it.
- The rising prices have caused unexpected *fluctuation* in our estimates of cost of production.

DECLARE

Synonyms : Announce, broadcast, proclaim, publish, advertise, enunciate.

Antonyms : Conceal, censor, withhold, deny.

Synonyms

- The government has *announced* its export policy for the next three years.
- The new policy was *broadcast* on the radio last evening in full detail.
- It *proclaims* some incentives for the manufacturers and exporters.

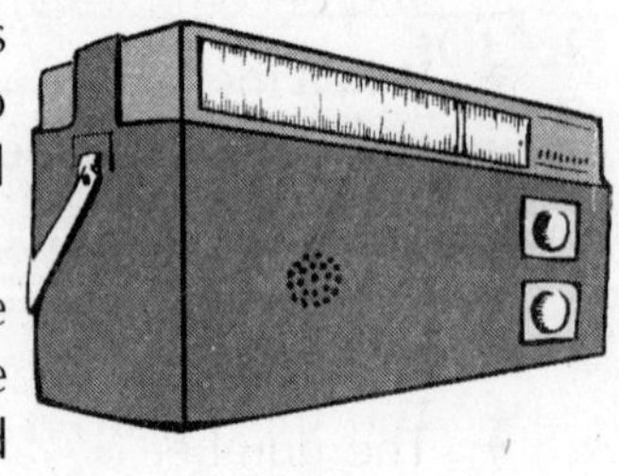

Antonyms

- She was overwhelmingly in love with him. No wonder she could not *conceal* her excitement on his arrival and hugged him.
- The government has the power to *censor* all news during an emergency like a war.

- The judge *withheld* his judgement on the case till the next date.

DECLINE

Synonyms : Reject, refuse, discard, renounce, sink, degenerate, decrease, lessen, fall, drop.

Antonyms : Accept, accede to, agree to, admit, grow, aggravate, enhance, increase.

Synonyms

- The court *rejected* his appeal for bail.
- The doctor *refused* to go and see the patient at midnight.
- All the traditions cannot be *discarded* outrightly.
- He has *renounced* the world and become a sanyasi.
- When the patient's pulse started *sinking* the nurse rushed to call the doctor.
- The decline of this *degenerate* empire is imminent.
- The number of students opting for science has *decreased* over the years.
- The drug *lessened* his pain and he slept well.
- Because of the slump in the market, the prices will *fall* further.
- He *dropped* his voice to a whisper.

Antonyms

- I *accepted* his offer of a long-term loan.
- The judge *acceded* to my request for fixing a new date for evidence in the case.
- She *agreed* to visit his mother in his absence.
- The principal has *admitted* my son into his college.

DECREASE

Synonyms : Reduce, decline, subside, diminish, lessen.

Antonyms : Increase, enlarge, enhance, extend, augment, advance, intensify.

Synonyms

- The doctor has advised her to *reduce* her weight.
- The crime rate in Delhi has been on the *decline* in last few months.
- The pain will *subside* but the disease cannot be cured.
- Lack of rainfall *diminished* the meagre water supply.
- The drug *lessened* his pain and he slept well.

Antonyms

- The recent *increase* in prices has upset many a family budget.
- The teacher asked the students to *enlarge* the paragraph into a full essay.

- India's role in the Non-aligned movement has greatly *enhanced* India's prestige in the comity of nations.
- Each of the super-powers is interested in *extending* its sphere of influence.
- The public sector in India can greatly *augment* the resources of the state.

DEED

Synonyms : Action, feat, exploit, work, achievement.

Antonyms : Inertness, unemployment, restful, passivity, dullness, fatigue, dormancy, delay.

Synonyms

- To every *action* there is an equal and opposite reaction.
- Playing several chess games simultaneously is a rare *feat*.
- Are you aware of the *exploits* of Daniel Boone?
- Some of his *works* are well known all over the world.
- He was awarded for distinguished scholastic *achievements*.

Antonyms

- He used to be very active in his young days. Old age has set in a sort of *inertness* and brought a decline in the quality of his poetry.
- The rate of *unemployment* has fallen in India with the libera-lisation of the economy.

- He is spending *restful* days since his retirement.
- The new incentives have woken up the private sector from its *passivity.*

DEFEAT

Synonyms : Overcome, rout, outwit, frustrate, fail.

Antonyms : Prevail, triumph, win, overthrow, vanquish.

Synonyms

- The brave *overcome* all difficulties to achieve their aim.
- They have started a new organisation to *rout* out the social evils.
- The thief *outwitted* the policeman and escaped.
- The coarse commercialism of some of the publishers has *frustrated* the talented playwrights.
- This year the crop has *failed* because of the usually hot summer.

Antonyms

- An atmosphere of fear and distrust *prevails* in the international sphere today.
- The crooks *triumph* easily in modern complex societies.
- Our college team *won* easily against Siddhartha College.
- The military general *overthrew* the civilian ruler and became a dictator.

DEFINITE

Synonyms : Exact, certain, specific, fixed, explicit, express, unconditional, unqualified, categorical, unequivocal.

Antonyms : Indefinite, unspecified, unspecific, vague, obscure, tentative, ambiguous, implicit, uncertain, conditional.

Synonyms

- The *exact* time at this moment is 1.05 pm.
- I am quite *certain* about the availability of this new apparatus from a specific firm.
- You have to give *specific* reasons.
- This train leaves at a *fixed* time every evening.

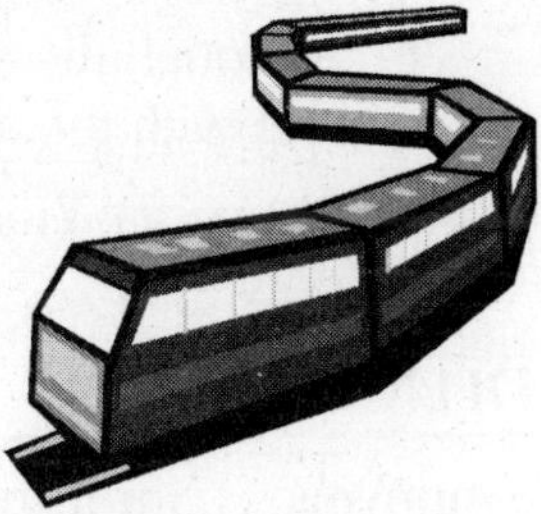

Antonyms

- My question brought forth only an *indefinite* answer from the official.
- The time for holding next meeting of the Board of Directors of the company has been left *unspecified.*
- The chairman seemed *unspecific* about the venue of the next meeting.

DELAY

Synonyms : Hold, keep, detain, retard.

Antonyms : Quicken, speed, send, further.

Synonyms

- ✦ The Congress party *held* its annual session recently.
- ✦ The police are *keeping* strict vigilance on the activities of the extremists.
- ✦ The accused was *detained* in police custody until the rise of the court.
- ✦ The population growth is responsible for *retarding* economic growth.

Antonyms

- ✦ He had to *quicken* the pace to finish in time.
- ✦ Although the car was going at a slow *speed* still it met with the accident.
- ✦ Please *send* me some money as I am totally broke now.

DELICACY

Synonyms : Smoothness, softness, nicety, elegance, refinement, slenderness, lightness.

Antonyms : Roughness, hardness, robustness, crudeness, heaviness.

Synonyms

- ✦ Reflection of light depends upon the *smoothness* of the surface.
- ✦ Some of the metals have extraordinary *softness.*
- ✦ Candlelight and linen napkins are the *niceties* of he classical dinner.

- ✦ The picture frame and modern furniture have added to the *elegance* of the room.
- ✦ The parents were very happy to see trends of *refinement* in the behaviour of their spoiled son.
- ✦ He was aware of the *slenderness* of chances of success, yet he decided to go.
- ✦ The gases are compared with each other in term of their *lightness*.

Antonyms

- ✦ The *roughness* of this cloth is in contrast to the softness of the nylon fabric.
- ✦ The *hardness* of the Indian farmer is now bringing good results, thanks to the improved provision of irrigation facilities.
- ✦ Dara Singh has become world champion in wrestling, thanks to his *robustness*.

DELIVER

Synonyms : Free, discharge, liberate, surrender, release, save, yield, relinquish, hand over, rescue.

Antonyms : Arrest, imprison, apprehend, capture, catch, seize, adopt, withhold, keep, appropriate.

Synonyms

- ✦ He was *freed* from jail before the expiry of his term for his good conduct and behaviour.

- The patient was *discharged* from the hospital although he was not fully well.
- Goa was *liberated* by India from the Portuguese in 1961.
- Ninety thousand soldiers *surrendered* to the Indian army in the 1971 war.
- After the war, India *released* all the prisoners of war.
- The boatman reached in time and *saved* him from drowning.
- The new variety of rice will *yield* very good results.
- The general will *relinquish* charge of his post to the new incumbent on the last day of this month.
- The court ordered him to *hand over* the property to his brother, the real owner.

Antonyms

- The thief was *arrested* by the police.
- He was *imprisoned* after the court had investigated and found him guilty.
- The police was able to *apprehend* and *capture* the head of the gang of robbers.

DENOTE

Synonyms : Mean, indicate, signify, mark, designate, imply.

Antonyms : Dissemble, suppress, conceal.

Synonyms

- He claims to *mean* one thing, but his choice of words suggests quite another.
- A flashing red light *indicated* that the stretch of the road was undergoing repairs.
- The legend of a map tells what each sign and abbreviation *signifies*.
- Nodding in an auction *marks* that the bidder has accepted the offer of the auctioneer.
- He has been *designated* the honorary secretary of the society.

Antonyms

- Cleaning of this machine involves *dissembling* it and again reassembling it.
- In early stages, every communist state has to *suppress* many personal liberties of the citizens.
- The doctor cannot diagnose correctly if the patient *conceals* some of the facts.

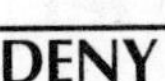

DENY

Synonyms : Withhold, reject, refute, disclaim, controvert, contradict, renounce, abjure.

Antonyms : Confirm, comply, ratify, verify, endorse, acknowledge, substantiate.

Synonyms

- Government has the right to *withhold* its permission to any foreign spy to leave the country.
- The principal has *rejected* most of the demands of the students.

- The enquiry has *refuted* all the charges levelled against him.
- Protestants *disclaim* the authority of the pope.
- The defendant tried to *controvert* the plaintiff's story.

Antonyms

- The principal has *confirmed* the dates for the holding of the annual examination.
- The candidate *complied* with all the requirements of the examination.
- The government has refused to *ratify* the non-proliferation treaty on grounds of its discrimination clause against the non nuclear powers.

- ✦ The employer *verified* the accuracy of the marks-sheet of the employee before issuing him the appointment letter.

DEPENDENCE

Synonyms : Slavery, helplessness, thraldom, reliance.

Antonyms : Delivery, permission, independence, discharge, licence, play, latitude, release, free trade, swing, full scap.

Synonyms

- ✦ America was the first country in the world to abolish *slavery*.
- ✦ The authorities showed *helplessness* in dealing with the hijackers of the plane.
- ✦ In villages, the zamindars keep some people in their *thraldom*.
- ✦ His too much *reliance* on his secretary was criticised by management.

Antonyms

- ✦ The *delivery* of post in the village has been delayed owing to the postman's sickness.
- ✦ The principal has granted *permission* to deserving students to take the scholarship test.
- ✦ Ever since *independence*, the government has *discharged* its responsibility in the field of economic development with proficiency.

✦ In India, one does not need a licence to start a small-scale industry.

DESCRIBE

Synonyms : Explain, relate, illustrate, define, narrate, recount, tell, draw.

Antonyms : Falsify, mystify, misrepresent, suppress, obscure, misinterpret.

Synonyms

✦ The science teacher *explained* the phenomenon with the help of *illustrations.*

✦ The politicians try to *relate* unconnected incidents to blame their opponents.

✦ He *illustrated* his point with a number of examples to convince the audience.

- One cannot *define* God as it is not possible to *define* what is supernatural.
- The hunter rejoiced in *narrating* his adventures.
- His heart filled with sorrow while *recounting* his unlucky childhood.

Antonyms

- His failure in the final examination *falsified* all his past record of brilliance.
- The phenomenal rise of the young man *mystified* the expectations of the old leader.
- The salesman booked the order by *misrepresenting* the virtues of the product.

DESPAIR

Synonyms : Despondency, dejection, desperation, hopelessness, discouragement.

Antonyms : Confidence, encouragement, elation, hopefulness, expectation, hope, optimism.

Synonyms

- The news of Mrs. Indira Gandhi's assassination sent a wave of *despondency* and rage in the whole of India.
- His dismissal from the high position has caused acute *dejection* in his family.
- "Pluck courage, my dear," said the father. "This look of *desperation* will take you nowhere".

Antonyms

- The leader spoke with *confidence*. No wonder he got elected with thumping majority.
- I must thank you for the *encouragement* your ideas have given me.
- I felt *elated* on topping the list of successful candidates.

DESPISE

Synonyms : Hate, abhor, scorn, loathe, disdain.

Antonyms : Admire, adore, like, love, respect, appreciate.

Synonyms

- To *hate* a human is inhumane.
- I *abhor* his negative thinking.
- He had a *scorn* for all weaklings.
- I *loathe* the company of bores.

Antonyms

- I *admire* your courage and sagacity.
- I cannot help *adoring* your spirit of selflessness.
- I *like* the very look of our Prime Minister.
- I *love* to see a movie every Sunday.

DESTROY

Synonyms : Ruin, raze, uproot, wreck, waste, demolish, annihilate, eradicate, exterminate, extinguish.

Antonyms : Make, repair, restore, reinstate, build, create, devise, establish.

Synonyms

- ✦ He *ruined* his career by showing impertinence to his new boss.
- ✦ The earthquake *razed* hundreds of houses to ground.
- ✦ The cyclone *uprooted* many old trees.

- ✦ It also wrecked numerous ships anchored on the sea coast.
- ✦ It was a great *waste* land.

Antonyms

- ✦ It is easy to destroy but difficult to *make.*
- ✦ My car needs *repairs.*
- ✦ This medicine *restores* my energy.
- ✦ The court passed orders *reinstating* the suspended employee.

DESTRUCTION

Synonyms : Devastation, demolition, desolation, annihilation, subversion.

Antonyms : Creation, production, making, construction,

Synonyms

- ✦ The storm has caused unprecedented *devastation* in the city.

- *Demolition* of unauthorised houses was withheld at the instance of the mayor of the city.
- *Desolation* of towns on the borders is a common sign of the coming war.
- *Annihilation* of Hiroshima and Nagasaki has put a great check on warlike tendencies in man.
- He was acquitted by the court because the charge of *subversion* and sabotage levelled against him could not be proved.

Antonyms

- All the beauty of nature, including mankind, is the *creation* of God.

- The *production* of food grains has picked up since independence.
- Education through doing helps *making* the character of the young.
- The local government has undertaken the *construction* of a new industrial estate.

DEVELOP

Synonyms : Expand, clear, unfold, disclose, lay open.

Antonyms : Obscure, conceal, wrap, envelop.

Synonyms

- The facilities for technical education are *expanding* year by year.

- There is no *clear* official policy yet on environment in India.
- Recent political events in Pakistan have *unfolded* fresh dictatorial tendencies.
- Neetu *disclosed* the secret to Mohit.

Antonyms

- The outcome of super power talks in Geneva is still very *obscure.*
- The thief *concealed* the stolen goods in an underground pit of his house compound.
- Better *wrap* the bread in the plastic bag to save it from moisture.

DEVIATE

Synonyms : Diverge, swerve, stray, ramble, wander, err, vary,. differ.

Antonyms : Converge, stay, perpetuate, continue, pervade, abide.

Synonyms

- She *diverged* from her usual route because of a traffic jam.
- The car *swerved* to avoid knocking the boy down.
- The driver lost his way and *strayed* with the passengers into a jungle track.

- The couple liked to *ramble* about the countryside in search of a seluded picnic spot.
- His speech *wandered* badly from one example to another without ever coming to the core point.
- To *err* is human, to forgive divine.
- The results of her new experiment very much *vary* from her earlier experiments.
- They *differ* in their approach but their aim is the same.

Antonyms

- Thousands of people *converged* on the banks of the river to bathe in the holy waters.
- The theme of the book *stays* within the prescribed syllabus.
- The socio-economic system in the country *perpetuates* the general poverty of the masses.
- The features of inequality continue to *pervade* the social fabric.

DEVOTED

Synonyms : Affectionate, assiduous, dedicated, fond, ardent.

Antonyms : Unfaithful, faithless, indifferent, cool, disloyal.

Synonyms

- ✦ The parents were ready to sacrifice anything for the happiness of their *affectionate* son.
- ✦ He got his Ph.D. degree after an *assiduous* research for seven years.
- ✦ He has *dedicated* his new book to his late mother.
- ✦ The young wife is *fond* of her husband. Her open gestures in public are, however, despised.
- ✦ An *ardent* patriot will not allow the cessionist tendencies to grow.

Antonyms

- ✦ His employee proved to be *unfaithful* in the emergent circumstances and deserted him.
- ✦ His *faithless* wife has applied for a divorce in order to pick up a new husband.
- ✦ The husband was *indifferent* to the divorce sought by his faithless wife.
- ✦ The husband and the wife were rather *cool* to each other right from the day of their marriage.

DILIGENT

Synonyms : Careful, laborious, attentive, busy, painstaking.

Antonyms : Slack, lazy, indolent, idle, slothful.

Synonyms

- The prime minister has asked the people to be *careful* of the divisive forces.
- The engineer was praised for the *laborious* job of cleaning up the river after the floods.
- The teacher flayed him for being not so *attentive* in the class.
- Nowadays he is *busy* in social work.
- It was the result of the *painstaking* efforts of the chairman that the society was saved from closure.

Antonyms

- My business is rather *slack* these days.
- He is a *lazy* fellow and does not get up before 9 am.
- He is a man of *indolent* habits. You cannot expect him to succeed in business.
- Don't *idle* away your time if you want to succeed in business.

DIPLOMATIC

Synonyms : Discreet, prudent, shrewd, sharp, astute, judicious, sagacious.

Antonyms : Indiscreet, imprudent, tactless, injudicious, silly, bungling.

Synonyms

- How can one be *discreet* if one does not know about the past career of one's opponent.

- It was not *prudent* to undertake climbing of the steep slope, it has put her life in constant danger.
- He was *shrewd* enough to understand how far he could go in criticising the existing regime.
- I like his *sharp* awareness of social niceties.
- The secretary made an *astute* assessment of the strengths and weaknesses of the plans for re-organising the department.
- His *judicious* judgement has saved the family from break up.
- In this matter you should ask a *sagacious* man for advice.

Antonyms

- His *indiscreet* haste made him to lose the contract.
- He was so *imprudent* in dealing with his boss that he could retain his job for just one month.
- His *tactless* behaviour lost him his best friend.

DIRTY

Synonyms : Foul, filthy, squalid, soiled, unclean, sordid, impure.

Antonyms : Clean, pure, unsoiled, unsullied, virginal.

Synonyms

- Sher Singh played a *foul* game and hence lost.
- The villain used *filthy* language against the hero but the hero remained unsullied.
- The chawl near Chowpaty had a *squalid* atmosphere owing to dirt and din of the poor.

- I don't want you *soiling* your hands with this sort of work.

Antonyms

- I can play a *clean* game of chess.
- Buddha preached for *pure* habits, *pure* thoughts, *pure* action and *pure* dealings.
- She is a mother of two children. But she still has *virginal* looks.

DISAPPOINT

Synonyms : Defeat, vex, baffle, foil, deceive, betray.

Antonyms : Satisfy, gratify, fulfil, justify.

Synonyms

- Ashoka *defeated* the Kalinga forces but the loss of life changed his heart.
- It left him *vexed* and betrayed.
- The military coup in Thailand was *foiled* in time.
- The rival king was *baffled* by the defeat.
- The commander *foiled* the attempt of a coup.

Antonyms

- Service to humanity in various ways *satisfied* his conscience.
- It *gratified* his ego and fulfilled the purpose of his existence as a human being.
- All the promises were *fulfilled*.
- It also *justified* his faith in God.

DISCLOSE

Synonyms : Reveal, unveil, confess, expose, uncover, betray, unfold.

Antonyms : Conceal, cover, suppress, hide, veil, dissemble, cloak.

Synonyms

- ✦ His business secrets were *revealed* to the income tax department by his own secretary.
- ✦ When he *unveiled* the statue, he was amazed at its beauty and artistic excellence.
- ✦ A true Christian *confesses* his guilt in the Church.

- ✦ The captain was blamed to have *exposed* the soldiers to the enemy's fire to save his own skin.
- ✦ When the police *uncovered* the box they found a dead body in it.
- ✦ The king was defeated because his own general had *betrayed* him.

✦ The grandmother *unfolded* a new story to the children every night.

Antonyms

✦ His expressionless face *concealed* the shock of the tragedy.

✦ He *covered* the face of the dead person.

✦ He could not finally *suppress* his shock and burst into tears.

DISGRACE

Synonyms : Degrade, humiliate, shame, disparage, discredit, dishonour, desert.

Antonyms : Honour, reverence, respect, exalt, dignify, elevate, venerate.

Synonyms

✦ The accusations were intended to *degrade* him and destroy his reputation.

✦ She felt thoroughly *humiliated* at her own lack of insight.

✦ They *shamed* him for timid behaviour in the emergency.

✦ No one liked their caustically *disparaging* each new production just to prove the playwright's worthlessness.

✦ He attempted to *discredit* his opponent by disparaging references from his personal life.

- The soldier was convicted of wilful *desertion* causing *dishonour* to the army.

Antonyms

- Mrs. Indira Gandhi was *honoured* with many awards and prizes.
- This was in *reverence* to her devotion to the cause of world peace throughout her life.
- It also showed the people's *respect* for the world's greatest woman of the century.

DISPLACE

Synonyms : Remove, dislocate, oust, supersede, supplant.

Antonyms : Establish, settle, secure, set, root, plant.

Synonyms

- The boss ordered the peon to *remove* the files from his table.
- The accident not only broke his leg but also *dislocated* his joints.
- The chief minister was *ousted* from party leadership by a no-confidence vote.
- He was *superseded* by his junior, he has therefore decided to resign from service.
- Trams are being *supplanted* by buses in this great city.

Antonyms

- My college was *established* in 1970.

- Let us *settle* our differences and live like friends.
- The factory is now well *set* to bring profits.
- We can now feel quite *secure*, thanks to the restoration of law and order in the city.

DISSOLVE

Synonyms : Divide, separate, break up, disperse, disconnect, part, disunite.

Antonyms : Unite, combine, concert, join, conjoin, amalgamate, connect.

Synonyms

- Britishers followed the policy of '*divide* and rule' to continue their occupation of the country.
- It seems quite certain Romy will *separate* from his father after his marriage.
- In modern society, joint families have a tendency to *break up* into smaller units.
- The thunderstorm *dispersed* the picnickers.
- If he joins the new office he will have to *disconnect* relations with his present friends.
- When the strings of the rope *parted*, the load fell to the ground.

Antonyms

- Divided we fall, *united* we stand.
- Let us *combine* our resources, if you want the firm to prosper.

- Unless we take *concerted* action, we cannot make our scheme a success.
- I have *joined* the bank as a probationary officer.

DISTANT

Synonyms : Far-away, inaccessible, remote, asunder.

Antonyms : Accessible, close, proximate, contiguous, adjacent.

Synonyms

- Our objective of making the firm pay for its past losses seems a *far-away* dream.
- The new governor has become *inaccessible* even to his close associates of the past.
- There is now a *remote* possibility of resurrecting the old relationship.

Antonyms

- Our principal is easily *accessible* for discussing reasonable demands of the students.
- Our college is quite *close* to my residence.
- The status of a bank manager *approximates* to that of a joint secretary in a government department.

DIVERSITY

Synonyms : Variegate, modify, alter, vary.

Antonyms : Solidify, unify, fix, conserve.

Synonyms

- Nehru had a *variegated* personality. He was a humanist, scientist, economist, politician all rolled into one.

- ✦ The government has *modified* its stand on economic issues. It is moving towards liberalisation of the private sector.
- ✦ I have asked the tailor to *alter* my trousers so as to adapt it to the new fashion.
- ✦ The design will *vary* in production as it is hand crafted.

Antonyms

- ✦ Modern educationists want to *solidify* all subjects at the primary level into one integrated whole.
- ✦ Economic institutions in modern societies help to *unify* all religions, races and sects.
- ✦ Political parties tend to develop *fixed* ideas on national and international issues.
- ✦ We must *conserve* the forest to survive.

DOUBT

Synonyms : Suspicion, scepticism, uncertainty, dubiety.

Antonyms : Certainty, confidence, conviction, assurance.

Synonyms

- ✦ I have no *suspicion* about your noble intentions but I expect early action in the matter.
- ✦ The present international atmosphere is surcharged with *scepticism* on the issue of nuclear disarmament.

- *Uncertainty* in law and order situation in Punjab has upset many a business house in the country.

Antonyms

- Only conditions of continued *certainty* and security can restore relations between different communities.
- The Prime Minister displayed positive *confidence* in his policies at his press conferences abroad.
- All his statements showed his deep *conviction* in international peace and cooperation among states.

DOUBTFUL

Synonyms : Uncertain, dubious, questionable, problematic, equivocal, ambiguous.

Antonyms : Clear, confident, definite, decided, sure, certain.

Synonyms

- Mohit is *uncertain* about his appointment in the Air Force.
- Jeewan is *dubious* about the intentions of his boss in the matter of his promotion.
- The speaker considered the behaviour of the opposition leader in the parliament as *questionable*.
- This child is very *problematic*.

Antonyms

- The new government has enunciated its politics in a *clear* manner.

- The government is *confident* of its ability to tackle the problem of law and order in the country.
- The new law is quite *definite* on the responsibility of political parties in maintaining law and order.

DREADFUL

Synonyms : Frightful, dire, afraid, terrific, alarming, awful, horrible.

Antonyms : Pleasing, pleasurable, propitious, reassuring, auspicious.

Synonyms

- *Frightful* howls pierced the air in the cemetery when the relations of the deceased arrived there.
- He threatened that refusal to meet his demands will result in *dire* consequences.
- We were *afraid* she might harm herself.
- A *terrific* explosion woke the whole town.
- The situation had become so *alarming* that the officer had to order firing on the violent mob.
- He was found guilty of the *awful* crime of murder.
- The sewer emitted a *horrible* smell.

Antonyms

- The sound of the soft music was very *pleasing* to the ear.
- Your dream is *pleasurable* but is it also practicable?
- The meeting between the disputed parties took place under *propitious* circumstances of international boom.

DRY

Synonyms : Parched, arid, barren, tedious, dehydrated, crisp, desiccated.

Antonyms : Damp, wet, moistened, fresh, lively, moist, soggy.

Synonyms

- The acute drought left the soil very much *parched* making it unfit for cultivation.
- The Institute of Agricultural Research has invented a new technique of farming for *arid* tracts of land.

- A good part of land on the high hills has to be left *barren* due to inaccessibility.

- The job assigned to him was very *tedious.*
- By the time we reached home we were absolutely *dehydrated.*

Antonyms

- Mumbai's climate is *damp* throughout the year owing to its proximity to the sea.
- This towel is *wet,* it may not soak the water of my body.
- Let me *moisten* my hands as they are too dry.

DULL

Synonyms : Monotonous, boring, tiresome, uninteresting, dreary.

Antonyms : Spirited, enthralling, lively, Interesting.

Synonyms

- The view from the train window grew *monotonous* after an a hour or two and I found myself dozing off.
- The film was so *boring* that I left the theatre hall an hour before the end.
- It was a *tiresome* day filled with a number of exhausting household tasks.
- For him even the job of a professor is *uninteresting.*
- She rented a *dreary* little room on the top floor of a building.

Antonyms

- The happy news *enthralled* her completely.

✦ Today's picnic was pretty *lively*. I enjoyed it to the full.

✦ This novel is too *interesting* to be left unread in one sitting.

✦ He delivered a *spirited* speech on the occasion.

EAGER

Synonyms : Desirous, keen, enthusiastic, anxious, fervent, impatient, zealous.

Antonyms : Cool, unconcerned, indifferently, apathetic, loath, disinterested.

Synonyms

- My friend is *desirous* of her hand in marriage.
- Children watched the clown with *keen* delight.
- He is very *enthusiastic* about the plans he has made for his higher studies.
- He is *anxious* to join the military service.

- The lawyer made a *fervent* plea for clemency.
- The class was *impatient* for the vacations to begin.
- Ram is the most *zealous* worker in the whole office.

Antonyms

- Mahatma Gandhi was a *cool* and calculated politician. He always found the non-violent way to his objective.
- The government cannot remain *unconcerned* about the atmosphere of violence let loose by the extremists.
- Of late Ramesh has become *indifferent* to studies.

EARN

Synonyms : Gain, win, achieve, acquire, merit.

Antonyms : Waste, spend, forgo, forfeit, lose.

Synonyms

- The students *gained* in knowledge from the lectures of the visiting professor from Boston University.
- Dara Singh has again *won* the wrestling championship.
- Our college has *achieved* very good results in recent years.

Antonyms

- Let's not *waste* time, but start the studies right now.
- The government must *spend* more money on the schemes meant for the upliftment of the poor.
- Work harder in life even if it means *forgoing* some leisure if you want better results.

✦ The doctor has advised the patient to *lose* weight by stages in order to normalise his blood pressure.

EBB

Synonyms : Wane, decline, decay, retire, sink, recede.
Antonyms : Flow, increase, abound, swell.

Synonyms

✦ High morals of the olden days are on the *wane* due to greater emphasis on material aspects in modern life.

✦ There is a *decline* in the real balanced values among the youth.

✦ *Decaying* is a natural process.

✦ He will *retire* next year that is why he is so much worried.

✦ The patient has been *sinking* fast since he developed symptoms of cancer.

Antonyms

✦ There is an *increased flow* of water in this canal owing to recent rains.

✦ The rate of crime is on the *increase* round the world.

✦ A number of criminal rackets *abound* in all metropolitan cities.

ELEGANT

Synonyms : Elaborate, luxurious, grandiose, sumptuous, deluxe.

Antonyms : Inexpensive, plain, mediocre, unadorned, simple, usual, vulgar.

Synonyms

✦ The organisers have made *elaborate* arrangements for the successful holding of the seminar.

✦ Modern aircraft have good *luxurious* seating arrangements.

✦ The new airport has a set of *grandiose* paintings collected from the best artists of the country.

Antonyms

- The new buses launched by the DTC have *inexpensive* yet comfortable fittings.
- I intend to have a simple *plain* talk with my girlfriend before deciding upon matrimony.
- Our new manager is *mediocre* in talent but has strong will-power to make up for this deficiency.
- Atul is top in every field — studies, sports and debates. He is like an *unadorned* prince of the college.

EMOTION

Synonyms : Agitation, tremor, passion, feeling, sentiment, desire.

Antonyms : Stoicism, insensibility, rationality, reason, indifference.

Synonyms

- The workers of the factory propose to launch an *agitation* for higher wages.
- The earthquake gave a strong *tremor* to the buildings in the city.
- His *passion* for his profession took him to glorious heights.
- He was *feeling* sad.
- His face showed his *sentiments.*

Antonyms

- Modern socialists are characterised by a strange sense of *stoicism* in their attitude.

✦ Modern management are marked by *insensibility* to galloping inflation so far as the question of increasing the wages of their workers is concerned.

✦ Worker's participation in management of factories is justified on the principles of *rationality* in human behaviour.

✦ There is every *reason* for managements to accede to workers' participation.

ENCHANTED

Synonyms : Charmed, fascinated, bewitched, captivated, enraptured, enamoured, entranced, spell-bound.

Antonyms : Disgusted, repulsed, repelled, nauseated.

Synonyms

✦ The scenic view glimpsed through the window of the train *charmed* me.

✦ The snake was *fascinated* by the charmer's music.

- Meena Kumari *bewitched* a generation of movie goers.
- The actor's talent and good looks *captivated* the audience.
- Her beautiful voice *enraptured* audiences everywhere.
- Most visitors are *enamoured* by the marble beauty of the Taj Mahal.
- A hypnotist looks for subjects which can be easily *entranced*.
- Everyone was *spellbound* by the music of Asha at the concert.

Antonyms

- The teacher was *disgusted* by the continued indifference of the student in studies.
- He was advised by the principal to attract the interest of students in studies by reforming his mode of speech which perhaps *repulsed* his students.
- Like poles *repel* while unlike poles attract.

ENCOURAGE

Synonyms : Back up, animate, urge, reassure, incite, cheer, embolden, foster, hearten, support, promote.

Antonyms : Dissuade, discourage, abash, dishearten, thwart, hinder.

Synonyms

- Every project needs to be *backed up* with finance before implementation.

- Cartoon films involve *animation* technique of still pictures.
- The vice chancellor has *urged* the lecturers to withdraw their strike in order to enable him to recommend higher salaries.
- The boss *reassured* him a raise very soon.

Antonyms

- The principal has *dissuaded* the lecturers from going on a strike.
- Nothing can *discourage* me from my resolve to proceed on a mountaineering mission.
- I hope bad weather will not *thwart* my mission.

ENCROACH

Synonyms : Infringe, violate, invade, intrude, trespass.
Antonyms : Desist, observe, respect, withdraw.

Synonyms

- I cannot tolerate anybody *infringing* my right to worship God the way I like.
- *Violation* of law is punishable in every state.
- The army *invaded* the enemy camps.
- The state does not *intrude* into the personal life of individuals in a democracy.

Antonyms

- I *desisted* from slapping him on the face, although he did his worst to annoy me.
- We can travel safely if we *observe* the rules of traffic seriously.

- With due respect to your sentiments, I beg to *withdraw* my comments.

ENDANGER

Synonyms : Hazard, risk, jeopardise, imperil.

Antonyms : Protect, safeguard, shield, defend, screen.

Synonyms

- Don't *hazard* your reputation by supporting that crook.
- He has insured his business against the *risk* of failure.
- It is not advisable to *jeopardise* your health for this petty gain of money.
- He *imperilled* his life to save a drowning boy.

Antonyms

- I can *protect* my rights, but do I protect the rights of others or of the society at large?
- Traditional weapons cannot *safeguard* a country against the evil designs of an atomic power.
- The ozone layer *shields* the earth against the sun's ultraviolet rays..

ENDLESS

Synonyms : Unceasing, boundless, eternal, infinite.

Antonyms : Temporary, brief, fugitive, limited.

Synonyms

- Mahatma Gandhi had *unceasing* patience to withstand opposition.
- Shivaji had *boundless* courage in war and peace.
- No enemy can break our *eternal* friendship.

Antonyms

- UN aid can give only *temporary* relief; what we need is hard work to become self-sufficient in food grains.
- What I need is a *brief* loan from the bank to tide over the present crisis.
- Great men do not behave like *fugitives.* They face the problems and solve them will courage.

ENDORSE

Synonyms : Approve, accredit, ratify, confirm, sanction.

Antonyms : Discredit, condemn, censure, disapprove, reject, apprehend.

Synonyms

- I whole-heartedly *approve* your stand on this issue.
- Samuel is an *accredited* representative of .the newspaper.
- India has *ratified* the Indo-Indonesian Trade Agreement of 1984.
- The dates for the tournament are *confirmed.*

Antonyms

- Communal disturbances in India bring *discredit* to the image of unity and integrity of the country.
- The communal elements anywhere need to be *condemned* in strong words.
- All political parties that stand for unity of the country should *censure* the divisive elements.

ENLARGE

Synonyms : Augment, expand, amplify, magnify, increase.

Antonyms : Contract, condense, narrow, shorten, reduce, decrease.

Synonyms

- A modern welfare state has to *augment* its financial resources to launch more welfare schemes for the common people.
- It needs to *expand* state activities on a larger scale.
- State policies are *amplified* for public discussion, so that in due course maximum cooperation in implementation of new schemes can be ensured.
- The glass will *magnify* the object.
- The *increase* in price affected the sale of the object.

Antonyms

- In terms of their trade agreement, India and Indonesia have signed a few *contracts* in the industrial field.
- This long paragraph can be *condensed* in two lines without losing its significant points.

- Recent meeting of the leaders of the super powers at Geneva has *narrowed* their differences over space disarmament.

ENMITY

Synonyms : Hostility, hate, discord, antagonism, animus, rancour, animosity.

Antonyms : Amity, love, harmony, fellowship, sympathy.

Synonyms

- Recent extremist activities in Punjab and other northern states are designed to create an atmosphere of *hostility* between communities.
- Some innocent members of the communities have fallen victim to this *hostility* with seeds of *hate* and *discord* bred in their relationships.
- Certain forces outside India are jealous of India's economic progress have fanned the spirit of *antagonism* by secret interference.

Antonyms

- There is enough *amity* between India and the USSR. 
- I *love* music and poetry as my hobbies.
- There is perfect *harmony* among the different communities of this state.

ENOUGH

Synonyms : Adequate, abundant, ample, plenty, sufficient.

Antonyms : Insufficient, inadequate, scarcity, deficient.

Synonyms

- ✦ Our hotel room was not luxurious, but it had *adequate* space for comfortable sleep.
- ✦ Despite the dry spell, there was *abundant* rain this year.
- ✦ We had *ample* time for a leisurely lunch today.
- ✦ We wish you peace and *plenty* in the New Year.
- ✦ We do not have *sufficient* fuel for the trip.

Antonyms

- ✦ This much evidence is *insufficient* for proving the case.
- ✦ The supply of electricity in this city is *inadequate* for industrial progress.
- ✦ *Scarcity* of power is responsible for the slow progress of industries in this district.
- ✦ He is quite healthy in physique but is *deficient* in brains.

ENRAGE

Synonyms : Anger, madden, incense, infuriate.

Antonyms : Pacify, mollify, soothe, tranquillise, placate.

Synonyms

- ✦ *Anger* is the enemy of success.
- ✦ His rough behaviour *maddened* me and I felt compelled to leave his premises.
- ✦ His illogical remarks *infuriated* me.

Antonyms

- ✦ His reconcialiatory attitude *pacified* my anger.
- ✦ The new medicine has *soothed* my nerves.
- ✦ Calmpose is a kind of tablet that acts as a *tranquilliser.*

ENTIRE

Synonyms : Whole, full, complete, intact, total.

Antonyms : Broken, partial, divided, damaged, destroyed, empty, imperfect, incomplete, limited.

Synonyms

- ✦ The *whole* world is at my disposal through the TV and radio.
- ✦ Today is *full* moon. How beautiful!

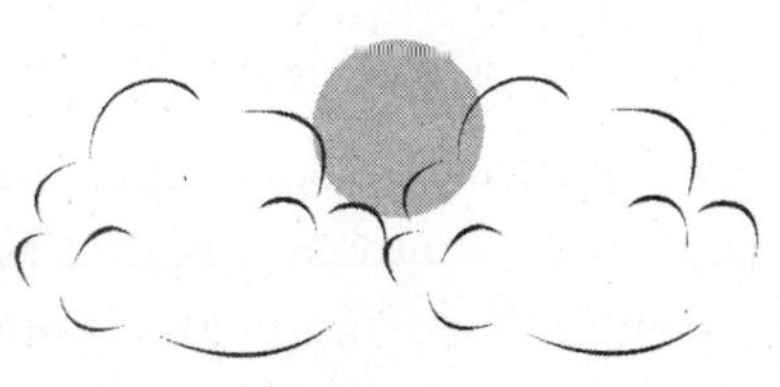

- Let us *complete* this task and then enjoy.

Antonyms

- Quickfix joins anything except a *broken* heart.
- This noon there is going to be a *partial* eclipse of the sun.
- United we stand, *divided* we fall.

ERASE

Synonyms : Efface, eradicate, obliterate, cancel, delete.

Antonyms : Impress, imprint, insert.

Synonyms

- It may take a long time to *efface* the wrong image of India created by communal riots.
- Poverty cannot be *eradicated* unless the working conditions of the farmers and workers are improved by legislation.
- The basic weaknesses in the economic structure are *obliterating* the concept of economic equality in our country.

Antonyms

- The system of education prevalent in this country *impresses* the foreign tourists as the most undemocratic in the world.
- There is an *imprint* of acute inequality among students of government schools and the so-called public schools.

- I have *inserted* an advertisement in the local newspaper for the sale of my old car.

ETERNAL

Synonyms : Perpetual, ceaseless, deathless, unending.

Antonyms : Temporal, fleeting, swift, passing.

Synonyms

- Poverty is a *perpetual* problem of India.
- The administration in the country is working *ceaselessly* to eradicate the root cause of poverty.
- The poor people are always engaged in a *deathless* struggle to subsist.

Antonyms

- The pope emphasised on the *temporal* nature of mankind and counselled his audience to avoid all kinds of conflicts.
- He said life was *fleeting* and each of us should make the best contribution to the good of society.
- Machine has made human life *swift* and colourful.

EVASION

Synonyms : Quibble, subterfuge, pretext, excuse, prevarication.

Antonyms : Refutation, reply, rejoinder, response, defence, answer.

Synonyms

- ✦ A *quibble* over exact wording of the bill delayed its passage in the parliament.
- ✦ Why didn't they tell us immediately instead of resorting to this *subterfuge*?
- ✦ The robber used the ringing of the door-bell as a *pretext* to the hold-up robbery.
- ✦ Ignorance of the law is no *excuse*.

Antonyms

- ✦ The minister's prompt *refutation* of the allegations made by a member of parliament saved the situation.
- ✦ I am awaiting a *reply* to my letter from the authorities.
- ✦ The opposition leader sent a *rejoinder* to the party in power on the issue of opposition involvement in the spy episode.

EVIDENT

Synonyms : Clear, visible, obvious, patent, manifest, distinct.

Antonyms : Hidden, obscure, secret, covert, latent, masked.

Synonyms

- ✦ He tried to give many examples but could not make his point *clear*.
- ✦ The airstrip was not *visible* because of the fog.

- It is an *obvious* gimmick to compensate for the playwright's jogging innovation.
- Every law has a *patent* as well as a latent meaning.
- The referee's *manifest* bias towards the home side was criticised by the audience.
- He failed to realise the *distinct* note of annoyance in her voice.

Antonyms

- Her charming face was *hidden* behind the veil but the impact of her beauty could not be contained.
- The new poems of the philosopher are rather *obscure* for the common man to comprehend.
- The government has kept the message received from the ambassador as top *secret.*

EXACT

Synonyms : Truthful, correct, precise, strict, careful.

Antonyms : Inexact, erring, incorrect, careless, negligent, untruthful.

Synonyms

- The witness gave a *truthful* account of the ac cident.
- She was wearing the *correct* dress for a formal dinner.
- The parts of a watch must be *precise,* or else it does not work.

- The laws on speeding have been made more *strict* for observance.
- Children should be taught to be very *careful* while crossing the road.

Antonyms

- The statistics used for this conclusion seem to be *inexact;* therefore they need rechecking.
- The *erring* figure spoilt the final result of the computer programme.
- It is *incorrect* to say that I deliberately evaded discussion on the controversial issue in the last meeting.
- You should not be *careless* in future.

EXCELLENT

Synonyms : Select, first-class, prime, first-rate, choice.

Antonyms : Mediocre, imperfect, faulty, poor, second-class.

Synonyms

- Look at his dress, manners, movements — he seems to belong to the *select* class.
- He is *first-class* MA in English from Delhi University.
- She is in the *prime* of her youth.

Antonyms

- Chandravarkar is a *mediocre* student. He secured only 40% marks in the last examination.

✦ This motor-bike is *imperfect* in many ways — its engine, ignition, brakes etc.

✦ The lighting system of this studio is rather *faulty*.

EXCITE

Synonyms : Stimulate, provoke, awake, arise, kindle, inflame, animate, irritate.

A1tonyms : Compose, soothe, allay, hush, mollify, quell, appease, quieten, pacify, lull.

Synonyms

✦ His remarks have *stimulated* my curiosity.

✦ The arbitrary police action *provoked* public outcry for an investigation.

✦ Arise, *awake* and stop not until you reach your goal.

✦ Poor sportsmanship in the stadium today *aroused* a sense of disgust among the spectators.

✦ A smouldering cigarette can *kindle* a devastating bonfire.

✦ The crowd was *inflamed* by the brutality of the police.

✦ A smile *animated* her face, when she met her boy friend after a long time.

- He is very short-tempered and gets *irritated* on trivial matters.

Antonyms

- *Compose* yourself, my dear, I have startling news for you!
- The new promises made by the leader *soothed* many a poor man.
- The mayor *allayed* the fears of the frustrated folk of the industrial estate.

EXERTION

Synonyms : Energy, strain, effort, stretch, pull, tug, endeavour, struggle, pain, trouble, spurt.

Antonyms : Rest, repose, peace, tranquillity, idleness, laziness.

Synonyms

- Einstein has proved that matter and *energy* are convertible into each other.
- I can realise your *strain* of working while suffering from a painful back ailment.
- Inspite of his best *efforts* he could not win any prize.
- He *stretched* his arm to the maximum but could not catch the moving train.
- He was praised for *pulling* the fallen climber out of the crevasse.
- He was *tugging* at my sleeve to ask directions.

- The Red Cross *endeavours* to alleviate the suffering of mankind.
- Fruits of one's *struggle* are most enjoyable.
- The president of the society has taken *pains* to save it from being wound up.
- He is always in *trouble*.

Antonyms

- I switched off the machine and it came to *rest*.
- Her face is a mirror of sweet *repose*.
- I have made *peace* with my boss by clarifying all the misunderstandings.

EXTEND

Synonyms : Lengthen, protract, widen, stretch, elongate, prolong.

Antonyms : Contract, shorten, narrow, shrink, terminate, truncate.

Synonyms

- As the sun goes down the horizon, shadows on earth have a tendency to *lengthen*.
- *Protracted* negotiations are being held between the US and USSR in Geneva on the disarmament issue.
- India and France have decided to *widen* the area of economic cooperation.
- This elastic will not *stretch* any further.

Antonyms

- ✦ In winter, metallic articles *contract*.
- ✦ *Shorten* this essay into a paragraph.
- ✦ The path leading to his house is too *narrow* to let this car pass.
- ✦ This cotton shirt will *shrink* on washing.

EXTRAVAGANT

Synonyms : Lavish, unreasonable, wasteful, excessive, immoderate, inordinate, prodigal, profuse, spendthrift.

Antonyms : Reasonable, judicious, moderate, temperate, economical, provident, thrifty, sparing,

Synonyms

- ✦ He consumed his inherited wealth with too *lavish* a hand.
- ✦ He is a spoilt son of a rich father, *unreasonable* in demands, not amendable to argument.

- ✦ The government is trying its best to economise on *wasteful* expenditure in day-to-day administration.
- ✦ His *excessive* love for money has brought him all these difficulties.

- The old man consumed an *immoderate* amount of wine and fell asleep, never to rise.
- *Inordinate* delay in the finalisation of minor details can cause failure of the project.
- The *prodigal* amount of eggs laid by the fish ensure the survival of the species.
- They gave *profuse* thanks to the industrialist for his contribution to the orphanage.
- He is a bit worried about his *spendthrift* brother who squanders a fortune on each outfit.

Antonyms

- The price of this handicraft seems *reasonable*.
- We must make *judicious* use of our voting right.
- The climate of Mumbai is *moderate* throughout the year.

FAME

Synonyms : Repute, honour, glory, renown, credit, reputation.

Antonyms : Disrepute, dishonour, notoriety, oblivion.

Synonyms

- Justice Bhagwati is a jurist of high *repute.*
- Children must be taught to show *honour* to their elders.
- The old soldier had won *glory* on the battle field.
- Jabriel Mehta is a musician of great *renown.*
- The photographer was given due *credit* for his participation in the programme.

Antonyms

- The involvement of the high official in the spy scandal brought him *disrepute.*

- *Dishonouring* the national flag is a serious crime punishable with imprisonment and fine.
- Dacoit Chandra Singh of Rajasthan has a *notoriety* for his ruthlessness and cruelty towards innocent citizens.

FAMOUS

Synonyms : Noted, celebrated, renowned, well-known.

Antonyms : Obscure, fugitive, inglorious, unknown.

Synonyms

- Ashok Kumar is not only a great actor but also a *noted* poet and writer.
- Ravi Shankar is a *celebrated* sitarist of India.
- He is *renowned* for creating sweet melodies on the sitar.
- Lata Mangeshkar is a *well-known* singer.

Antonyms

- His writings are uninteresting and *obscure*.
- Some of the offenders who caused riots have recently become *fugitives*.
- They are obviously feeling sorry for their *inglorious* behaviour.

FANCIFUL

Synonyms : Imaginary, capricious, unreal, whimsical, imaginative, fantastic.

Antonyms : Positive, realistic, existent, substantial, factual, veritable.

Synonyms

- ✦ He is always haunted by his *imaginary* fear of failure in business.
- ✦ The actions of diplomats must never be *capricious.*
- ✦ She lives in an *unreal* world of make-believe.
- ✦ His essay on the care and feeding of husbands is pleasantly *whimsical.*
- ✦ The artist's *imaginative* use of colour delighted the critics.
- ✦ The director received *fantastic* praise from the audience for his new play.

Antonyms

- ✦ His *positive* role in organising the meeting so successfully was greatly appreciated.
- ✦ His role in this film is highly *realistic.* It seemed he actually lived the character he played.
- ✦ A *substantial* amount of oil has been dug and drilled in this terrain.

FASTEN

Synonyms : Join, bind, fix.

Antonyms : Loose, undo, unfix.

Synonyms

- ✦ Seth Dina Nath *joined* the movement for economic freedom of the bonded labour, after distributing a good part of his own land to his old workers.

- India has refused to *bind* itself to any of the power blocs in the world. It prefers to remain non-aligned.
- Smith's salary has been *fixed* at Rs. 2000/- per month.

Antonyms

- This belt is too *loose* for your slim waist.
- It is very difficult to *undo* a wrong done to the poor.
- If you do not approve this draft agreement, I will *unfix* the whole deal.

FAT

Synonyms : Stout, portly, obese, plump, adipose, chubby, buxom.

Antonyms : Emaciated, thin, slim.

Synonyms

- Winston Churchill had a *stout* impressive body.
- He had a *portly* gait in his movements like those of a king.
- She gives an impression of an *obese* personality. She is known to be a glutton.

Antonyms

- Continued poverty has brought him *emaciated* looks.

✦ He is so lean and *thin*, I am always afraid the next cyclone will blow him away.

✦ This frock is too wide for her slim waist.

FATAL

Synonyms : Lethal, mortal, deadly, destructive, pernicious, baneful.

Antonyms : Life-giving, helpful, beneficial, constructive.

Synonyms

✦ Cyanide is a *lethal* poison.

✦ Because of an ancient family feud, the two cousins grew up as *mortal* enemies from birth.

✦ Leukaemia is a *deadly* disease.

✦ Nuclear energy should not be wasted for *destructive* purposes.

✦ Nowadays he is involved in the *pernicious* business of selling heroin.

Antonyms

✦ This medicine has a *life-giving* constituent.

✦ His attitude was greatly *helpful* in the achievement of my objective.

✦ Panchsheel is a *beneficial* concept for the solution of many international conflicts.

FEAR

Synonyms : Fright, horror, alarm, panic, terror, dread.

Antonyms : Trust, courage, calmness, equanimity.

Synonyms

- ✦ Nuclear armament gives many a nation grave *fright.*
- ✦ The *horror* of the third World War keeps modern civilisation in suspense.
- ✦ The doorbell rang in the middle of the night and *alarmed* her.

Antonyms

- ✦ Super powers must learn to *trust* each other, if they wish to dispel the fear of war.
- ✦ They must display *courage* in placing their cards on the table in order to reach a settlement on armament issues.
- ✦ Their leaders must show *calmness* and *equanimity* in dealing with each other.

FEEBLE

Synonyms : Weak, impotent, frail, infirm, debilitated, languid.

Antonyms : Strong, vigorous, muscular, athletic, stalwart, robust, sinewy.

Synonyms

- ✦ The strong should help the *weak.*
- ✦ His wife has sought divorce from him because she thinks he is *impotent.*

- He has put forth a *frail* theory which even an average person can challenge.
- The *infirm* conclusion was based on deliberate distortion of the evidence.
- Their health has *debilitated* due to long exposure to the elements.
- A *languid* movement of the hand pointed towards the beautiful vase.

Antonyms

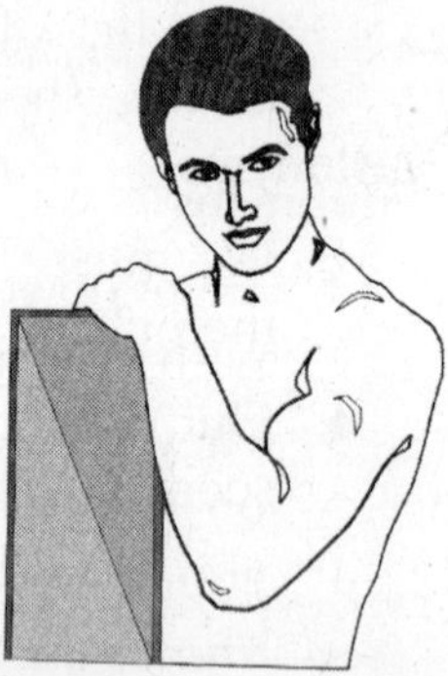

- A *strong* man needs no arms to fight his way up.
- The country has to make *vigorous* efforts to solve the unemployment problem.
- His *muscular* body enables him to perform numerous feats.
- He is a political *stalwart.* He has retained the Lok Sabha seat since the very first elections after independence.

FILTHY

Synonyms : Dirty, squalid, foul, unclean, sullied, impure.

Antonyms : Pure, clean, immaculate, spotless, unsullied, unsoiled.

Synonyms

- A pile of *dirty* clothes is to be sent to the laundry.

- The hippies live a *squalid* life.
- The policeman used *foul* language against a suspect without due confirmation of guilt.
- People, *unclean* in mind and spirit, generally try to harm others.
- I will not let my lips be *sullied* by the use of such words.
- Failure of rains compelled people to drink *impure* water.

Antonyms

- We must first boil the water and then claim it is *pure*.
- Our classroom is so *clean*, not a speck of dust can be seen anywhere.
- Your friend John always wears *immaculate, spotlessly* clean clothes.
- This shirt is old but *unsoiled* so far.

FINAL

Synonyms : Last, ultimate, concluding, finishing.

Antonyms : First, beginning, opening, initial.

Synonyms

- I did reach an agreement with him in the *last* round of talks.

- The *ultimate* result of the negotiations was the retention of the premises by the company against an additional payment of Rs. 1 lakh only.
- In his *concluding* remarks, the principal counselled the students to do selected reading rather than unplanned study of too many books.

Antonyms

- My *first* advice to you is to develop the habit of listening to what others have to say and then giving your own views.
- Geneva negotiations on disarmament are yet in their *beginning* stage.
- The *opening* remarks of the president on the occasion were devoted to the importance of religion in day-to-day life.

FIND

Synonyms : Locate, learn, unearth; detect, ascertain, discover.

Antonyms : Forget, mislay, miss.

Synonyms

- Kanniya Kumari is *located* in the extreme south of India.
- We should *learn* the essentials of healthy living by heart.
- The police was finally able to *unearth* the headquarters of the spy ring.

- I have *detected* quite a few factual errors in this book.

Antonyms

- It is good to *forget* the unlucky past and start a new era with sincere effort.
- Sam *mislaid* his purse during his journey and had to face lot of inconvenience.
- I *missed* the train by just a few seconds.

FINISH

Synonyms : Close, shape, end, conclude, complete, perfect, finalise.

Antonyms : Begin, start, open, initiate.

Synonyms

- Unless we *close* our ranks in society, we can not hope to achieve socialism.
- India and the United States are likely to have greater economic cooperation in future, looking at the way India's liberalisation policy is *shaping*.
- This policy may *end* the long-standing differences between the two countries.

Antonyms

- ✦ Prime Minister's visit to Washington may *begin* a new era in Indo-US friendship.
- ✦ The leaders of the two countries have already *started* parleys on important issues.
- ✦ The parleys if successful will *open* the way to manifold increase in economic exchanges of different sort.

FORESIGHT

Synonyms : Foreknowledge, forethought, prescience, prudence, presentiment, foreshadowing.

Antonyms : Narrow-mindedness, bias, shortsightness, prejudice.

Synonyms

- ✦ Augustine's treatment of God's *foreknowledge* and man's free will makes an interesting reading.
- ✦ He could have avoided the accident by using *forethought*.

- ✦ God's *prescience* is only one aspect of his general omniscience.
- ✦ The king's *prudence* saved him from falling prey to his minister's designs.

- The saint had a *presentiment* that his pupil will poison him one day.
- These incidents are a *foreshadow* of the civil war.

Antonyms

- *Narrow-mindedness* is one of the main causes of conflict among humans at all levels.
- The teacher had a *bias* against Mary. He, therefore, deducted her marks in general behaviour, though she showed great improvement in overall performance.
- Jane's *short-sightedness* in business brought her early profit but huge loss in the end.

FRIGHT

Synonyms : Apprehension, panic, dread, dismay, trepidation, fear, terror.

Antonyms : Tranquillity, calmness, coolness, equanimity, placidity, composure.

Synonyms

- His *apprehensions* about the difficulties inherent in the new job proved correct.
- The terrorists are trying to create *panic* by killing innocent people.

- During the international crisis, everyone was filled with the *dread* of nuclear war.
- Their utter refusal to compromise *dismayed* him and left him at a loss.
- All the members of the family were in a state of *trepidation* when the dacoits attacked the house at midnight.

- Countless *fears* leaped up whenever she had to face any new situation in life.

Antonyms

- Installation of military guards has brought about *tranquillity* in the state.
- The leaders have shown *calmness* in handling the law and order situation.
- His *coolness* in human relations cannot be termed as his mental *equanimity*.

FRAUD

Synonyms : Deceit, deception, duplicity, stratagem.

Antonyms : Honesty, probity, integrity.

Synonyms

- Many were involved in this web of *deceit*.

- She referred to the pills as sweets in a harmless *deception*; this made it easier to administer them to the child.
- She confessed her guilt of *duplicity* of another engagement that evening.
- His *stratagem* for winning her comprised of agreeing to everything she said.

Antonyms

- *Honesty* always pays its way in due course.
- He puts his cards always face up. He is, therefore, known for his *probity*.
- He believes in straight forward dealings in society. He is, therefore, known for his *integrity* of character.

FUNDAMENTAL

Synonyms : Essential, important, primary.

Antonyms : Secondary, unimportant, non-essential.

Synonyms

- Always speaking the truth is an *essential* qualification for this job of great financial responsibility.
- Fertilisers have become an *important* feature of agricultural productivity.
- Irrigation facilities are a *primary* consideration for determining the value of an agricultural farm.

Antonyms

- Human labour has come down to *secondary* position in this age of automation.
- His attendance at today's meeting is *unimportant.*
- Many of the *non-essential* commodities like motor car and TV have been upgraded to essential category in all modern advanced countries.

GATHER

Synonyms : Congregate, collect, muster, convene, assemble.

Antonyms : Disband, scatter, separate.

Synonyms

- All the leaders of the country belonging to different religious organisations and associations *congregated* at the All India Religious Conference held in Vigyan Bhavan, New Delhi.
- We should first *collect* the funds and then plunge into action.
- The general *mustered* courage and plunged his army into the war.

Antonyms

- As soon as the mission was over, the leader *disbanded* the gang.
- The sun sends out the rays, *scattering* them throughout the horizon.
- We can *separate* oxygen from water; the left over is an invisible gas hydrogen.

GAY

Synonyms : Cheerful, jovial, vivacious, jolly, joyous, sprightly, buoyant, blithe.

Antonyms : Mournful, cheerless, unhappy, depressed, gloomy, sorrowful, sad, dismal.

Synonyms

- Although he was to undergo an operation, he was looking *cheerful.*
- Albert Johnson was a kind *jovial* old man of this neighbourhood.

- The *vivacious* girl made a good sales executive for the advertisement agency.
- We had a *jolly* time at the party.
- Our grandfather's 80th anniversary was a *joyous* occasion for the whole family.
- He is unusually *sprightly* for a man of 80.
- Rita's *buoyant* personality attracts many new friends to her.

✦ The child had a wonderful *blithe* personality.

Synonyms

✦ He is so serious in life; his looks become *mournful* as soon as he concentrates on a difficult problem.

✦ Visiting his office is no pleasure. He is rich but *cheerless.*

✦ *Unhappy* is one who is rich but unhealthy.

✦ The low percentage of marks in the examination has made him too *depressed.*

GENERAL

Synonyms : Common, popular, public, universal, accepted.

Antonyms : Uncommon, unusual, queer, specific.

Synonyms

✦ It is *common* knowledge that wine is unwelcome in religious premises.

✦ It is well-known that Kolkata has produced many *popular* revolutionaries.

✦ An agreement contrary to *public* policy is unenforceable.

✦ Gandhiji's greatness is *universally* accepted.

Antonyms

✦ Taj Mahal has *uncommon* beauty.

✦ A penguin is a *queer* bird.

- I can answer all your *specific* enquiries without hesitation.

GENEROUS

Synonyms : Liberal, lavish, noble, bountiful, magnanimous.

Antonyms : Niggardly, selfish, greedy, light, chary, sparing,

- It befits a gentleman to be *liberal.*
- He is *lavish* in his charity.
- There are very few who deserve to be called *noble* in this materialistic selfish world.
- Nature is *bountiful* in India but men are lazy and lethargic due to heat or cold.

Antonyms

- One whose heart is made of lead cannot but be *niggardly.*
- *Selfish* parents seldom care for their children.
- Businessmen always and everywhere tend to be *greedy* for profit.
- He is a *light*-weight person, both in body and mind.

GENUINE

Synonyms : Authentic, pure, real, true, sincere, actual.

Antonyms : Fictitious, spurious, artificial, forged, fake, imaginary.

Synonyms

- This news is *authentic.*
- *Pure* unadulterated ghee is available at that shop.
- This pearl is *real.*
- His statement is *true* as per my knowledge.
- Our guests always receive a *sincere* welcome.

Antonyms

- The characters in this story are *fictitious.*
- This drug is *spurious,* hence, it should not be taken.
- That body of water is an *artificial* lake.

- He *forged* the managing director's signature but was caught in time.

- Both the roots of this quadratic equation are *imaginary* but quite illustrative of the point at issue.

GLORIFY

Synonyms : Extol, exalt, commend, appraise.

Antonyms : Abuse, depress, reject, condemn.

Synonyms

- The teacher *extolled* his student for standing first.
- He took great pains to *exalt* the glory of ancient India.
- The students *commended* the greeting message of the principal.
- The examiner unbiasedly *appraised* the papers of the students.

Antonyms

- One of the accused started *abusing* his friends in the presence of the police.
- The scene of the accident *depressed* me.
- The principal has *rejected* my application for leave.
- The workers *condemned* the management for throwing some of their colleagues out of job.

GIFTED

Synonyms : Intelligent, able, apt, skilful, sagacious, talented.

Antonyms : Foolish, stupid, idiotic, stolid.

Synonyms

- Ape is an *intelligent* animal.
- Though he is *able*-bodied he is lazy.
- The doctor made a few *apt* remarks about nutrition and health.
- Only the most *skilful* pilots are deployed for bombing the enemy positions.
- Mrs. N. Kapur is the most *sagacious* of all the biology teachers in our school.
- Atul is one of the few *talented* students of the class.

Antonyms

- It would be *foolish* on your part to change the profession at this late age.
- The *stupid* fellow! He annoys his friends by making sill comments at the wrong movement.
- His *idiotic* utterances now and then leave a bad impression on his colleagues.
- He is basically *stolid*. His face remains expressionless against anger or irritation.

GORGEOUS

Synonyms : Sumptuous, magnificent, splendid, grand.

Antonyms : Colourless, simple, unadorned, sombre.

Synonyms

- Our host provided a *sumptuous* feast on his birthday.

✦ Mozart's Don Giovanni is a *magnificent* opera.

✦ His reputation as a physicist is *splendid*.

✦ The president received his guests in a *grand* manner.

Antonyms

✦ The inauguration of the shop by the minister happened to be a rather *colourless* affair.

✦ Sonia is too *simple* a girl to work in an advertising agency, where clever and smart girls will not even let her breathe freely.

✦ The manager is the *unadorned* king of this department store.

✦ His *sombre* attitude always let him down as a salesman.

GOVERN

Synonyms : Rule, control, manage, direct, supervise, administer, command.

Antonyms : Misrule, mismanage, misgovern.

Synonyms

✦ A dictator thinks he can be successful only when he *rules* with an iron hand.

✦ The police failed in its attempt to *control* the unruly mob.

- He has appointed a new man to *manage* his business.
- Mrs. Indira Gandhi personally *directed* the nation's foreign policy.
- Our new office manager will *supervise* the work of several departments.
- The vice-chancellor of our university personally *administers* the establishment's financial affairs.
- The king *commanded* the guards to raise the new bridge.

Antonyms

- The military general *misruled* his country; no wonder he had to abdicate in favour of a civilian government.
- Some of the public sector undertakings are still *mismanaged*.
- The new governor has taken personal responsibility to set right the *misgoverned* departments.

GRADUAL

Synonyms : Slow, continuous, regular, progressive.

Antonyms : Rapid, momentary, unanticipated, unforeseen.

Synonyms

- *Slow* and steady wins the race.
- The *continuous* outflow of blood led to his untimely death.

- He is very *regular* in his studies.
- Only a few of the young politicians are *progressive*.

Antonyms

- *Rapid* flow of river waters causes soil erosion, unless the extra flow is used for hydro-electricity.
- His response to the boss's instructions was only *momentary*.
- Quite often *unanticipated* circumstances beyond one's control upset the planned procedures.

GRAND

Synonyms : Noble, lordly, stately, majestic, resplendent, august, superb, exalted, illustrious.

Antonyms : Inferior, colourless, ignoble.

Synonyms

- Attainment of nirvana is a *noble* idea.
- His *lordly* manners angered everyone present in the meeting.
- All the members of the nonaligned movement were awed by Mrs. Gandhi's *stately* grandeur and innate humanism.

- In the north of India stands the *majestic* Himalayas as its saviour.

- Her *resplendent* necklace became the focus of attention of all her female guests.
- Ashoka is the foremost *august* personality of Indian history.
- The performance of Chinese swimmers was *superb.*
- Poet John Milton wrote in an *exalted* style.
- He has won many medals for his *illustrious* service in the Indian Army.

Antonyms

- A lieutenant has *inferior* status compared to a captain.
- The opening ceremony of the exhibition was rather *colourless.*
- His *ignoble* performance at the meeting led to his dismissal.

GRASP

Synonyms : Hold, seize, snatch, grip, grab, clutch, clasp.

Antonyms : Loose, lose, abandon, release, relinquish.

Synonyms

- I will *hold* the mirror; you look into it.
- One who *seizes* the opportunity when it comes makes a success in life.
- The thief *snatched* the golden necklace from the lady's neck and ran away.
- They tightened the *grip*.
- But the policeman *grabbed* the thief by the arm and recovered the necklace.

Antonyms

- This shirt is too *loose* for my slim body.
- Don't *lose* patience; I will set it right.
- I have *abandoned* the idea of going abroad for the time being.
- He *relinquished* his job on being criticised by the general manager.

GRIEF

Synonyms : Pain, sorrow, trouble, affliction, bereavement, distress.

Antonyms : Glee, joy, contentment, satisfaction, happiness, pleasure.

Synonyms

- ✦ The doctor gave me a tablet to relieve the *pain* in my stomach.
- ✦ *Sorrow* will pay no debt, sorrows are our best educators.
- ✦ His spoilt son has become a source of great *trouble* to him.
- ✦ Faith prompted him to endure every *affliction*.
- ✦ His *bereavement* was shared by his relatives and friends.
- ✦ The *distress* caused by her son's death can make her insane.

Antonyms

- ✦ The child experienced great *glee* on breaking the toy.
- ✦ Taking a cold drink gives *joy* and *contentment* in summer.
- ✦ It gives me satisfaction, *pleasure* and *happiness* in declaring a net dividend of 15% on the ordinary shares of the company.

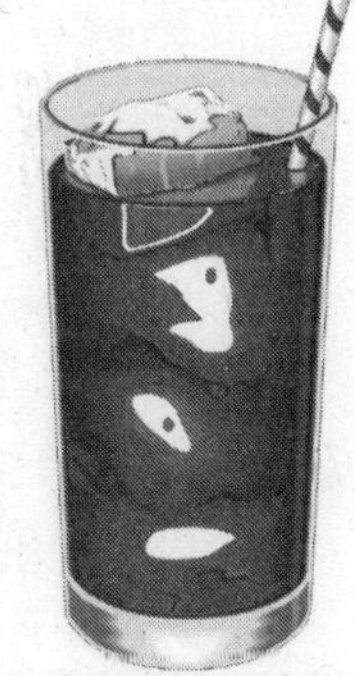

GROUNDLESS

Synonyms : False, baseless, unauthorised, fanciful, gratuitous.

Antonyms : Actual, material, well-founded, substantial, positive, real, solid.

Synonyms

- We should not make a *false* statement in a legal document come what may.
- His allegations were founded on a *baseless* rumour.
- His *unauthorised* absence from office will be treated as a break in service.
- She has a *fanciful* way of calling her plants by human names.
- His *gratuitous* insult flabbergasted me.

Antonyms

- I have made a statement of *actual* facts and figures.
- There is *material* evidence available to prove our case.
- My arguments in this case are based on *well-founded* legal precepts.
- There is *substantial* weight in your new theory.

HANDY

Synonyms : Skilled, skilful, expert, adroit, dexterous, close, convenient, proficient, near, ready.

Antonyms : Unskilled, unskilful, bungling, clumsy, unhandy.

Synonyms

- It is better to pay more to a *skilled* man than exploring an unskilled man.
- The bricklayer did a *skilful* job in building this wall.
- The rider was an *expert* horseman; that is why he escaped the accident.
- Most of the leaders in this political party are *adroit* speakers.
- Her *dexterous* fingers moved effortlessly over the piano keys.
- Come *closer* so that I can see you.
- The parking lot is *convenient* to the office.

- Although he is a *proficient* typist, he takes little interest in his work.
- A storm is *near,* I am afraid.
- Keep your dress *ready* because we can start from here any time.

Antonyms

- This factory will do better if it were to replace *unskilled* workers by trained mechanics.
- He claimed proficiency on machines, but his handling of this machine seems *unskilful.*
- The new management is *bungling* with the whole mechanism of the production process.

HANDLE

Synonyms : Hold, wield, touch, carry out.

Antonyms : Throw, bungle, miscarry.

Synonyms

- I can *hold* this bag in the bus without much difficulty.
- The chief engineer *wields* great authority in the Public Works Department.
- If I *touch* a task, it has to be done.
- I *carried out* the orders of my boss without hesitation.

Antonyms

- I sold my land at a *throw*away price.
- If you *bungle* with my money in future, I will throw you out.

- ✦ The pregnant woman fell from the staircase and *miscarried* her baby.

HARD

Synonyms : Arduous, difficult, laborious, troublesome, trying.

Antonyms : Easy, simple, plain

Synonyms

- ✦ This is an *arduous* task involving lot of time and travelling.
- ✦ It is extremely *difficult* for a service man to make his both ends meet in these days of inflation.
- ✦ This job is *laborious*. My wages may be quite high.
- ✦ Handling the kids is a *troublesome* job.
- ✦ Ram is passing through *trying* circumstances.

Antonyms

- ✦ It is *easy* to say but difficult to perform.
- ✦ It is a *simple* machine, capable of being run by an unskilled person.
- ✦ He made the objective of his visit quite *plain*.

HARSH

Synonyms : Jarring, raucous, strident, discordant.

Antonyms : Musical, concordant, tuneful, melodious, mild.

Synonyms

- ✦ The news of their elopement was *jarring* to their parents.

- The *raucous* yelling of the crowd could be heard over blocks.
- The *strident* voice of my wife quite often bores me.
- Many a couple have *discordant* views on the art of raising children nowadays.

Antonyms

- The sweet atmosphere inspired the couple to make *musical* notes.
- The meeting helped to create *concordant* views on the controversial subject.
- My piano made *tuneful*, *melodious* sounds in the hall.
- Use a soap that is *mild* on the skin.

HAZARD

Synonyms : Chance, danger, peril, risk, venture, threat, contingency, jeopardy.

Antonyms : Assurance, certainty, necessity, protection, safeguard, security, surety.

Synonyms

- She *chanced* to find her sister at home.
- He had stayed up so late that he felt the *danger* of oversleeping and being late for work the next morning.

- ✦ Many species are already in *peril* of extinction because of our destruction of their natural habitat.
- ✦ He has insured his assets against the *risk* of fire and theft.
- ✦ Such a gamble against odds would put their whole *venture* in *jeopardy*.
- ✦ They have *threatened* to wipe him out if ever he thought of leaving the gang.
- ✦ We must be prepared for any *contingency*.

Antonyms

- ✦ I wanted an *assurance* from my boss for security of job.
- ✦ There is no *certainty* of a lasting career in the private sector.
- ✦ There is no particular *necessity* for me to linger on this job.
- ✦ A house is the first *protection* from the vagaries of nature.

HEALTHY

Synonyms : Vigorous, sound, hale, well, strong, robust.

Antonyms : Sickly, ill, unhealthy, weak, weakly, unsound, sick.

Synonyms

- ✦ The *vigorous* climate of European countries makes its people strong and *robust.*
- ✦ A *sound* mind can exist in a *sound* body.
- ✦ I found our neighbour *hale* and hearty at 78.
- ✦ He has the knack to keep *well* under any circumstances.

Antonyms

- ✦ Sam has started feeling *sickly* of late.
- ✦ I fell *ill* due to extreme cold.
- ✦ The atmosphere of this locality is very *unhealthy.*
- ✦ That is why you find children here *weak.*
- ✦ This plan of business is rather *unsound.*

HESITATE

Synonyms : Waver, pause, falter, vacillate, demur, tarry, totter.

Antonyms : Determine, settle, end, decide, resolve.

Synonyms

- ✦ She hesitated only so long as he *wavered.*
- ✦ He *paused* long enough before each painting in order to note the painter's name.
- ✦ She *faltered* in her denunciation of him as she remembered the good points of her man.

- While she hesitated, he *vacillated* between positive and negative thoughts of her.
- The majority were in favour of the plan, but a few *demurred.*
- Don't *tarry* too long in coming to a decision.
- The vase *tottered* and fell on the hard ground.

Antonyms

- I am *determined* to make a success of this project.
- The differences between the husband and wife need to be *settled* once and for all.
- The controversy over political issues should be *ended* without delay.
- We should *decide* about the course of action to be taken in this behalf.
- The problems could then be *resolved* with ease.

HEAVY

Synonyms : Crushing, burdensome, onerous, oppressive.

Antonyms : Trivial, easy, light, mild.

Synonyms

- Prakash Padukone gave a *crushing* defeat to his opponent in the finals of World Badminton.
- It is a *burdensome* task to prepare a good pitch for the coming cricket match in this rainy season.
- The heat this summer is quite *oppressive.*

Antonyms

- Do not quarrel with your friend on this *trivial* matter, sort it out immediately.
- There is nothing so *easy* as talking and gossiping.
- He is basically *light*-footed.
- He has a *mild* temperament and has never made an enemy.

HIGH

Synonyms : Elevated, tall, lofty, towering.

Antonyms : Base, low, short, degraded.

Synonyms

- A joint secretary in the ministry of external affairs is generally *elevated* to the position of an ambassador.
- Palm tree is usually very *tall*.

- ✦ I am possessed of very *lofty* ideals; but I don't know whether I will ever get the necessary opportunities to achieve them.
- ✦ Our new manager is a great intellectual and orator, he has a *towering* personality.

Antonyms

- ✦ The *base* of all evil in the world is selfishness of individuals.
- ✦ The standard of living of the common people in India is still rather *low*.
- ✦ I have joined a *short* term course in computer programming.
- ✦ By talking in terms of special rights of regions and religions, we are *degrading* the national viewpoint.

HIGHEST

Synonyms : Topmost, uppermost, supreme.

Antonyms : Undermost, lowest, deepest, bottom.

Synonyms

- ✦ The president holds the *topmost* position in the United States.
- ✦ Disarmament is the *uppermost* controversy in the international discussions today.
- ✦ Under the constitution of India, the president is the *supreme* commander of the country's defence forces.

Antonyms

- The peon is the *undermost* member of the administrative system in India.
- He is at the *lowest* rung of the departmental hierarchy.
- The Pacific is the *deepest* ocean in the world.
- At the *bottom* of the ocean lie many unknown treasures of Nature.

HIRE

Synonyms : Engage, employ, rent, enlist, recruit.

Antonyms : Purchase, buy, fire, retire, discharge.

Synonyms

- I am *engaged* in the construction of my house these days.
- I have *employed* 60 workers to do the construction work.
- I may *rent* out one portion of my house when it is completed,
- I have already *enlisted* a few candidates for the proposed renting of the portion concerned.

Antonyms

- I had to *purchase* the cement at a very high price.
- I have yet to *buy* the wood for the almirahs, doors and windows.
- He *fired* the unreliable worker.
- I will *retire* from my present job this October.

HOLY

Synonyms : Religious, godly, divine, saintly, hallowed, sacred.

Antonyms : Irreligious, ungodly, irreverent, sacrilegious, profane.

Synonyms

- ✦ In Hindu law marriage is a *religious* ceremony.
- ✦ The old patriarch was a wise and *godly* man.
- ✦ Swami Vivekananda tried to establish relationship between the *divine* and material worlds.
- ✦ Not only the audience but the priests were also influenced by the *saintly* sermons of Swami Vivekananda.
- ✦ John's last wish was that he may be buried in *hallowed* ground.
- ✦ Giriraj is a mountain near Mathura thought to be *sacred* by the Hindus.

Antonyms

- ✦ By declaring India a secular state, you cannot say that Constitution-makers wanted to make the countrymen *irreligious*.
- ✦ A communist society cannot be called *ungodly* as the actions of the people of such a society are perfectly godly.
- ✦ The common people are not *irreverent* to clergymen and churches are not used for *sacrilegious* or *profane* activities.

HORRIBLE

Synonyms : Frightful, appalling, dire, ghastly, fearful, dreadful, awful, hideous, repulsive, terrific, ugly.

Antonyms : Agreeable, pleasant, delightful, pleasurable, charming, pleasing.

Synonyms

- ✦ As the full moon rose, *frightful* howls pierced the air around the cemetery.
- ✦ The plight of the victims of the railway accident was *appalling*.
- ✦ Hijackers threatened that refusal to meet their demands will have *dire* consequences.
- ✦ It was the *ghastliest* accident I have ever seen.
- ✦ He was *fearful* of her psychological situation, lest she should harm herself.
- ✦ Though he was going slow, he met with a *dreadful* accident.
- ✦ He was found guilty of the *awful* crime of poisoning his wife.
- ✦ Everyday we read about *hideous* crimes in the Western countries.
- ✦ He is a well-educated man but his table manners are *repulsive*.
- ✦ A *terrific* explosion woke up the whole town.

Antonyms

- ✦ He has an *agreeable* attitude to every friend.
- ✦ His *pleasant* manners have won him a large circle of friends.
- ✦ Meeting him is always a *delightful* experience.

HOT

Synonyms : Burning, feverish, scorching, torrid.

Antonyms : Cold, calm, cool, soothing.

Synonyms

- ✦ The hot sun is *burning* my skin.
- ✦ The government is *feverishly* trying to come to a settlement with Western leaders.
- ✦ In mid-June, Delhi has *scorching* heat.

Antonyms

- ✦ This winter is exceptionally *cold*.
- ✦ This tablet will *calm* down your nerves.
- ✦ It is quite *cool* today.
- ✦ This music is highly *soothing*.

HUMANE

Synonyms : Humanitarian, philanthropic, sympathetic, tender, kind, benign, human, charitable, compassionate.

Antonyms : Inhuman, unkind, cruel, uncharitable, malignant.

Synonyms

- ✦ World Health Organisation is an international organisation doing a lot of *humanitarian* work.
- ✦ Some of the industrialists perform a few *philanthropic* activities just to hoodwink the income tax authorities.
- ✦ Our management has a *sympathetic* attitude towards the labour.

Antonyms

- ✦ Bonded labour practice is considered *inhuman* in a democracy.
- ✦ It was *unkind* of the manager to push out Nandani from employment just because she did not attend the birthday party of his son.
- ✦ Some tumours are *malignant* while others are benign.

HUMID

Synonyms : Wet, moist, close, sticky, oppressive.

Antonyms : Parched, dry, arid.

Synonyms

- ✦ Don't *wet* my carpet. Better leave your soggy shoes outside.
- ✦ This lipstick not only colours the lips but also *moistens* them.
- ✦ Today the weather is rather *close* and *sticky* as there is no breeze.

- The government of South Africa is indulging in *oppressive* acts against the coloured population.

Antonyms

- The drought has made even fertile land dry and *parched*.
- The scientists have now invented chemicals which help vegetation in *arid* lands.

HUMOUR

Synonyms : Wit, fun, drollery, amusement, jocularity, pleasantry.

Antonyms : Solemnity, gravity, sobriety, seriousness.

Synonyms

- She showed a great deal of *wit* in handling the delicate situation.
- *Fun* is like life insurance: the older you get, the more it costs.
- We are so happy with the *drollery* of the game that we play it every night.
- There is a time for work and a time for *amusement*. 
- He is popular for his *jocularity* in the company of friends.
- There was not much conversation, only an exchange of *pleasantries*.

Antonyms

- We have to maintain the *solemnity* of the occasion. Reserve your nice jokes for some other time.
- It took us some time to let him wake to the *gravity* of the situation.
- This topic needs an atmosphere of *sobriety* for a healthy discussion.
- The politician realised the *seriousness* with which the matter needed to be pursued.

HUMOROUS

Synonyms : Funny, witty, comic, comical, droll, jocose, jocular, waggish.

Antonyms : Serious, grave, dull, sedate, gloomy.

Synonyms

- This story is quite *funny*. Let us read it again.
- The main character is so *witty*, his dialogues can make even a priest laugh.
- We can convert the play into a *comic* story without much difficulty.

- There are a number of *comical* scenes in this feature film.

Antonyms

- I have a *serious* interest in this business.

- ✦ The situation in Beirut is very *grave* owing to civil war in the country.
- ✦ My duties in this organisation involve *dull* and drab study of statistical data.

HYPOCRISY

Synonyms : Deceit, pretence, cant, falsify, deception.

Antonyms : Honesty, uprightness, straightforwardness.

Synonyms

- ✦ There is too much *deceit* practised by private companies in India to make extra profits.
- ✦ The detective managed to infiltrate into the smuggling ring by *pretence*.
- ✦ The thief's claim that he was going to give the money to the poor was just an act of *cant*.
- ✦ He *falsified* his birth certificate in order to get a new passport.
- ✦ The stage murder looked real, but it was only a visual *deception*.

Antonyms

- ✦ He has risen in life by dint of his strict adherence to the principle of *honesty*.
- ✦ He lays his cards on the table. He had nothing to hide. He believes in *uprightness*.
- ✦ His dealings are marked by *straightforwardness*. He does not indulge in hypocrisy.

IDEAL

Synonyms : Archetype, model, prototype, example, standard, original pattern.

Antonyms : Factual, realistic, practical.

Synonyms

- Satan is the *archetype* of the evildoers.
- The architect has prepared a *model* of our housing scheme.
- The government has formulated a *prototype* scheme for constructing the houses for miners.
- The teacher quoted many *examples* to make the lesson interesting.
- Critics with different *standards* often disagree.
- The scientist Newton gave many *original* ideas to science.
- A good seamstress can make a dress without a *pattern*.

Antonyms

- This is the *factual* outlook of our scheme.
- It is *realistic* rather than ideal, but it can be achieved and depended upon.
- Let us be *practical*, not utopian, if you wish to be popular among the common people of average intelligence.

IDLE

Synonyms : Inert, unoccupied, lazy, inactive, sloth, sluggish, unemployed, indolent.

Antonyms : Active, busy, diligent, industrious, assiduous.

Synonyms

- Helium is an *inert* gas, as it neither moves nor causes any motion.
- Indian farmer is *unoccupied* for about eight months in a year.
- The waiters seem *lazy* in this restaurant as there is not much rush of visitors. 
- Many machines have been *inactive* in this office since the computer was installed last year.
- Her *sloth* manners keep her from getting ahead in her job.
- People from the eastern part of Uttar Pradesh are generally *sluggish*.

- Today the *unemployed* youth is our biggest national problem.
- The teacher rebuked the *indolent* student but could not pull him up.

Antonyms

- John is a very *active* boy. He is good in both sports and studies.
- He keeps himself *busy* in one activity or the other all his waking hours.
- He takes *diligent* interest in extra-curricular activities.
- He is quite *industrious* in his studies and *assiduous* in sports.

IMITATE

Synonyms : Burlesque, echo, follow, copy, impersonate, mock, mimic, counterfeit, forge, parody.

Antonyms : Alter, convert, modify, vary.

Synonyms

- The cultural evening programme had a drama in which *burlesque* scenes on absent-minded professors were exhibited.
- The temple bells *echoed* across the valley every evening.

- Religion teaches us to *follow* the footsteps of our saints.
- Don't *copy* everything your elder brother does.
- Narcotic agents usually *impersonate* drug addicts.
- Back in the barracks he would *mimic* the platoon sergeant.
- Nowadays-*counterfeit* currency is in large circulation.
- He was jailed for possessing a *forged* passport.
- Everyone laughed when the comedian *parodied* the minister's brag.

Antonyms

- He has very much *altered* with age. He is no more the sprightly gentleman.
- He has *converted* his religious attitude into a purely materialist one.
- The tailor *modified* the suit to keep up with modern styles.

IMPROVE

Synonyms : Amend, reform, rectify, correct, ameliorate, better, increase.

Antonyms : Spoil, deteriorate, corrupt, mar, impair, pollute, damage, deprecate, rot, worren.

Synonyms

- The procedure to *amend* the Constitution is laid down in the constitution itself.
- How can an indifferent society *reform* its desperate men?
- The accounting error was *rectified* before the ledgers were sent for audit.
- The results to his experiment proved wrong as he had not *corrected* his earlier findings.
- We have constituted a Welfare Fund to *ameliorate* the living and working conditions of the rural poor.
- Modern technology has made *better* the working condition of the average worker.

Antonyms

- You will *spoil* the child by increasing his pocket money.
- His condition had *deteriorated* in this nursing home owing to negligence of the doctors.
- The movement for regional autonomy has caused *deterioration* in the nationhood of Indian society.
- The officials of this department are rather *corrupt*.
- They are *marring* the reputation of the whole organisation by their *corrupt* habits.
- The relations among different communities stand *impaired* in the Punjab owing to violent acts of terrorists.

✦ Too much smoke from the automobiles has *polluted* the atmosphere of the cities.

INCAPABLE

Synonyms : Incompetent, inefficient, unqualified inadequate, unable, unfit.

Antonyms : Gifted, capable, qualified, accomplished, competent, efficient.

Synonyms

✦ The workers went on strike as the new manager was found *incompetent* to efficiently control productive activities of the firm.

✦ The *inefficient* workers cannot be paid as much as the efficient ones.

✦ The acceptance of a deal should be *unqualified* to be valid in law.

✦ *Inadequate* supply of essential commodities in the district has caused general dissatisfaction among the people.

- He is *unable* to walk properly owing to a recent accident.
- The operation left her *unfit* for months.

Antonyms

- He is a *gifted* child and invariably tops in the class.
- He is a *capable* and just leader.
- He is a *qualified* engineer. No wonder he makes the machine work accurately.
- He is an *accomplished* personality in every sense of the term — knowledgeable, smart, sociable and healthy.

INCLEMENT

Synonyms : Rough, stormy, unfavourable, unpleasant.

Antonyms : Genial, mild, favourable, pleasant.

Synonyms

- His *rough* manners repel many a good friend.
- His speech was so *stormy*, the mob proceeded to the office of the chairman to express their strong protest against the corrupt practices of the officials.

- The weather tod ay is rather *unfavourable* for the playing of badminton.
- The weather was rather *unpleasant.*

Antonyms

- His *genial* personality makes everybody a well-wisher.
- Today the weather is *mild* enough to let us go on a picnic.
- His *pleasant* manners win everybody to his side.

INCLINE

Synonyms : Dispose, lean, fall upon, tend, towards, slope.

Antonyms : Indispose, rise, go upwards, repel.

Synonyms

- He *disposed* of the old furniture.
- This creeper tends to *lean* downwards in a vertical fashion.
- The common people have a tendency to *fall upon* the right kind of leadership, patriotic and strong.

+ This valley *slopes* downwards on the west side of the hill.

Antonyms

+ When I went to meet him, I found him *indisposed* and lying in bed.
+ The sun *rises* around 5.20 am in summer in Delhi.
+ The smoke of the automobiles *goes* up in the environment.
+ His cold temperament *repels* me from any intimate talk.

INCLUDE

Synonyms : Involve, comprise, contain.

Antonyms : Exclude, omit, leave out.

Synonyms

+ The manufacture of washing soap *involves* the use of many a chemical.

- This country *comprises* of a few hills, valleys and sea coasts.
- This classroom *contains* a number of benches, desks, a blackboard and a teacher's chair and table.

Antonyms

- We can easily *exclude* the girl students from this picnic, as it is going to be too hazardous.
- Don't *omit* the use of commas and full stops while answering your question paper in the English language. These are pertinent to accuracy.
- *Leave out* the inks from the list of stationery as I am going to buy it wholesale from Mumbai.

INCUR

Synonyms : Meet, bring danger, blame.

Antonyms : Shun, avoid, escape, defect.

Synonyms

- The loss will have to be *met* by raising a new loan.
- The commitment to import a new machine *brings danger* of further temporary loss in the books of the company.
- We cannot *blame* the management for this situation as the machine will add to the profits in due course.

Antonyms

- We cannot *shun* new investments for the future prosperity of the company.

- We can not *avoid* new schemes for workers' welfare.
- The culprit *escaped* from the place of accident without being noticed.

INDECENT

Synonyms : Shameless, lewd, indelicate, indecorous, improper, filthy, foul, unchaste.

Antonyms : Decent, decorous, pure, moral, virtuous, seemly, proper, chaste.

Synonyms

- The *shameless* woman flirted with many a man she met.
- The *shameless* fellow passed *lewd* glances at every passing woman.
- It is thought by many to be *indelicate* to discuss how much money one makes.
- She always felt it *indecorous* when she was obliged to adjust a slipped shoulder-strap in public.
- It is considered *improper* for a lawyer to discuss cases with his clients outside his office.
- Even educated persons may use *filthy* language while talking to excited illiterates.
- The slaughter house was filled with *foul* odour.

Antonyms

- His ways with women are considered always *decent* and *decorous.*
- He is a man of *pure, moral* character above the unchaste atmosphere of modern youth clubs.

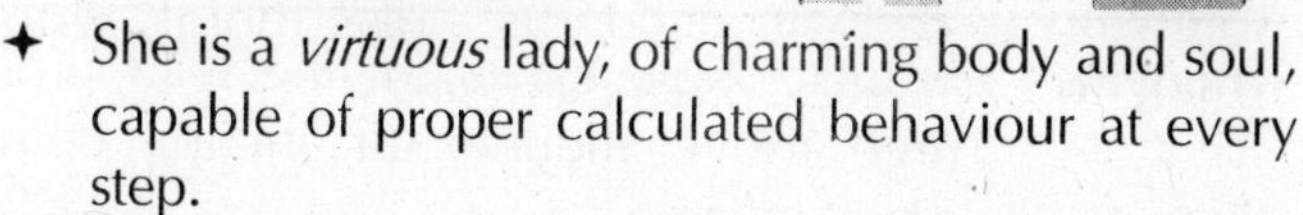

- She is a *virtuous* lady, of charming body and soul, capable of proper calculated behaviour at every step.

INDUCE

Synonyms : Impel, persuade, cajole, urge, coax, wheedle, move.

Antonyms : Hinder, repel, discourage, subdue.

Synonyms

- Your role in the creation of the present circumstances in the company have *impelled* me to demand your resignation.
- The managing director *persuaded* the supervisor to resign in the interests of the company.
- I *cajoled* Romy to resign but as he refused to do so, I had to dismiss him.
- Sunil *urged* the committee to give sanction.

Antonyms

- The manager's intemperate decisions *hindered very* much the progress of the company.
- He *repelled* many a good worker by his violent temper.
- He *discouraged* efficient supervisors by refusing due promotions.

INFLUENCE

Synonyms : Actuate, draw, excite, incline, lead, prompt, urge, move, induce, stir, incite, compel, drive, inflame.

Antonyms : Retard, dissuade, hinder, deter, prevent, inhibit, restrain.

Synonyms

- Most of his acts are *actuated* by greed and selfish interests.
- The strands of rubber were *drawn* to test their strength.
- The professor's lecture on 'murder' *excited* our interest to know more about criminal law.
- The roof *inclines* over the porch without distorting its view.
- The candidate's integrity and strength *led* the voters to support him.
- He was *prompted* by his friends to quarrel with his neighbour.
- She *urged* the members to pay their dues promptly.

- Curiosity *moved* me to open the box.
- Alcohol can *induce* a loosening of the tongue.
- The coach's emotional pep talk *stirred* the teams.
- The dictator's cruel decree *incited* the people to open rebellion.
- Bad health *compelled* him to resign from his job.

Antonyms

- His poor health *retarded* his progress in his career.
- I *dissuaded* him from his illegal activities like smuggling, bribery to officers and the like but to no avail.
- His lust for money *hindered* his slow but steady rise in career.
- There was nothing that could *deter* him from achieving his objective. 
- Even my lecture on honesty could not *prevent* him from becoming rich the fast way.
- He sidetracked the normal *inhibitions* and could not be *restrained* in his illegal proclivities.

INNER

Synonyms : Inward, interior, internal, real.

Antonyms : Outer, exterior, external, superficial.

Synonyms

- ✦ Your *inward* thoughts make your total personality.
- ✦ I have engaged an architect to make a plan for the *interior* decoration of my house.
- ✦ India does not interfere in the *internal* affairs of her neighbours.
- ✦ This necklace is made of *real* pearls.

Antonyms

- ✦ The *outer* atmosphere of the earth has many natural features which help mankind to survive and develop.
- ✦ The *exterior* covering of the human body is called skin.
- ✦ The *external* affairs of India are governed by Panchsheel, i.e., five principles of mutual co-existence among sovereign countries.
- ✦ He is a *superficial* personality without real talent or character.

INNOCENT

Synonyms : Blameless, sinless, untainted, virginal, guiltless, irreproachable.

Antonyms : Blameworthy, culpable, guilty, immoral, lewd, impure, unchaste, depraved, dirty, indecent.

Synonyms

- ✦ His strict adherence to lofty principles of truth and honesty has bestowed on him a *blameless* personality.

- His whole life can be regarded as a continuity of *sinless, untainted* achievement.
- Her face is a mirror of *virginal* innocence.
- His poise and solitude manifest his *guiltless* soul.
- Raju's behaviour in society has always been *irreproachable.*

Antonyms

- His bad company right from childhood has made him a *blameworthy* character.
- The police has found him *guilty* of *culpable* homicide.
- His life is a network of numerous *immoral* and *lewd* deeds, although he may have escaped the clutches of law for long.
- His involvement with smugglers and dacoits tells of his life of *impurity, unchastity,* and *depravation.*

INSERT

Synonyms : Introduce, interpose, interject, interpolate.

Antonyms : Abstract, excerpt, extract, detach, release, remove.

Synonyms

- This doctor has *introduced* a new medicine to cure a patient in early stages of cancer.
- This sentence is all right but it will read better if you *interpose* inverted commas before and after the word cheerful.
- A foreign correspondent *interjected* many new questions during the prime minister's press conference in Washington, to clarify India's position on various issues of foreign policy.

Antonyms

- This painting deals with an *abstract* idea and only the painter can elaborate its significance.
- This book has a number of *excerpts* from Shakespeare to give it a more interesting touch.
- This medicine contains *extracts* of rose.
- After a flight of 3000 km. upwards, the space station *detached* the module from its base.

INSIST

Synonyms : Urge, persist, contend, demand, maintain, persevere.

Antonyms : Relinquish, forgo, waiver, renounce, abandon.

Synonyms

- The secretary *urged* the members to pay their dues promptly.

- Despite hardship he *persisted* in his ambition to get college education.
- The lawyer *contended* before the judge that the witness was not factually present at the scene of the incident.
- Courtesy *demands* us to be polite to our seniors.
- The two friends have *maintained* their friendship for the last thirty years.
- Talent is worthless unless you *persevere* to develop it.

Antonyms

- The retiring manager *relinquished* charge of his job after delivering the portfolios to the new manager.
- I can *forgo* my share of profits in his favour.
- The judge announced a *waiver* of penalty against defaulters.
- Buddha *renounced* the kingdom to take to meditation and to study the objective of human life.
- I have *abandoned* the idea of going to England this summer.

INTEGRITY

Synonyms : Honesty, probity, sincerity, truthfulness.

Antonyms : Unfairness, dishonesty, disunity, diversity.

Synonyms

- *Honesty* adopted as a policy in business pays huge dividends in the long run.

- *Probity* involves deep thinking about each and every aspect of a problem.
- *Sincerity* brings its reward by the very law of natural relationships.
- *Truthfulness* may cause trouble to start with but always has a happy ending.

Antonyms

- Business losses fast exposed the *unfairness* of its management.
- The firm disreputed by *dishonesty* can seldom survive.
- The sense of national integration among citizens is essential to avoid *disunity* and break-up in a federation.
- India is a land of *diversity* in religion and language but unity in economy and polity.

INTENSIFY

Synonyms : Aggravate, magnify, increase, enhance, heighten.

Antonyms : Lessen, diminish, attenuate, reduce, alleviate, assuage.

Synonyms

- Wrong medicine will *aggravate* the pain.
- This lens can *magnify* the object 40 times.
- It is very easy to *increase* the expenditure but very difficult to decrease it.

- Her splendid dress *enhanced* her beauty.

Antonyms

- This tablet will *lessen* the pain in your back.
- The number of students in our school has *diminished* since last year.
- Your donation to the orphanage will *attenuate* your guilt to some degree.
- This exercise will help you *reduce* your weight.
- The only thing that can *alleviate* your financial burden in the long run is taking to mechanisation and automation at the earliest.
- Resumption of duty alone will *assuage* your worries.

JEST

Synonyms : Joke, fun, jeer, taunt, amuse.

Antonyms : Seriousness, thoughtful, earnest, sober.

Synonyms

- ✦ There is nothing to *joke* about the present hard financial position that I am in.
- ✦ It is no *fun* being a complete broke.
- ✦ Don't *jeer* at my helplessness today for I may be a rich man tomorrow.
- ✦ He has no right to *taunt* on my failure in business.

Antonyms

- ✦ I can say with all the *seriousness* at my command that you can rise to the top in acting.
- ✦ He is quite *thoughtful* in his investments. No wonder they always bear good dividend.
- ✦ I am *earnest* in my endeavour to pass this examination.
- ✦ He can maintain a *sober* temperament under any circumstances or situation.

JOYOUS

Synonyms : Ecstatic, elated, jovial, genial, jolly, glad, happy.

Antonyms : Morose, gloomy, miserable, solemn, sad, unhappy.

Synonyms

- Rafi's poems are generally set to *ecstatic* tunes.
- His songs can *elate* the morbid lovers.
- Kishore Kumar can sing the *jovial* songs much better.
- Sunny can maintain a *genial* atmosphere in any gathering by his *jovial* talks.
- Who is that *jolly* man in the corner?.

Antonyms

- His *morose* presence makes even a bright atmosphere *gloomy*.
- He feels *miserable* in the company of girls.
- Let us take a *solemn* pledge to perform our fundamental duties sincerely.
- He is very *sad* to know about the untimely demise of his uncle.

JUSTIFY

Synonyms : Absolve, defend, clear, explain, perform.

Antonyms : Condemn, accuse, censure, blame, denounce.

Synonyms

- ✦ After examining all evidence, the judge *absolved* the accused of all charges.
- ✦ The lawyer who *defended* the accused felt elated at the judgement.
- ✦ The issues in the case were cleverly *cleared* by the defence advocate.
- ✦ The accused *explained* the circumstances of his involvement in detail.

Antonyms

- ✦ The government strongly *condemned* the extremists for their violent activities.
- ✦ The opposition leaders *accused* the government of partiality towards notable politicians.
- ✦ The judge *censured* the prosecution for illegal detention of the accused.
- ✦ He *blamed* the police for hasty action.
- ✦ The government *denounced* the opposition for open support to regional parochialism.

KEEN

Synonyms : Acute, eager, sharp, shrewd, penetrating.

Antonyms : Slow, stupid, bland, languid, dull, indifferent.

Synonyms

- I have an *acute* headache at the moment.
- I am *eager* to take a tablet to get rid of my headache.
- This razor is still *sharp* for my shave. 
- He is a *shrewd* politician and knows the art of diplomacy and accurate judgement of human affairs.
- His *penetrating* eyes observed the criminal with professional thoroughness.

Antonyms

- He is a *slow* thinker, but a fast worker.
- He was *stupid* enough to miss the chance of an interview with the Prime Minister.
- After the meeting, a *bland* statement was issued.

✦ She looked *languidly* at her boyfriend, but discouraged the latter from any rash advance.

KILL

Synonyms : Assassinate, massacre, murder, slaughter, slay, execute, butcher, dispatch, put to death.

Antonyms : Create, produce, fashion, cause, originate.

Synonyms

✦ Nathu Ram Godse *assassinated* Mahatma Gandhi when the latter had just finished his prayer.

✦ Hitler ordered the *massacre* of innocent Jews to satisfy his racial whims and fancies.

✦ He was sentenced to death for *murdering* his boss.

✦ The herd was taken to the *slaughter* house.

✦ In the fairy-tale, Jack *slew* the giant.

✦ The murderer deserves to be *executed.*

✦ Even the milch animals were *butchered* due to shortage of meat for the soldiers.

✦ The injured horse was *dispatched* by its owner.

✦ The king *put* his minister *to death* when he came to know of the conspiracy hatched by the latter.

Antonyms

✦ God has *created* humans to love each other, not to hate and kill.

- Satyajit Ray has *produced* another new-wave picture.
- She *fashioned* the clay into a pot.
- Deforestation has *caused* soil erosion in many parts of the country.

KIND

Synonyms : Compassionate, benign, affable, generous, lenient, sympathetic, charitable, merciful, tender, philanthropic, complacent.

Antonyms : Cruel, callous, unfeeling, unkind, hard-hearted, insensible, harsh.

Synonyms

- After the death of his father, he was appointed as a salesman in the same company on *compassionate* grounds.
- His *benign* attitude to the subordinates is appreciated by the top echelons of the company's management.
- He has *affable* manners towards the fair sex.
- Mary is very *generous.* and gives the children lovely presents on her birthday.
- His *lenient* attitude has made his subordinates irregular in attendance.
- His neighbours were quite *sympathetic* to his family during Ram's illness.
- The *charitable* institutions have been exempted from the new tax.

- Your Honour is counted as a *merciful* man.
- We had a *tender* chicken for dinner.
- Our organisation has benefitted from the *philanthropic* attitude of the business magnate.
- The *complacent* boy did not study and, therefore, failed in his examination.

Antonyms

- The *cruel* king along with his *cruel* nobles had to surrender to the mob.
- The king was *callous* to the genuine demands of the people. No wonder he was made to abdicate.
- His attitude to the sick was marked by *unfeeling* and lack of human consideration.
- He was *unkind* to the slaves and the poor peasantry.

KINDLE

Synonyms : Ignite, inflame, light, fire.

Antonyms : Extinguish, put out, satisfy, satiate.

Synonyms

- The malicious propaganda of the communal parties *ignited* a fresh wave of violence.
- The speeches of the leaders *inflamed* the already high passions of the mob.

- Sunita *lighted* five candles on her fifth birthday.
- The house caught *fire* due to electrical short circuit.

Antonyms

- The police used new equipment to *extinguish* the fire in the house.
- It took them five hours to *put out* the fire.
- Of all the cold drinks, Campa Cola *satisfies* my thirst the best.
- Though journalism may be financially less paid, it does *satiate* one's thirst for knowledge and adventure.

KNOWLEDGE

Synonyms : Perception, science, wisdom, intuition, comprehension, information, cognition, lore, light, intelligence.

Antonyms : Ignorance, unfamiliarity, misunderstanding, misapprehension, inexperience, illiteracy.

Synonyms

- A good driver must have a good *perception* of distance.
- Systematic knowledge acquired after experiments is called *science*.
- Learning facts does not necessarily give one *wisdom*.
- My *intuition* turned out to be correct.

- The teacher had no *comprehension* of the boy's problems at home.
- The *information* was gratefully received.
- The judge gave no *cognition* to the verbal plea of the prosecution without thorough evidence.
- The *lore* of Naga tribes includes many fascinating stories about their habits.

- He could not throw any *light* on the issue.
- Mohan shows great *intelligence* though he is still very young.

Antonyms

- *Ignorance* of law is no excuse to commit a crime.
- Mohan showed complete *unfamiliarity* with the topic though he was given notice of a full week.
- A *misunderstanding* has crept up between the two brothers regarding their father's will.
- Their *misapprehensions* against each other need to be cleared by a mediator.

LABOUR

Synonyms : Work, toil, exertion, drudgery, industry.

Antonyms : Repose, rest, relaxation, stillness.

Synonyms

- ✦ He *works* till late hours every night.
- ✦ The farmer *toils* in the field from dawn to dusk but the landlord enjoys the fruit of his labour.
- ✦ This *exertion* will be good for him for reducing his excessive fat.

- ✦ Preparing these monthly reports is nothing but *drudgery*.
- ✦ The new supervisor was rewarded for his *industry* and intelligence.

Antonyms

- ✦ He has *reposed* confidence in me despite my first default.

- I have taken two days' leave for *rest* and recreation.
- Mental *relaxation* is a must for any original creation by an artist.
- The *stillness* of the atmosphere awed me and reminded me of the noisy scenes of the previous evening.

LACK

Synonyms : Need, shortage, deficiency, want.

Antonyms : Sufficiency, prosperity, wealth, riches.

Synonyms

- Besides the nourishing food, he *needs* complete physical and mental peace.
- *Shortage* of money compelled him to stop further construction of his house.
- *Deficiency* of iron in the body leads to anaemia.
- One *wants* more vegetables, fruits and good diet to cure anaemia.

Antonyms

- *Sufficiency* of essential items for a reasonably good living is necessary for the growth of a balanced personality.
- India is on her way to *prosperity*, thanks to the plans of economic development launched by Jawaharlal Nehru.
- Natural resources like forests, mines, water, vegetation, etc., are called the basic *wealth* of a nation.

- The *riches* of the rich and the poverty of the poor are the basic contradictions in the Indian economy.

LARGE

Synonyms : Big, mammoth, great, monumental.

Antonyms : Small, minute, delicate, sophisticated.

Synonyms

- The administration of a country is responsible for solving all its problems, *big* or small.
- The prime minister addressed a *mammoth* crowd at the Red Fort to explain in brief the national policies on matters of internal and external nature.
- Ashoka and Akbar are two *great* outstanding names in India's history of ancient and medieval periods.
- This book is a *monumental* work on the s)cial system in India.

Antonyms

- The writing of a book on 'Society in India' is not a *small* job.
- It requires going into *minute* details, before putting in black and white the facts about Indian society.
- Some of the topics dealt with are of *delicate* nature and hence time consuming.
- It requires a *sophisticated* approach to make a success of the project.

LAWFUL

Synonyms : Rightful, legal, fair, legitimate.

Antonyms : Illegal, unlawful, illicit.

Synonyms

- ✦ Sonia is the *rightful* heir to this property as the only survivor of the family.
- ✦ Property is no more a fundamental right of the individual in society; it is only a *legal* right which means one can acquire it by payment of cost of such property and not otherwise.
- ✦ The principal's decision on the dispute between the two students was *fair* and reasonable.
- ✦ The demand of the labour for participation in the management of a firm is considered *legitimate* in modern philosophy.

Antonyms

- ✦ Use of violence to solve mutual disputes among individuals is *illegal*.
- ✦ It is *unlawful* to use violence against other individuals in society except for self-defence.
- ✦ There are numerous underground firms in the country producing *illicit* drugs.

LAZY

Synonyms : Idle, sluggish, indolent, unemployed, slow, slothful.

Antonyms : Active, smart, agile, up and doing.

Synonyms

- Indian farmer is *idle* for about six months in a year.
- The turtles ran a *sluggish* race.

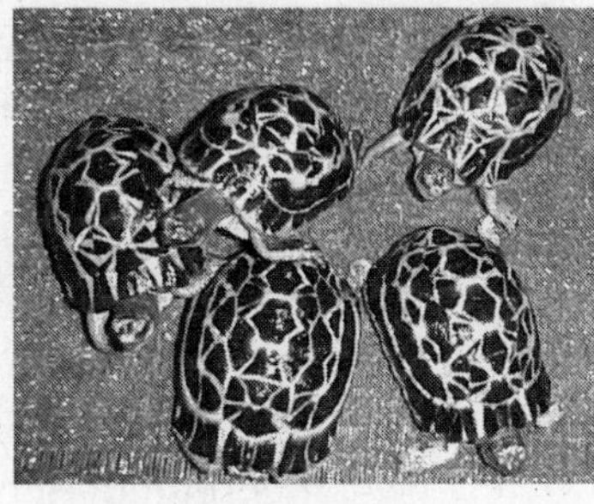

- Mohan used to be an *indolent* boy but now he works quite hard.
- *Unemployed* youth is a serious problem of our times.
- *Slow* and steady wins the race.
- His *slothful* attitude keeps him from getting ahead in his job.

Antonyms

- Growth of industries in cities around the villages can make the Indian farmer *active* throughout the year. Sam, a *smart* boy, is good in studies as well as in sports.
- His *agile* mind has brought Jim the desired success.
- He is always *up and doing* whether at home or outside.

LEADER

Synonyms : Guide, guru, teacher, director, conductor, principal, politician.

Antonyms : Follower, trainee, apprentice, pupil, henchman.

Synonyms

- The Geeta is the greatest *guide* of the Hindus.
- The *guru* should be given as much respect as was given by our forefathers.
- Did your *teacher* tell you how to do your sums?
- The club needs a vigorous recreation *director.*
- He had served as a *conductor* for ten years before getting his promotion.
- My father retired as the *principal* of Ramjas School.
- Today some *politicians* treat elections as a business.

Antonyms

- Lal Bahadur Shastri was a strict *follower* of Mahatma Gandhi.
- Atul has been selected as an executive *trainee* by a multinational.
- He started his career as an *apprentice* in a chemical enterprise.
- Srivastava is respected and revered by his *pupils* for his noble character.
- A politician generally has to develop a good number of *henchmen* to keep his popularity alive.

LEARN

Synonyms : Acquire, memorise, discover, detect, trace.

Antonyms : Forget, unlearn, miss, misunderstand, ignore.

Synonyms

- Indian scientists have already *acquired* advanced knowledge of space technology.
- Gita can *memorise* the numbers very fast.
- Columbus *discovered* America in 1498.
- The plumber soon *detected* the fault of the gas-pipe.
- The police combed the whole village to *trace* the dacoits.

Antonyms

- Forgive and *forget* is a common trait in a successful personality.
- The time lag between initial lessons and the intensive course in a foreign language has made me *unlearn* its basic theory.
- Though I read the lesson twice, I *missed* an important point.
- Lack of thorough knowledge about each others' viewpoint usually creates *misunderstanding* among clients.
- I cannot *ignore* the disrespect heaped on me by the new subordinate.

LEARNING

Synonyms : Scholarship, erudition, knowledge, understanding.

Antonyms : Ignorance, illiteracy, misunderstanding, unlearning.

Synonyms

- The new pope is a man of great *scholarship.*
- His manner of prayer and the content of speeches show his *erudition* and wisdom.
- He has a good *knowledge* of physics.
- His social behaviour is always designed to create an atmosphere of *understanding.*

Antonyms

- *Ignorance* of law is no excuse for its evasion.
- Over 60% of people in India are still *illiterates.*
- *Misunderstandings* between any two countries can be removed by negotiation and international arbitration.

LENGTHY

Synonyms : Tedious, diffused, detailed, spread.

Antonyms : Short, concise, brief.

Synonyms

- This text book seems to be a *tedious* one for young students.
- The prime minister has *diffused* the differences among the leaders of the district by discussing the focal problems in full *detail.*
- The task has been *spread* out into sections and subsections to make its implementation easy.

Antonyms

- This pair of trousers is too *short* for me.

- ✦ Let us be *concise* in our discussion; I have my next appointment in ten minutes.
- ✦ I have given you a *brief* description of the incident.

LESSEN

Synonyms : Lighten, assuage, allay, mitigate, soften, temper.

Antonyms : Heighten, toughen, enlarge, escalate, extend, intensify.

Synonyms

- ✦ Automation has *lightened* the manual work of our workers.
- ✦ We have tried to *assuage* the feelings of our retrenched employees by offering to absorb them in the next phase of the expansion programme.
- ✦ We have to *allay* the fears of the existing staff in respect of any further retrenchment.
- ✦ The management has announced an increase in dearness allowance to *mitigate* the adverse effect of recent inflation.
- ✦ This has *softened* the attitude of hard-core union leaders.
- ✦ It has also helped to *temper* the quality of the new staff.

Antonyms

- ✦ Promotions among the existing officers have greatly *heightened* the reputation of the company.

- ✦ But the attitude of the lower staff has *toughened* threatening to reduce productivity at the lower levels.
- ✦ We should *enlarge* the sphere of cooperation among the officers and the subordinates somehow to achieve better performance.

LIBERAL

Synonyms : Plentiful, tolerant, profuse, free.

Antonyms : Scanty, grasping, mean, low.

Synonyms

- ✦ The current monsoons assure a *plentiful* crop of foodgrains next year.
- ✦ Unless Hindus and Sikhs show the old *tolerant* attitude, the age-long oneness may not be fully restored.
- ✦ She shed *profuse* tears on hearing of her son's death in a bomb blast. 
- ✦ The new economic policy announced by the prime minister gives a *free* hand to private enterprise in its day-to-day functioning.

Antonyms

- ✦ The *scanty* rains this year in some of the states in India may adversely affect the total availability of foodgrains.
- ✦ Our manager has a *grasping* temperament.

- It was very *mean* on his part to confront his father.
- I am feeling very *low* today as the news of the air crash has upset my spirits.

LIBERTY

Synonyms : Emancipation, freedom, independence, licence, permission.

Antonyms : Captivity, compulsion, constraint, imprisonment, slavery, serfdom, servitude, oppression, obligation, thraldom.

Synonyms

- 1807 was the year of *emancipation* of slaves in the British Isles.
- Eternal vigilance is the price of *freedom*.
- India got its *independence* after a long-drawn struggle for two centuries.
- He has applied for a *licence* to keep fire-arms.
- The teacher will give him *permission* to attend the class provided he has done his home work.

Antonyms

- Many landlords in India openly violate the new law on bonded labour by keeping many of their labourers in *captivity*.
- The workers are made to bear captivity on *compulsion* of mere subsistence.
- The landlords need to be put under *constraint* by strict enforcement of the new law.

- Defaulting landlords should be duly punished by prescribed *imprisonment.*
- The age-long *slavery* of the bonded labour must be ended in practice and not only in theory.
- The country must rise above the *serfdom* of the 19th century political environment.

LIE

Synonyms : Falsehood, untruth, prevarication, quibble, collusion.

Antonyms : Truth, honesty, veracity.

Synonyms

- *Falsehood* never pays in the long run.
- Prosperity based on *untruth* can never bring happiness as your conscience always pricks you.
- I am afraid your firm will have to rise above *prevarication* if you wish to deal with my firm.
- Better stop *quibbling* over small issues and come to the basic problem.

Antonyms

- *Truth* always wins.
- *Honesty* is the best policy in every walk of human life.
- He is a great businessman. The secret of his success lies in his *veracity.*

LIFT

Synonyms : Exalt, erect, raise, elevate, hoist.

Antonyms : Drop, lower, sink, let fall.

Synonyms

- The Queen holds a very *exalted* position in Britain.
- The town has *erected* a monument to its war heroes.
- The management has *raised* new hopes for us in the matter of salaries.
- The vice president was *elevated* to the presidency of the company.
- The prime minister *hoists* the flag at the Red Fort on Independence Day every year.

Antonyms

- I have *dropped* the idea of taking to politics.
- This may *lower* my prestige in business circles in the long run.
- The steel ball *sinks* when thrown in sea water but the ship does not.
- Hold on properly, don't *let* it *fall*.

LIKELY

Synonyms : Apt, reasonable, liable, credible, possible, conceivable, presumable.

Antonyms : Doubtful, improbable, questionable, unlikely, dubious, unreasonable.

Synonyms

- Our puppy is *apt* to knock his dish over.
- Mother bought this chair at a *reasonable* price.
- If you don't agree with her, she is *liable* to get angry.
- He told quite a *credible* story of his adventure.
- The prisoner saw only one *possible* way of escaping.
- There is no *conceivable* way to unite the opposition parties in India.

Antonyms

- I am *doubtful* of his sincere endeavour next time.
- His arrival today in Delhi seems *improbable* due to bad weather.
- His solution to this problem is *questionable* owing to inability to dig real facts and figures.
- My visit to Mumbai in the near future seems *unlikely*.
- His approach to this ticklish problem is rather *dubious*.

- The company has rejected the demand of the peons for further raise in salaries as *unreasonable.*

LIVELY

Synonyms : Vivid, animated, brisk, keen, vivacious, spirited.

Antonyms : Listless, languid, lethargic, langorous.

Synonyms

- Mr. Smith gave a *vivid* picture of his visit to Germany.
- His description of the luxurious living of the average citizen in Germany was rather *animated.*
- There was *brisk* business today in the shares of our company at the Stock Exchange.

Antonyms

- His recent sickness has left him rather *listless.*
- His movements are *languid* and feverish.
- He falls occasionally sick as he has a *lethargic* routine.

LONELY

Synonyms : Solitary, lonesome, forlorn.

Antonyms : Escorted, attended, accompanied.

Synonyms

- I was the *solitary* passenger in the early morning bus to the railway station.
- The house was situated at a *lonesome* area.

✦ He is a *forlorn* personality, seldom seen in the company of friends.

Antonyms

✦ The manager was *escorted* to his place of work by his assistant.

✦ Nancy *attended* the marriage ceremony of her brother with great enthusiasm.

✦ She was *accompanied* by a large number of her friends.

LOOK

Synonyms : Behold, inspect, see, watch, stare, gaze, observe, regard, survey, view, discern.

Antonyms : Ignore, reject, veil, bypass.

Synonyms

✦ I was enchanted to *behold* the beauty of the Taj.

✦ The engines of a new ship have to be carefully *inspected* before she sets out on voyage.

✦ Did anyone *see* the accident?

✦ *Watch* the magician and try to figure out how he makes the rabbit disappear.

✦ Her icy *stare* gave me a chill.

✦ When the baby is in her pram she *gazes* up at the sky.

- ✦ The doctor will *observe* the patient only when he visits him at the clinic.
- ✦ The condemned prisoner *regarded* the jury with a look of outraged innocence.
- ✦ We *surveyed* the countryside from the top of the hill.

Antonyms

- ✦ Jonathan *ignored* the presence of his rival at the ceremony.
- ✦ I am sorry I cannot *reject* the valuable remarks of the esteemed viewers.
- ✦ He tried to *veil* the circumstances of the accident by giving a different story.
- ✦ You cannot *bypass* the reality by closing your eyes.

LOUD

Synonyms : Noisy, vociferous, clamorous, boisterous.

Antonyms : Peaceful, silent, soft, taciturn, subdued.

Synonyms

- ✦ The railway station presented a very *noisy* scene.
- ✦ He is *vociferous* in his views on political issues.
- ✦ The workers cannot help making *clamorous* demands for increased wages in these days of galloping inflation.
- ✦ He can keep the atmosphere around him highly gay with his *boisterous* personality.

Antonyms

- I like to run away from the noisy atmosphere of Mumbai to the *peaceful* environment of a hill station.
- This fan moves *silently* even at full speed.
- My brother is too *soft* to work as a policeman where one has to deal with criminals and gangsters.

LOVE

Synonyms : Affection, fondness, charity, liking, regard, friendship, tenderness, attraction.

Antonyms : Dislike, abhorrence, animosity, disgust, repugnance, antipathy, abomination, loathing, aversion, destestation.

Synonyms

- Mother's *affection* for her child knows no bounds.
- I have a *fondness* for children.
- *Charity* is one of the five duties imposed on man by the Koran.
- The husband should take care of the *likings* and dislikings of his wife.

- The people have great *regard* for their leader.
- Adversity is the real test of *friendship*.

- The new medicine will maintain the *tenderness* of your skin during winter.
- The hero and heroine were an *attraction* to the crowd at the airport.

Antonyms

- I *dislike* the idea of getting up too early in the morning.
- I have an *abhorrence* for the noisy atmosphere of Mumbai's life.
- Their friendship has turned into *animosity* owing to some recent developments in business.
- I am *disgusted* with this life of poverty and deprevation.
- I have *repugnance* for untimely jokes cut by Nancy.

LUCK

Synonyms : Fortune, chance, prosperity, good stroke.

Antonyms : Bad luck, misfortune, bad stroke, unfavourable.

Synonyms

- It was his good *fortune* that he missed the plane that later crashed.
- He got many *chances* to become rich but he did not avail of them as he has no love for money.
- He is not jealous of the *prosperity* of his brothers.
- One *good stroke* and your life is made.

✦ A *stroke* of good luck turned the beggar into a rich man.

Antonyms

✦ He is such an enterprising young man. His failure in business is mere *bad luck.*

✦ I have been denied many good chances in the career as I have the *misfortune* of being the nephew of a notorious politician.

✦ I was booked for a nice career abroad, but the breaking out of the war proved a *bad stroke.*

✦ My circumstances are now rather *unfavourable* for a career in business.

LOVING

Synonyms : Affectionate, devoted, fond.

Antonyms : Bitter, cold, unaffectionate.

Synonyms

✦ Sunny is one of my *affectionate* friends on whom I can depend.

✦ Joseph is so much *devoted* to his wife, he will never go abroad without her.

✦ I am *fond* of my hobby of gardening.

Antonyms

- ✦ There is no need to feel *bitter* over my remarks as they are meant for your good.
- ✦ Ronald is a *cold* person who goes by logic not emotions.
- ✦ Of late, I have noted our uncle has become rather *unaffectionate* so far as I am concerned.

MAJORITY

Synonyms : Adulthood, excess, superiority, preponderance.

Antonyms : Minority, smallness, inferiority.

Synonyms

- ✦ If a girl is married before 16 years of her age she can declare her marriage null and void on attaining *adulthood*.
- ✦ *Excess* of everything is bad.
- ✦ He does not mix up gracefully with his classmates because he is suffering from a *superiority* complex.
- ✦ This deal was decided according to the theory of *preponderance* of probability.

Antonyms

- ✦ Only a small *minority* of students is interested in politics these days.

- His tall talk about himself shows his *smallness.*
- Children from poor families wherever admitted in public schools are bound to carry the *inferiority* complex owing to obvious reasons.

MANNER

Synonyms : Style, mode, custom, method, system, way, fashion, conduct, behaviour.

Antonyms : Mannerlessness, discourteous, unsocial, unsystematic, unmethodical.

Synonyms

- The new golfers have an awkward *style* of hitting the ball.
- The *mode* of repayment of debt was duly described in the agreement.
- A *custom* must be very old in order to be valid in the eyes of law.
- I like his *method* of doing the office work.
- Scientists have helped the farmers to try out new *systems* of growing crops.
- Hard work is the only *way* to success.
- She moves in a graceful *fashion.*
- The students were fined for their disruptive *conduct* in the class.
- The biologist studied the *behaviour* of lions in their natural habitat.

Antonyms

- His *mannerlessness* caused disgust among the highbrows.
- He was so *discourteous* to the principal that the managing committee had to rusticate him despite his high connections with the deputy commissioner.
- He is extremely intelligent, but his *unsocial* behaviour stands like a wall in his career.
- He is intelligent but *unsystematic.*
- Were he not so *unmethodical,* he would have by now become the manager.

MELODY

Synonyms : Unison, tune, music, harmony, air, symphony.

Antonyms : Discord, distortion, disruption, noise.

Synonyms

- The children showed complete *unison* in their dance and music items.

- R.D. Burman has composed many interesting *tunes.*

- Shall we have some *music* during dinner?
- Sally and I worked together in complete *harmony* for several years.
- The rich child carries an *air* of extravagance around him.
- This *symphony* is part of his new composition.

Antonyms

- Religion is no more the root of *discord* in modern societies.
- Many a dispute in society are based on *distortion* of facts by vested interests.
- Once the society is divided among classes, *disruption* consequentially follows.
- The music presented at the concert was pure and simple *noise* meant for the animal taste and not for the gentry invited for the occasion.

MERCY

Synonyms : Benevolence, favour, pardon, clemancy, compassion, leniency, pity, gentleness, mildness, grace, kindness.

Antonyms : Cruelty, harshness, hardness, vigour, severity, penalty, punishment.

Synonyms

- The playground coach smiled with *benevolence* at the noisy children but tamed them in a few minutes with his sportsmanship.
- He is always ready to do anyone a *favour*.

- May God grant you *pardon* for your sins.
- The defendant was grateful for the judge's *clemancy.*

- The nurse had great *compassion* for her patients.
- The members took undue advantage of the *leniency* of the chairman.
- We feel *pity* at the inhuman living conditions of the slums.
- His *gentleness* moved his opponents to appraisal.
- The *mildness* of a spring day can be best appreciated out of doors.
- By the king's *grace,* the traitor was permitted to leave the country.
- He can never forget the *kindness* shown by his neighbors during the communal riots.

Antonyms

- *Cruelty* to animals must be condemned.
- The *harshness* of the teacher failed to reform the student.
- The *hardness* of the metal was not in consonance with the needed quality of the motor.

- ✦ Let us serve our motherland with all the *vigour* at our command.
- ✦ The *severity* of this winter has bruised my skin.
- ✦ The delay in return of the books compelled me to pay the *penalty*.
- ✦ Violation of traffic rules can lead one to *punishment* by fine or imprisonment.

MERIT

Synonyms : Worth, value, excellence, virtue.

Antonyms : Fault, error, flaw, weakness, worthlessness.

Synonyms

- ✦ The present *worth* of a rupee is hardly 50% of last year.
- ✦ It means the *value* of money in relation to goods has fallen to almost half.
- ✦ On the whole, however the economy of the country has shown its *excellence* in terms of total national product.
- ✦ The engineering exports of the country have doubled by *virtue* of scientific advancement.

Antonyms

- ✦ This steno grapher has many *faults* in his behaviour.
- ✦ He is amenable to *errors* of over-sophistication and artificiality.
- ✦ There is, however, no *flaw* in his character.

- ✦ Every man has some *weaknesses*, and he is no exception.
- ✦ The *worthlessness* of certain ideologies in modern societies has been proved beyond any doubt.

MILD

Synonyms : Bland, soft, gentle, kind, docile, tender, meek, placid.

Antonyms : Wild, ferocious, blood-thirsty, fierce, brutish, savage.

Synonyms

- ✦ These *bland* spring days are good for picnics.
- ✦ The *soft* green grass of the Mughal Gardens is a special attraction for the visitors to Rashtrapati Bhavan in New Delhi.
- ✦ She gave the baby a *gentle* pat on the back.
- ✦ Although he tried to act rough, he was basically a *kind* man.
- ✦ He was criticised for being too *docile* to be an administrator.
- ✦ The mother took good care of the *tender* child, yet the baby fell ill.
- ✦ Even the *meek* students could not help speaking against the history teacher for his anti-social approach.
- ✦ She has an amazingly *placid* disposition which appeals to one and all.

Antonyms

- With growing civilisation, *wild* animals are going extinct one by one.

- Tiger is a *ferocious* animal but humans can tame him all right.
- The frustrated criminal became *blood-thirsty* after release from long imprisonment.
- Kalinga war which was *fierce* and took a toll of thousands of lives, ultimately converted Ashoka into a great Buddhist.
- The policeman's *brutish* appearance terrified the criminal.

MIND

Synonyms : Wit, thought, sense, reason, intellect, disposition, brain, intelligence, understanding, spirit.

Antonyms : Body, matter, brawn, brute force, material, substance.

Synonyms

- His essays are full of *wit* and humour.
- He had to change his plan of action when he gave a second *thought* to the problem.
- The teacher tried to inculcate into his pupils a *sense* of beauty.

- His arguments did not appeal to *reason.*
- Man's *intellect* distinguishes him from the beasts.
- She has a very frank and friendly *disposition.*
- He died because his *brain* was wounded in the accident.
- Objective type questions are a new method of testing the *intelligence* of the candidates.
- Few people have an *understanding* of international law.
- He was deeply depressed and no one could lift his *spirits.*

Antonyms

- The hypnotist mesmerised my *body* and soul.
- The *matter* in nature is divided into solids, liquids and gases.
- In this kind of job you need *brawn* as well as brains.
- It needs *brute force* to kill an enemy.
- The government favours the policy of importing raw *materials,* finishing them into products and exporting them.
- There is little *substance* in the facts and figures to support your argument.

MISCELLANEOUS

Synonyms : Assorted, mingled, motley, unlike, various, varient; dissimilar, discordant, confused, promiscuous.

Antonyms : Homogeneous, identical, like, pure, uniform, same, similar.

Synonyms

- ✦ The gift pack contained *assorted* biscuits.
- ✦ A few cows *mingled* with the sheep in the same field.
- ✦ It is amazing that such a *motley* group has got along for such a long time.
- ✦ It is the only club which gives membership to *unlike* persons.
- ✦ This song is just a *variant* of a folk tune.
- ✦ We have *various* types of cars in this showroom for sale.
- ✦ The two girls are so *dissimilar* that you won't believe they are real sisters.
- ✦ The speakers had entirely *discordant* views on the subject. Hence they could not help quarrelling with each other.
- ✦ He was so *confused* that he could not answer even simple questions.
- ✦ The closet contained a *promiscuous* array of ornaments.

Antonyms

- ✦ India is composed of *homogeneous* races.
- ✦ The interests of all the states in India are *identical.*
- ✦ Very often he behaves *like* an uneducated person.

- ✦ This is *pure* diamond, not artificial.
- ✦ A *uniform* law on citizenship prevails in most of the European countries.

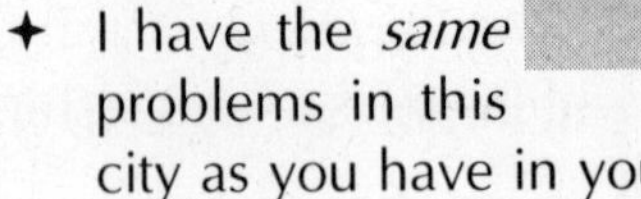

- ✦ I have the *same* problems in this city as you have in yours.

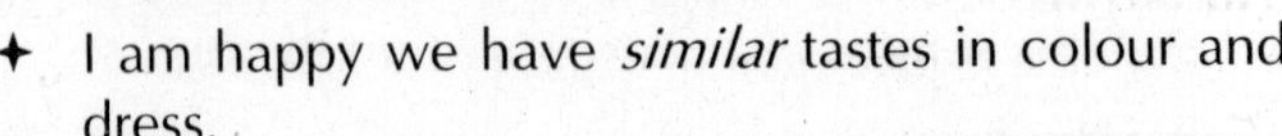

- ✦ I am happy we have *similar* tastes in colour and dress.

MISERABLE

Synonyms : Forlorn, unhappy, dismal, sorry, wretched.

Antonyms : Happy, cheerful, joyous, contented.

Synonyms

- ✦ Don't look so *forlorn* without your girlfriend.
- ✦ *Unhappy* is the head that wears the crown.
- ✦ His achievement abroad was rather *dismal* as he fell in the company of drug addicts.
- ✦ I am so *sorry* I cannot help you in your financial problems.
- ✦ African Negros are leading a *wretched* life in South Africa where the white minority continues to reign supreme.

Antonyms

✦ Ederson and Jane are a *happy*-go-lucky couple.

✦ Johny is always *cheerful* come what may. I always feel *joyous* in his company.

✦ Thomson is *contented* with his lot due to his over spiritual attitude.

MISERY

Synonyms : Distress, woe, wretchedness, heartache, anguish, torment, torture, agony, discomfort.

Antonyms : Bliss, pleasure, happiness, ecstasy, elation, joy.

Synonyms

✦ I am *distressed* at the *woe* of poorer sections of society in the country.

✦ Poverty is the biggest *wretchedness* for mankind.

✦ Incidents like the Kanishka air-crash cause many a would-be-passengers *heartache*.

✦ The majority of the people in Asia and Africa suffer from *anguish* of one type or the other, natural or man-made.

✦ We could not bear the *agony*.

✦ His loss in business put him in great *discomfort*.

Antonyms

✦ It is a *bliss* to be ignorant of mankind's agonies.

✦ People who get *pleasure* out of other people's sufferings are called sadists.

- Real *happiness* lies in doing something which eradicates human suffering.
- Their cultural affinity helped them feel real *ecstasy* during their honeymoon.

MISLEAD

Synonyms : Misguide, deceive, delude, beguile, misdirect.

Antonyms : Pilot, guide, direct, steer, lead.

Synonyms

- The members of the committee were *misguided* by the secretary.
- The beggar *deceived* us by pretending he was blind.
- I may be *deluding* myself, but I think I am losing weight.
- He *beguiled* the woman into thinking that he could not pay for his night's lodging.
- The stranger was *misdirected* by the naughty boys.

Antonyms

- I *piloted* the plan of the new project at the general meeting of the members of the company.
- The minister simply *guides* the policy of the ministry while the real work is done by the members and staff of the Secretariat.
- The supervisors at the local level *direct* the activities at the grassroots.

- Only a bold leader can *steer* the affairs of the country to peace and progress.
- A big nation needs to be *led* by love and devotion, intellect and wise judgement.

MODERN

Synonyms : New, present, contemporary, current, recent, timely, present-day.

Antonyms : Bygone, past, ancient, old-fashioned.

Synonyms

- The *new* policy lays down more incentives for the private sector.
- The *present* leadership is quite liberal in its attitude to different sectors in the economy.
- It keeps in mind *contemporary* political thought round the world while formulating its basic philosophy.
- You must keep abreast of the *current* topics to succeed in competitive exams.
- Implementation of the new rule was a *timely* action taken by the government.

Antonyms

- Let *bygones* be bygones and restore our old friendship.
- India's nationalism developed very strongly in the *past* century.
- India's glorious *ancient* history keeps inspiring traditions and culture.
- This dress has now become *old-fashioned.*

MODEST

Synonyms : Lowly, humble, shy, unassuming, unpretentious.

Antonyms : Conceited, pretentious, showy, over-bearing, immodest.

Synonyms

- ✦ Although a millionaire today, he is *lowly* born.
- ✦ He is *humble* in habits but rich in intellect.
- ✦ She is beautiful in appearance but *shy* in public.
- ✦ In spite of her great achievement in music, Lata Mangeshkar is so *unassuming*.

Antonyms

- ✦ His high status in wealth has little meaning so long as he is self-*conceited* and *pretentious*.
- ✦ He is more *showy* than he really does.
- ✦ Jolly is a fantastic story-teller but he becomes *over-bearing* after a few minutes.
- ✦ His riches, unaccompanied by real talent, have made him rather *immodest*.

MORAL

Synonyms : Honourable, upright, just, strict, right, ethical, virtuous.

Antonyms : Immoral, dishonourable, vicious, licentious, unprincipled, uprighteous.

Synonyms

- ✦ The *Honourable* Prime Minister will deliver a speech on this subject next Monday.

- He is an *upright* man of strong character.
- The rules made by the government on this subject are *just* and fair.
- Our English teacher is very *strict* and allows no talking in his class.

- He is the *right* man for the chairmanship of the company.

Antonyms

- Everything is fine in society except greed for money which raises all kinds of *immoral* social problems.
- Greed of money makes many an honourable person *dishonourable.*
- The *vicious* look in the criminal's eyes made the unarmed policeman shiver with fear.
- The *unprincipled* leader had to face defeat in election at the hands of his voters.

MOURN

Synonyms : Bemoan, bewail, sorrow, lament, regret, grieve, deplore.

Antonyms : Joy, rejoice, triumph.

Synonyms

- Stop *bemoaning* the loss of your job and go look for a new one.
- He *bewailed* the disappearance of his little dog.
- It is a matter of great *sorrow* that he has lost his son in an accident.
- He *lamented* the loss of his kitten for a long time.
- Everyone *regretted* the death of Smt. Indira Gandhi.
- Try not to *grieve* too much for the puppy that has died.
- The boatman *deplored* the roughness of the sea.

Antonyms

- The child gets a strange *joy* from playing with the toys.
- Let's *rejoice* the silver jubilee of our company by holding a grand party.
- You should have seen that look of *triumph* on Som's face when he won the gold medal.

NATIVE

Synonyms : Aboriginals, innate, natural, natal, original, indigenous.

Antonyms : Foreign, extraneous, alien, acquired, supplemented, extrinsic.

Synonyms

- ✦ The *aboriginals* of this district still live in small huts.
- ✦ An *innate* flaw doomed the plan from the start.
- ✦ The loss of some persons even in a small war is *natural* and inevitable.
- ✦ Ante-*natal* care of the children forms a part of the new family welfare schemes of the government.

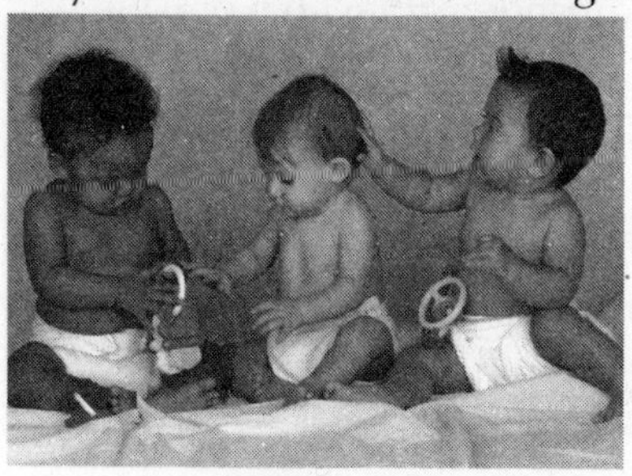

- The *original* plan was good but of late it has become too complicated for implementation.
- Our industrial policy lays great emphasis on *indigenous* production of machinery.

Antonyms

- *Foreign* policy of India lays due emphasis on five principles of co-existence called Panchsheel.
- The doctor found an *extraneous* matter in his blood; so he referred him to a specialist.
- *Aliens* are kept under constant watch in India these days to stop the smuggling of heroin.
- The government can *acquire* any private property for public good by paying due compensation to the owner.
- My uncle *supplemented* his income by working overtime to cover an extra family liability.
- The *extrinsic* value of a currency is the one which matters in international dealings.

NECESSARY

Synonyms : Essential, needful, required, requisite, undeniable, unavoidable.

Antonyms : Casual, worthless, needless, non-essential, optional, unnecessary, useless.

Synonyms

- Food, shelter and clothing are *essential* for life.
- The court has directed the police to do the *needful* immediately.

- He was *required* to be present before the court in person.
- We have reminded them to send the *requisite* information expeditiously.
- Freedom of speech is an *undeniable* right of man.
- He was under such compelling circumstances that his neighbour's help became *unavoidable* for him.

Antonyms

- Engineering appliances are no more a *casual* need of the townsman. These are becoming almost essential for a decent day-to-day life.
- All talk of luxuries for the poor is *worthless* unless you meet their ordinary needs first.
- *Needless* to say I will be present at the meeting only if it is held on a Sunday.
- Bus transport and electricity are no longer *non-essential* items of daily use in the cities.
- I have chosen philosophy as my *optional* subject in college.
- Leave out the *unnecessary* details and come to the brasstacks.
- It is *useless* to cry over spilt milk.

NEGLECT

Synonyms : Carelessness, neglectfulness, negligence, omission, oversight, scorn, slackness, heedlessness, default, failure, disregard, disrespect, slight, inadvertance.

Antonyms : Care, attention, heed, observation, adventure.

Synonyms

- His *carelessness* will cause him great loss one day.
- His boss rebuked him for his *neglectfulness.*
- The subordinates took full advantage of the *negligence* of the boss.
- He was regretful of his *omissions* and errors.
- The typist has made this error due to *oversight.*
- The boatman *scorned* his son for his perpetual fear of paddling in the sea. 
- The *slackness* of the clerk irritated the boss.
- The father was worried about the *heedlessness* of his son for studies.
- I am confident he will not *default* in repaying your loan.
- One should not be disappointed on *failures,* as they ultimately lead to success in life.
- The king *disregarded* the counsel of his minister and waged the war.
- He married a poor girl *disrespecting* the wishes of his parents.

Antonyms

- If you *care* for others, others will certainly *care* for you.
- I drew the *attention* of the minister to the sources of corruption in his ministry.
- The minister *heeded* my *observations* while drafting his proposals for eradication of corrupt practices.
- My new scheme is an *adventure* in the country's economy.

NERVOUS

Synonyms : Hesitant, timid, agitated, shaky, timorous, afraid.

Antonyms : Courageous, bold, manly, undaunted, doughty, valiant, brave.

Synonyms

- He was *hesitant* to go outstation in the first instance. His father, however, encouraged him to join the offered post in Kolkata.
- Tommy feels very *timid* when he sees a big dog.
- He was much *agitated* when he heard of the accident.
- His recent failures have made him so *shaky* he is not ready to start even a sound business.
- He is *afraid* of lightning.
- The beggar begged for alms in a *timorous* voice.

Antonyms

- ✦ There are very few *courageous* persons like Atul.
- ✦ Atul has launched many *bold* projects this year.
- ✦ His *manly* courage is responsible for his great success in business.
- ✦ Rajiv Gandhi showed *undaunted* courage by concluding an agreement on Punjab.
- ✦ The circusman, a *doughty* fellow, was feeding the lions as if these were cats.
- ✦ *Valiant* are those that carry on the struggle until they achieve their objective.
- ✦ Kim is a *brave* boy. He can walk the whole city at night all alone.

NEW

Synonyms : Unused, fresh, novel, recent, modern.

Antonyms : Old, ancient, aged, obsolete, antique, antiquated.

Synonyms

- ✦ He deals in used as well as *unused* cars and scooters.

- ✦ This is the only market in this area where one can get *fresh* vegetables and fruit.
- ✦ Mrs. Indira Gandhi was praised all over the world for her *novel* ideas on international issues.
- ✦ He has given the details of his *recent* visit to Antarctica region in his adventure story.
- ✦ Father does not like *modern* music, but Asha and I do.

Antonyms

- ✦ I am twenty years *old*.
- ✦ The major *ancient* civilisations are: Indus Valley, Egyptian, Chinese and Roman.
- ✦ Emerson was accompanied by an *aged* person when I saw him.
- ✦ This machine is *obsolete* yet highly valuable.
- ✦ It is an *antique* of the Indus Valley civilisation.
- ✦ I am fed up with my mother's *antiquated* ideas.

NIMBLE

Synonyms : Active, agile, prompt, flexible, quick, speedy, spry, swift.

Antonyms : Clumsy, unready, sluggish, inert, inactive, dull, dilatory.

Synonyms

- ✦ Even at the age of 67, Mrs. Indira Gandhi was very *active* and *agile*.
- ✦ He is very *prompt* in replying to my letters.

- His attitude towards life is quite *flexible.*
- The *quick* reply given by the child surprised all of us.
- *Speedy* action on the part of the fire brigade saved the house from destruction.
- She is very *spry* for a woman of her age.
- The thief made a *swift* exit leaving no trace of his identity.

Antonyms

- Poor children of a slum cannot help looking *clumsy*. They are after all underfed and shabbily dressed.
- The police was *unready* to chase the dacoits. No wonder the dacoits decamped with the loot.
- My habits have become *sluggish*. This is the result of my recent sickness.
- The boy lay *inert* on the road after being hit by a car.
- Anil is rather *inactive* for the type of quality education he is enjoying.
- Our new teacher is rather *dull* and drab in his lectures.

NOBLE

Synonyms : Dignified, lofty, eminent, honourable, great, illustrious, elevated, peer, lord, aristocrat, grand, magnificent.

Antonyms : Ignoble, mean, humble, common.

Synonyms

- The Queen received the guests in her usual *dignified* manner.
- The Himalayas is a *lofty* mountain.
- I met several *eminent* leaders in a conference yesterday.
- *Honourable* deeds are far better than empty words.
- Rabindranath Tagore was a *great* poet of India.
- Shakespeare is England's most *illustrious* poet. 
- An *elevated* house is one that has been built on a high platform.
- The defendant was tried by a jury of *peers*.
- He keeps *lording* over his subordinates day in and day out.
- Membership of this club is limited to *aristocrats* only.
- The duke looked *grand* in his naval uniform.

Antonyms

- His *ignoble* attitude has spoiled the image of his political party.
- He is rather *mean* in his dealings with his colleagues.

- ✦ Mahatma Gandhi was *humble* in demeanor but noble in ideas and action.
- ✦ The *common* man in India still lives below the poverty line.

NOTION

Synonyms : Conception, impression, imagination, opinion doctrine, belief, supposition, thought.

Antonyms : Truth, reality, fact, variety, actuality.

Synonyms

- ✦ The architect's *conception* of the building was a glass sky-scraper.
- ✦ He imbibed a deep *impression* of the Taj's lovely moonlight beauty when he viewed it for the first time.
- ✦ With a little *imagination* we should be able to find a solution to this vexed problem.
- ✦ His teacher has a very high *opinion* about Atul.
- ✦ The Church teaches the *doctrine* of free will.
- ✦ His firm *belief* in God helps him overcome all difficulties in life.
- ✦ He acted on the *supposition* that the public would applaud his political manouvres.
- ✦ What are your *thoughts* on this subject?

Antonyms

- ✦ *Truth* always triumphs; falsehood never pays.

- Terrorism has of late become one of the menacing *realities* round the world.
- The *fact* of poverty in the developing countries continues to persist.
- There is a great *variety* of religions in India: Hinduism, Islam, Sikhism, Christianity, Buddhism, Jainism, Zoroastrianism, etc.
- The *actuality* of divisive tendencies in the Indian social firmament cannot be denied.

NUMEROUS

Synonyms : Various, several, manifold, sundry, diverse.
Antonyms : Few, scarce, scanty, rare.

Synonyms

- *Various* views have been expressed on the agreement relating to the Arab-Israeli conflict.
- God is one but the ways of realising him are *several*.
- The city counsel has a *manifold* plan to beautify the city.
- I had to buy *sundry* things to equip myself for the forthcoming trip abroad.

- The crowd scattered in *diverse* directions when the police opened the tear-gas.

Antonyms

- Only a *few* individuals graced the silver jubilee celebrations of the political party owing to the tense atmosphere in the city.
- The commodities which are *scarce* in supply carry more value in the market.
- The southern region has had only *scanty* rainfall this year.
- This piece of handicraft has been declared a *rare* object.

OBEDIENT

Synonyms : Submissive, subservient, dutiful, tractable, yielding.

Antonyms : Mutinous, stubborn, intractable, disobedient, refractor.

Synonyms

- His *submissive* nature leads others to believe he is a coward.
- A good leader's policies must be *subservient* to the needs of the people.
- For many years he was a *dutiful* soldier before he turned a rebel.

- A dude ranch needs *tractable* horses for its guests.
- The government has been *yielding* to even undue demands of the minorities.

Antonyms

- The northern command headed by Gen. Okello became *mutinous* and deposed President Milton Obete in Uganda.
- My husband is a *stubborn* character and it is rather difficult for me to change his habits.
- My ideas on the political system needed for India are *intractable* as they are based on strong logic.
- It is not wrong to be *disobedient* to the elders if your cause is noble and lofty.
- Cancer is a *refractory* disease in India so far.

OBLIGATORY

Synonyms : Necessary, unavoidable, needful, imperative, compulsory.

Antonyms : Desired, willing, voluntary, self-chosen.

Synonyms

- It is *necessary* to go to college if you want to be well-educated.
- Paying taxes is *unavoidable* if your income is beyond Rs. 50,000 in a year.
- I am sure he will do the *needful* in this matter if he possibly can.
- It is *imperative* that communal violence be suppressed immediately and with iron command.
- Yoga has been made *compulsory* in many schools in Delhi and Mumbai.

Antonyms

- We should work our utmost to achieve the *desired* objectives.
- Sorry, I am not *willing* to relax the rules for the sake of your son's admission in my school.
- My father has taken to *voluntary* retirement after 20 years of service in the government, though he could still continue for five more years.
- The career followed by my son is *self-chosen* as I have never given him serious advice or guidance.

OBLIVIOUS

Synonyms : Forgetful, absent-minded, inattentive.

Antonyms : Attentive, aware, observant.

Synonyms

- He is a *forgetful* type, so one cannot entrust him serious assignments.
- Our professor of philosophy is so *absent-minded* that he entered his neighbour's house instead of his own yesterday.
- John is *inattentive* in his class. That is why he is so backward in studies.

Antonyms

- My son is very *attentive* in his lessons and always near the top in his class.

- ✦ The people are gradually becoming *aware* of their rights and responsibilities as citizens, thanks to the ever-spreading TV media.
- ✦ Our managing director is quite *observant* of the activities of his rival businessmen.

OBVIOUS

Synonyms : Clear, evident, visible, distinct, palpable, patent, discernible, perceptible.

Antonyms : Hidden, masked, veiled, covert, secret, obscure, concealed, latent.

Synonyms

- ✦ He is very *clear* in his thoughts as well as actions.
- ✦ It became quite *evident* that he was not willing to undertake the assignment.
- ✦ Nothing was *visible* at a distance of even 10 metres because of the thick fog. 
- ✦ The woodpecker makes a *distinct* tapping noise.
- ✦ There is a *palpable* difference in their ages.
- ✦ His *patent* reply to every question is a big No.
- ✦ The mediator made a *discernible* analysis of the problem.
- ✦ The difference in their heights is hardly *perceptible*.

Antonyms

- ✦ Every idea has a *hidden* meaning besides the obvious one.
- ✦ The leader's views seemed *masked* by a deeper meaning.
- ✦ The creditor gave a *veiled* threat to his debtor to expedite his recovery.
- ✦ Despite the ban on gambling, the crooks found a *covert* place to play cards.
- ✦ He made no *secret* of his lofty ambitions.

OBSCURE

Synonyms : Dark, doubtful, dim, dense, muddy, unintelligible, involved, deep, cloudy, dusky, hidden, turbid, darksome.

Antonyms : Apparent, intelligible, lucid, unadorned, obvious, evident, plain, straightforward, transparent, distinct.

Synonyms

- ✦ He always kept his parents in the *dark* regarding the weakness in his studies.
- ✦ His friends were *doubtful* about his sincerity to them.
- ✦ I could scarcely read by the *dim* light of the candle.
- ✦ After looting the bus the dacoits ran into a *dense* jungle.
- ✦ They had to pass through the *muddy* water before reaching the temple.

- The behaviour of the host was *unintelligible* to the guests and they left for their homes.
- The government has prescribed such an *involved* procedure for grant of subsidy that hardly a few can make use of the scheme.
- His sermons carry too *deep* a philosophy. It is beyond my understanding.
- All of a sudden the sky became *cloudy* and it started raining heavily.
- I hardly recognised him in the *dusky* light.

Antonyms

- The *apparent* reason for his failure in the examination is his sickness during the examination days.
- His accent is not so *intelligible* to the class.
- His thinking is very *lucid* but action rather complicated.
- Joseph is the *unadorned* king of the school sports.
- Smith was the *obvious* choice of the school for representing it in the state sports.
- That he is intelligent in studies is *evident* from his power of speech together with the vast vocabulary at his command.

ODD

Synonyms : Queer, uneven, strange, irregular.

Antonyms : Usual, match, matching, even, parallel.

Synonyms

- ✦ This philosopher has very *queer* habits of always performing day-to-day routines in the *irregular* way.
- ✦ His *uneven* moods make him completely unpredictable.
- ✦ Do you recognise that *strange* man in the blue cap?
- ✦ My *irregular* habits of diet have wrecked my health.

Antonyms

- ✦ This is my *usual* time for lunch.
- ✦ These ducks very much *match* in colour.
- ✦ This colour is not *matching* with the original.
- ✦ Two, four, six, eight, ten are all *even* numbers in arithmetic.

ONEROUS

Synonyms : Burdensome, troublesome, oppressive, difficult, wearing.

Antonyms : Easy, fluent, harmless, comfortable.

Synonyms

- ✦ The old man was glad to get rid of his *burdensome* furniture.

- A successful teacher knows how to handle the *troublesome* students.
- Democracy cannot tolerate *oppressive* leaders.
- Facing a corrupt bureaucracy is one of the most *difficult* problems of the new government.
- The members of the society are tired of the *wearing* manners of the secretary.
- Carrying the furniture to the attic was an *onerous* task.

Antonyms

- The language paper was rather *easy*. I had nothing to worry.
- Modern moving belt system at the airports and big railway stations has made *fluent* the problem of luggage placement in the planes/luxury cars.
- Taking of bed tea is *harmless* only if you keep the consumption within limits.
- The new luxury coach is as *comfortable* as your well-cushioned drawing room.

OOZE

Synonyms : Drip, drizzle, drop, let fall.

Antonyms : Rush, pour, gush, flow, rain.

Synonyms

- The bottle of glucose was *dripping* very small drops into the tube for transmission into the patient's veins.

✦ The light *drizzle* changed the weather from hot to pleasant.

✦ The earthen pitcher filters the water *drop by drop.*

Antonyms

✦ During floods this river has a sudden *rush* of water.

✦ *Pour* some sauce over the pasta.

✦ The syphon allows a *gush* of water in the can if you suck off the air and use a wide connecting tube.

✦ This tributary has a uniform *flow* of water throughout the year.

OPINION

Synonyms : Thought, idea, judgement, theory, dogma, mind, notion, speculation, verdict, tenet.

Antonyms : Silence, dictation, non-committal, execution, order.

Synonyms

✦ You must give a serious *thought* before resigning this cosy job.

✦ I got a good *idea* last night for my mother's birthday present.

✦ The *judgement* of the umpire cannot be questioned by the players.

✦ His *theory,* if accepted, will open new vistas in the field of public health.

- With the advent of science the religious *dogmas* have lost their sway.
- It is very difficult to know his *mind* because he speaks very little.
- His colleagues had a wrong *notion* about him but he is basically a very kind-hearted man.
- My *speculation* about the election results has come out true.
- The jury will give its *verdict* in this case next week.

Antonyms

- There was a pin-drop *silence* in the hall when the pope delivered his sermon.
- He is a versatile steno; he can take down notes from the *dictation* of a tape-recorder.
- The reply of the management to the demands of the labourers was *non-committal*.
- The project is now ready in all respects for being taken up tor *execution*.
- The prime minister has *ordered* for fresh elections in the state.

OPPORTUNITY

Synonyms : Chance, occasion, turn, expedient.

Antonyms : Omission, lapse, neglect, leave undone,

Synonyms

- Real success lies in availing of the right *chance* at the right moment.

- The present state of affairs is no *occasion* for rejoicing.
- Now it is my *turn* to distribute the cards.
- It is now *expedient* to hold the election in the Punjab.

Antonyms

- There are many errors of *omission* in this book.
- The time for payment of the income tax has *lapsed.*
- The case reflects extreme *neglect* on the part of the dealing officer.
- At many places the analysis of data has been *left undone.*

OPTIMIST

Synonyms : Hopeful, confident, brave, bright, cheerful, happy.

Antonyms : Pessimist, dejected, drooping, disappointment, cheerless, hopeless.

Synonyms

- India is *hopeful* of big strides in space technology very soon.
- He is *confident* of his success in the competition.
- The coast guard men *braved* the storm to reach the sinking ship.
- The *bright* girl is well-liked by her teachers.

- ✦ It will make Mary *cheerful* if you go over and talk to her.
- ✦ It makes me *happy* to think of the golden college days.

Antonyms

- ✦ Anil is basically a *pessimist.* He looks at the dark side of things more than at the bright.
- ✦ When I entered the house, I found my brother *dejected* owing to a bad interview he had in an examination.
- ✦ With her marriage proposal breaking half way, she lay *drooping* on her bed.
- ✦ Her *disappointment* was acute.
- ✦ Her demeanour was *cheerless.*

ORDERLY

Synonyms : Neat, tidy, trim, uniform, graceful.

Antonyms : Chaotic, disorderly, untidy, messy,

Synonyms

- ✦ Our firm has an entirely *neat* system of filing.
- ✦ Ramesh is always found in *tidy* apparels.
- ✦ The gardener was asked to *trim* the hedges.
- ✦ His body and mind are generally marked by *uniform* smoothness of sorts.
- ✦ She had a very *graceful* disposition.

Antonyms

- ✦ Our library is in a *chaotic* condition since the librarian is on a long leave.

- ✦ The books of the library are lying in a *disorderly* way.
- ✦ The whole room is *untidy*.
- ✦ The students and teachers who come and look for books on their own have created a *mess*.

ORDINARY

Synonyms : Average, common, usual, commonplace, regular, medium, inferior, undistinguished, low.

Antonyms : Extraordinary, uncommon, one-in-a-million, above average, abnormally high, first rate, superior, distinguished.

Synonyms

- ✦ He is student of *average* calibre but secures a high position in the examinations due to hard work.
- ✦ The *common* man is hit hard by the price rise but the government has taken no steps to raise his wages in equal proportion.
- ✦ Father has gone out for his *usual* evening walk.
- ✦ Horses and buggies were a *commonplace* sight of Delhi in 1920s.
- ✦ Getting up very early in the morning is his *regular* routine.
- ✦ She is neither short nor tall; she has a *medium* height.
- ✦ A captain is *inferior* in rank to a major in the Indian Army.

+ His military career was an *undistinguished* one but after retirement he has done some business and made tons of money.

Antonyms

+ My brother is an *extraordinary* boy, both in studies and sports.
+ Amitabh Bachhan is an actor of *uncommon* calibre, *one-in-a-million.*
+ Anil is far *above average* in intelligence but a middling in all-round performance.
+ His intelligence quotient is *abnormally high.*
+ An MP is called a *first rate* citizen in a democracy.
+ Ramesh has a *superior* position in the company.
+ Nilkanth is a *distinguished* lawyer of this country.

ORGANISE

Synonyms : Classify, arrange, order, sort, marshal.

Antonyms : Disorganise, muddle, bungle, dishevel.

Synonyms

+ A dictionary is a *classified* arrangement of words.
+ Please *arrange* these words alphabetically.
+ These goods need to be placed in the showroom in an aesthetic *order.*
+ *Sort* out the commercial letters from this mail.

- I have *marshalled* the facts of the case in this notebook for your ready reference.

Antonyms

- Our college library is very much *disorganised* these days due to stock-taking.
- Henry has *muddled* the whole sales programme owing to his eccentric behaviour with his clients.
- The new treasurer has *bungled* with the accounts of the society.
- Never mind my *dishevelled* hair; come to the point.

OUTBREAK

Synonyms : Commotion, tumult, insurrection, outburst.

Antonyms : Order, quiet, subsidence, peace.

Synonyms

- The crowd waiting outside was causing a *commotion*.
- The labouring class has caused a *tumult* in a number of factories by their agitation against rising prices.
- Discontentment against the king was so great that the common people rose in an *insurrection* and dethroned the king.
- She was alarmed by his violent *outburst*.

Antonyms

- The new leadership created *order* out of chaos.
- The dissidents achieved what they wanted and the result was return of peace and *quiet*.
- Continuous soil erosion resulted in the *subsidence* of many houses.
- Universal *peace* is an impossibility.

PACIFY

Synonyms : Appease, mitigate, quench, lull, allay, compose, quiet, tranquillise, assuage.

Antonyms : Irritate, inflame, annoy, incense, enrage, exasperate, vex.

Synonyms

- ✦ He *appeased* his hunger with sweet dishes.
- ✦ Government has taken several steps to *mitigate* the hardships of the shopkeepers of this area.
- ✦ Coca Cola will not *quench* your thirst.
- ✦ There was a *lull* before the thunderstorm.
- ✦ The doctor was able to *allay* the patient's anxiety.
- ✦ She remained well *composed* during the hot controversy.
- ✦ The teacher tried to *quieten* the students.
- ✦ This medicine will *tranquillise* the restless baby and put him to sleep.

- The medicine may *assuage* the pain, but soaking in lukewarm water will do your injury more good.

Antonyms

- His criticism *irritated* me very much.
- The fiery speech of the trade union leader *inflamed* the passions of the workers.
- The subordinate's impertinence *annoyed* the boss.
- The arbitrary decision *incensed* the workers.
- The peasant's rude behaviour *enraged* the landlord.
- The neglect of the civic problems in the city has *exasperated* the local population.
- The municipal commissioner has *vexed* the problem by his indifference.

PAIN

Synonyms : Throes, pang, ache, grief, agony.

Antonyms : Health, pleasure, well-being, ecstasy, relief.

Synonyms

- Child-birth is no joke as it causes immense *throes* in a would-be-mother.
- The beloved could hardly bear the *pangs* of separation from her lover.
- My head *ache* has been greatly relieved by this medicine.

- Sunny has come to great *grief* by his constant unemployment.
- Scooter accident has put him in a state of *agony*.

Antonyms

- *Health* is the first requisite of a good personality.
- "Duty first, *pleasure* next" is the motto of good citizens.
- A welfare state does a lot of work nowadays for the *well-being* of the common people.
- Ram felt *ecstasy* in the company of Sita.
- It gives me great *relief* to be told about an increase in my salary.

PARDON

Synonyms : Condone, forgive, acquit, excuse, overlook.

Antonyms : Condemn, convict, punish, penalise.

Synonyms

- The principal has *condoned* my late fee.
- *Forgive* me God for my bad deeds, if any!
- The judge *acquitted* the accused after preliminary hearing.
- *Excuse* me, may I borrow your pen for a minute?
- We should not *overlook* our faults while appraising our good achievements.

Antonyms

- This racket needs to be *condemned* and brought to the notice of the government.

- The court *convicted* the accused for his guilt.
- Law *punishes* the people who commit social crimes.
- God *penalises* those who escape the legal penalties by hook or by crook.

PARDON

Synonyms : Absolution, mercy, remission, amnesty, forgiveness, acquittal.

Antonyms : Penalty, retaliation, punishment, retribution, vengeance.

Synonyms

- His *absolution* from his partner's debts gave him great relief.
- The prisoner begged for *mercy* but to no avail.
- His application for *remission* of fine was rejected by the principal.
- The king granted *amnesty* to the rebels.
- We must forgive our enemies if we ourselves expect *forgiveness.*
- His *acquittal* by the jury has saved an innocent from being punished.

Antonyms

- The government has imposed a new *penalty* for evasion of taxes.
- *Retaliation* is no solution to the verbal attacks made in individual relationships.
- All crimes against society carry a *punishment* under law.

- ✦ Some traditions lay down *retribution* as a punishment for social misdeeds, intentional or otherwise.
- ✦ The idea of *vengeance* is repugnant to the philosophy of Buddhism.

PART

Synonyms : Atom, member, portion, share, segment, section, particle, fragment, piece, disconnect, fraction, disjoin.

Antonyms : Connect, join, tie, attach, link, combine, couple, cement.

Synonyms

- ✦ At one time it was thought an *atom* could not be split.
- ✦ Only the *members* of the club can participate in the annual function.
- ✦ Only some *portion* of an iceberg is visible above the water.
- ✦ Each of the partners tried to appropriate a bigger *share* of the profits.
- ✦ A chord is a line which divides a circle into two *segments.*
- ✦ The government has formulated a new policy for the upliftment of the economically weaker *sections* of the society.
- ✦ She got a *particle* of dust in her eye while sweeping the room.

- The cup was smashed and lay in *fragments* on the floor.
- She tore his letter into *pieces* and threw it in the waste paper basket.
- The guard's van was *disconnected* from the train.

Antonyms

- By *connecting* the wire of the positive charge with the negative one, we simply create a big spark.
- *Joining* of two dots by a footrule makes a straight line.
- We can *tie* the knots on the rope and make a net.
- His name has been *attached* with a spy ring.
- His *link* with an important smuggling concern has been established.

PARTIAL

Synonyms : Unfair, incomplete, limited, biased, restricted, predisposed, one-sided, inequitable.

Antonyms : Fair, entire, complete, equitable, disinterested, whole, just, impartial.

Synonyms

- He has resorted to *unfair* means to win the election.
- This clerk is in the habit of leaving his work *incomplete*.

- Inspite of the *limited* resources, the Indian scientists have made great inventions.
- Some people have *biased* views against their colleagues.
- His *restricted* approach can lead to his failure in this noble mission.
- His mother's work as a nurse *predisposes* him for aspiring to be a doctor.
- A judge cannot do justice if he takes *one-sided* view of the case.

Antonyms

- The new minister has a *fair* view of society and its problems.
- He has travelled the *entire* length and breadth of the country to obtain a practical insight of social problems.
- He intends a *complete* study of the society of India.
- There is need for a more *equitable* distribution of wealth in India.
- An internationalist is one who can take a *disinterested* view of international problems.
- A triangle covers only a part of the *whole*.
- I can lay down my life for a *just* cause.
- I cannot take an *impartial* view in a case where my brother may be involved.

PASSION

Synonyms : Love, anger, fury, emotion, fever, desire, excitement, zeal, fervour.

Antonyms : Idea, conception, belief, thought.

Synonyms

- Everything is fair in *love* and war.
- My *anger* grew as he continued his invectives.
- He wondered if she would turn into a noisy *fury* like her mother. 
- The film did generate enough *emotion* among the audience.
- The examination *fever* makes him nervous.
- His only *desire* was to see his son married before his death.
- She had to calm down herself after all the *excitement*.
- He has started his new business with great *zeal* and *fervour*.

Antonyms

- It is simply an *idea*. Whether we can make it practicable will depend upon your fervour.
- The plan was brilliant in *conception* but failed due to lack of funds.
- Our success would depend on the deeper *belief* you place in this idea.

- ✦ The political *thought* round the world is taking a reverse gear from communism to individualism.

PASSIVE

Synonyms : Patient, inert, submissive, resistant.

Antonyms : Active, alert, vigilant, watchful.

Synonyms

- ✦ Rajiv gave a *patient* hearing to my problem and promised to help.
- ✦ Anil has become rather *inert* since his last illness.
- ✦ Anil is *submissive* in his business dealings.
- ✦ He has lost the power of *resistance* to wrong decisions.

Antonyms

- ✦ Atul is an *active* and smart boy.
- ✦ He is *alert* to his surroundings both in business and private life.
- ✦ Income tax authorities have of late become more *vigilant* of economic offences by business houses.
- ✦ Rajiv advised me to be *watchful* of the tricks of my partner.

PATERNAL

Synonyms : Fatherly, careful, patronising, kind-hearted.

Antonyms : Careless, rough, rude, indifferent.

Synonyms

- ✦ My boss has a *fatherly* attitude towards me.

- ✦ My father is *careful* in his business dealings. He never signs a paper without proper judgement.
- ✦ He is *patronising* so long as my business proposals are profitable to him as well as to me.
- ✦ He is also *kind-hearted* in his social dealings.

Antonyms

- ✦ I try not to be *careless* in accounts which I consider are basic to success in any business.
- ✦ Before taking a business decision I make *rough* estimates and then prune them before implementation of projects.
- ✦ I am never *rude* to my employees.
- ✦ I am not *indifferent* to the welfare of my subordinates.

PATIENCE

Synonyms : Forbearance, passiveness, sufferance, resignation, endurance, fortitude, calmness.

Antonyms : Wrath, enrage, annoy, infuriate, vex, displease, inflame, incite, indignation, irritation, provoke.

Synonyms

- ✦ It takes considerable *forbearance* to overlook his faults.
- ✦ The *passiveness* of the Indian farmer can be partly attributed to his religious traditions.
- ✦ He cannot help but praise the *sufferance* of the audience who saw the full drama.

- He accepted his defeat with *resignation.*
- Sailing the Atlantic singlehanded requires great *endurance.*

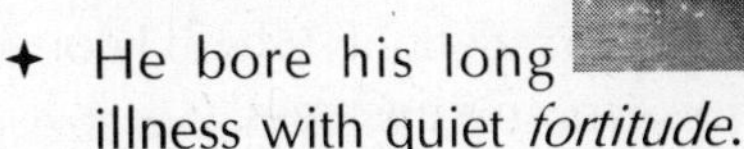

- He bore his long illness with quiet *fortitude.*

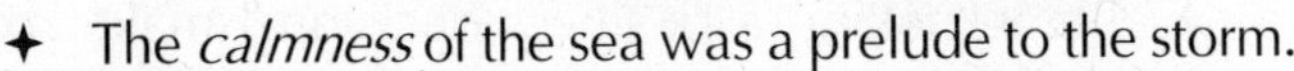

- The *calmness* of the sea was a prelude to the storm.

Antonyms

- The cyclone pounded the whole coastal area as God's own *wrath.*
- The behaviour of the servant *enraged* the master.
- Let's first finish our home task lest we *annoy* our teacher.
- The boss felt *infuriated* on the failure of the subordinate in tackling such a simple problem.
- Let's simplify rather than *vex* the problem.
- The boss was *displeased* with his subordinate.
- The political leader *inflamed* the mob without proposing *patience.* Hence the incident of stone-throwing.

PAUSE

Synonyms : Respite, interval, break, halt, cessation, intermission, lull, suspension, stoppage, wait.

Antonyms : Continue, continuation, continuity, continuance.

Synonyms

- ✦ The director gave the hero a short *respite* before the next scene.
- ✦ There was an *interval* of ten minutes at the concert, to give the orchestra a rest.
- ✦ His absence from office was treated as a *break* in his service.
- ✦ *Halt* at the cross-roads.
- ✦ The warring nations agreed on a *cessation* of hostilities.
- ✦ Many from the audience left the hall in the *intermission*, so boring was the picture.
- ✦ There was a *lull* before the thunderstorm.
- ✦ His *suspension* has been revoked by the new secretary.
- ✦ *Stoppage* of work by the union leaders for their trivial demands was condemned by the press.
- ✦ Time and tide *wait* for none.

Antonyms

- ✦ We *continued* our journey without break.
- ✦ We should inform of our new order to the firm in *continuation* of the earlier order.
- ✦ We must ensure the *continuity* of schemes undertaken by the foregoing ministry.

✦ This business is a *continuance* of the old one.

PECULIAR

Synonyms : Strange, extraordinary, remarkable, odd, queer, unusual, rare, abnormal, uncommon, irregular, singular.

Antonyms : Natural, customary, normal, commonplace, usual, ordinary.

Synonyms

✦ He told us a *strange* story.

✦ A snowflake as seen under a microscope is of *extraordinary* beauty.

✦ Our party has made *remarkable* progress in the current elections.

✦ The giraffe is an *odd*-looking animal.

✦ We heard a *queer* story about how a dog was changed into a monkey.

✦ The shape of this tree is *unusual*.

✦ He has a good collection of *rare* art pieces.

✦ An *abnormal* growth of tissues leads to cancer.

✦ A solar eclipse is an *uncommon* occurrence.

✦ Our clock is *irregular* and cannot be trusted.

✦ We saw a *singular* sight of a dog pulling a small cart.

Antonyms

- Hot summers are a *natural* phenomenon of tropical countries.
- Dessert is a *customary* dish after dinner in European hotels.
- The *normal* temperature of Mumbai in June is between 34°C and 24°C.
- T.V is a *commonplace* source of recreation for the town folk nowadays.
- My *usual* summer dress is a bushirt and terricot trousers.
- Many extraordinary luxuries in India are *ordinary* necessities in Europe.

PERFECT

Synonyms : Flawless, faultless, ideal, consummate.

Antonyms : Deficient, imperfect, flawed.

Synonyms

- This scheme seems *flawless* if well operated.
- Your thesis is *faultless* in language and ideas.
- Your approach to the problem seems *ideal.*
- This technique will certainly lead to *consummation* of the task.

Antonyms

- India is still *deficient* in mineral oil.
- Mary's performance in the play was *imperfect* to say the least.

- ✦ Mohan *flawed* in the debate at many points.

PERMANENT

Synonyms : Stable, enduring, lasting, durable.
Antonyms : Brief, temporary, short-lived.

Synonyms

- ✦ India's *stable* foreign policy since Nehru's time has brought international applause.
- ✦ An *enduring* programme of rural development is necessary to boost India's economy.
- ✦ His sermons have a *lasting* effect on the disciples.
- ✦ This machine has been made *durable* enough to last a decade without repairs.

Antonyms

- ✦ He made a *brief* speech on the occasion.
- ✦ This arrangement is meant for a *temporary* period of a month or so.
- ✦ We need not devote such huge investment of time and money on this *short-lived* problem.

PERMISSION

Synonyms : Leave, allowance, license, permit, liberty, authority, consent
Antonyms : Prevention, refusal, resistance, prohibition, denial, hinderance, opposition, objection,

Synonyms

- ✦ The teacher gave him *leave* to go home early.

- ✦ The daily *allowance* paid to the government servants on tour does help them to save something after expenses.
- ✦ His *licence* to keep a dog has been cancelled by the municipal authorities.
- ✦ He was given a *permit* to go through the private park.
- ✦ Eternal vigilance is the price of *liberty*.
- ✦ The Headmaster has no *authority* to administer a school in whatever way he likes.
- ✦ Mother *consented* to me spending the day with my friends.

Antonyms

- ✦ *Prevention* of a disease is better than cure.
- ✦ His *refusal* to lend me a small amount of Rs. 50/- shocked me very much.
- ✦ His *resistance* to my tempting invitation to a sumptuous dinner was very unusual.
- ✦ The government of Tamil Nadu has withdrawn *prohibition* of alcoholic drinks.

PERMIT

Synonyms : Let, allow, authorise.

Antonyms : Forbid, prevent, prohibit.

Synonyms

- ✦ Please *let* me go into the ward to see my ailing mother.

- ✦ The government should not *allow* any fissiparous tendencies to raise their ugly head.
- ✦ The deputy commissioner was *authorised* to nip the riots sternly.

Antonyms

- ✦ The court gave its ruling *forbidding* the use of religious places for political campaigning.
- ✦ We can *prevent* the spread of this disease by general inoculation of children.
- ✦ The principal had to *prohibit* demonstrations of any kind in college premises.

PERSIST

Synonyms : Continue, last, remain, stay, endure, insist, preserve.

Antonyms : Discontinue, conclude, quit, finish, terminate, end, desist, cease.

Synonyms

- ✦ He *continued* his speech despite hooting.
- ✦ He was afraid that his money would not *last* to the end of his holidays.
- ✦ The weather will *remain* cold for the next few weeks.
- ✦ How long did you *stay* there?
- ✦ The Bible says that God's mercy *endures* for ever.
- ✦ Father *insisted* that mother must rest in the afternoon.

- It is our duty to *preserve* our national monuments.

Antonyms

- My sister has *discontinued* her studies after graduation.
- His studies *concluded* after 15 years under the 10 + 2 + 3 year graduation course.
- Satish has *quit* his job as he could not pull on with his boss.
- He has *finished* his practical training in a couple of good firms.
- The boss *terminated* the services of his inefficient subordinate.
- This feature film will *end* at 9 pm.
- Anil has *desisted* further assaults on his reputation.
- I will *cease* to be a member of the club from next month.

PERSISTENT

Synonyms : Ceaseless, continuous, unceasing, unremitting.

Antonyms : Occasional, periodic, temporary.

Synonyms

- It requires a *ceaseless* struggle to eradicate casteism in Indian society.

- They had to undertake a *continuous* journey for three months by road to reach their destination.
- It was through *unceasing* planning and effort that he topped in the class.

Antonyms

- It was one of the *occasional* chances that brought him to limelight.
- *Periodic* checkup is always good for children.
- Fever near the exams brought a *temporary* set-back in his career.

PERSUADE

Synonyms : Allure, urge, lead, incite, entice, coax, convince, incline, move, induce, impel, bring.

Antonyms : Hold back, restrain, deter, repel, dissuade, hinder, discourage.

Synonyms

- He was *allured* by her wealth and sophistication.
- Mother *urged* Ram to go to the dentist.
- The tug will *lead* the liner into the harbour.
- His speech *incited* the mob to violence.
- Father did everything to *entice* mother to go to the party.
- Ram *coaxed* his father to let him use the family car.
- The politician's speech *convinced* the voters he was the man deserving to be elected.

- ✦ The whole family is *inclined* to rise early in the morning.
- ✦ He was deeply *moved* on hearing his cousin's death.
- ✦ I tried to *induce* Mohan to come with us, but he would not.
- ✦ Wild animals and birds are often *impelled* by hunger to come near the human beings, especially in winter.
- ✦ I just can't *bring* myself to apologise.

Antonyms

- ✦ I cannot now *hold back* my offer of a job to him in my organisation.
- ✦ His remarks greatly disparaged my reputation, but I *restrained* myself from giving him a blow on his jaw.
- ✦ Such a blow could have *deterred* him from making such remarks in future.
- ✦ Similar poles *repel* each other.

PHYSICAL

Synonyms : Bodily, carnal, fleshy.

Antonyms : Mental, spiritual, intellectual.

Synonyms

- ✦ He was *bodily* healthy but intellectually inferior.
- ✦ *Carnal* necessities compel many a young man to stoop low.
- ✦ His approach in day-to-day life is rather *fleshy*. There is nothing poetic about him.

Antonyms

- His *mental* make-up is so strong, he invariably tops in the class.
- Unless the modern youth reduce their luxurious habits, they cannot take to *spiritual* outlook.
- They could not relate to each other on *intellectual* level.

PITIABLE

Synonyms : Sad, distressing, sorrowful, moving, grievous, doleful, woeful, mournful.

Antonyms : Pleasant, desirable, enviable.

Synonyms

- What has happened to make you look so *sad*?
- It was *distressing* to see him suffering from pain.
- Hearing the *sorrowful* news she wept loudly.
- This story has no *moving* parts.
- The death of Martin Luther King in 1968 was a *grievous* loss to humanity.
- The funeral involved a long, *doleful* ceremony.
- The *woeful* news grieved the nation.
- The pupils and teachers are *mournful* today because the headmaster has died.

Antonyms

- ✦ The weather is very *pleasant* today.
- ✦ Our college encourages numerous *desirable* extracurricular activities after study hours.
- ✦ Our new manager is an *enviable* personality — what gait, manners, speech, vocabulary, health!

PLAIN

Synonyms : Clear, evident, obvious, conspicuous, apparent.

Antonyms : Hidden, concealed, secret, imperceptible.

Synonyms

- ✦ It is better we *clear* our accounts before it is too late.
- ✦ His desire for friendship with you is *evident* from his offering a bouquet of flowers on your birthday.
- ✦ That Jorden is intelligent is *obvious* from the result of his exam.
- ✦ The flaws in this book are *conspicuous.*

Antonyms

- ✦ The thief's face was *hidden* in a mask.
- ✦ Romy *concealed* many of his business dealings from his partner. No wonder their partnership broke off.
- ✦ They wanted to implement their *secret* agenda.
- ✦ The leader's clarification made only an *imperceptible* impact on the public who continued to carry the grudge against his earlier stand on the issue.

PLEAD

Synonyms : Pray, sue, supplicate, entreat.

Antonyms : Command, demand, order.

Synonyms

- The advocate *prayed* to the court to take a compassionate view about his client.
- Jim *sued* Sam for damages.
- The student *supplicated* to the principal to take a lenient view of his misadventure.

Antonyms

- Nehru *commanded* great respect in international circles for his intellect and humanity.
- Workers *demanded* a raise in their wages.
- The principal *ordered* the dissenting students to quit the college.

PLEASANT

Synonyms : Pleasing, agreeable, attractive, enjoyable, nice.

Antonyms : Obnoxious, unpleasant, repulsive, displeasing, unattractive.

Synonyms

- The *pleasing* demeanour of the wife cancelled the anger of her husband.
- The *agreeable* temperament of the salesman won him many an order from the market.
- *Attractive* manners always bring good reward.

- The movie was a very *enjoyable* one.

Antonyms

- The *obnoxious* demeanour of the wife added to the wrath of the husband.
- The husband-wife clash caused an *unpleasant* atmosphere in the house.
- *Repulsive* manners bring untoward misery, however harmless the objectives of a person.

PLEASURE

Synonyms : Delight, enjoyment, joy, ecstasy.

Antonyms : Agony, pain, displeasure, sorrow, suffering.

Synonyms

- It gave Mohan great *delight* to receive an invitation to dinner from the governor.
- Physical health is as important as mental health for the *enjoyment* of life.
- *Joy* and suffering are two sides of a life.
- The study of poetic fiction gave him great *ecstasy*.

Antonyms

- ✦ The death of his mother caused him *agony* and sorrow.
- ✦ The fracture of his arm gave him unbearable *pain*.
- ✦ It is always advisible to avoid *displeasure* of elders.
- ✦ The old man was filled with *sorrow* on his son's death.

PLENTIFUL

Synonyms : Abundant, lavish, luxuriant, plenteous, sufficient, replete, bountiful, teeming, ample.

Antonyms : Scarce, limited, niggardly, sparing, skimpy, scanty, insufficient.

Synonyms

- ✦ Oranges are *abundant* in Spain.
- ✦ Uncle Hari was always *lavish* in giving presents.
- ✦ Her *luxuriant* black hair were the envy of many girls.
- ✦ There is a *plenteous* supply of wheat in India this year.
- ✦ These fishes are *sufficient* for the foreign market.
- ✦ The cabinets were *replete* with valuable antiques.
- ✦ The crops are *bountiful* this year.
- ✦ Agra *teems* with tourists on full moon nights.

Antonyms

- ✦ Apples are a *scarce* commodity in summer.

- ✦ Their supply is extremely *limited*, hence their price rises very high.
- ✦ He belongs to a rich family, yet the housewife is *niggardly* to its guests and visitors.
- ✦ There is hardly a *sparing* capacity in our workshop these days.
- ✦ You should not wear that *skimpy* dress to college.

POLITE

Synonyms : Elegant, genteel, gallant, courtly, courteous, civil, complaisant, chivalrous, cultivated, polished, urbane.

Antonyms : Awkward, bluff, untaught, unpolished, uncouth, brusque, ill-bred, clownish, raw, insolent, insulting, discourteous, coarse.

Synonyms

- ✦ The table was covered with an *elegant* lace cloth.
- ✦ My aunt Mary was the most *genteel* woman I ever knew.
- ✦ Foche's army made a *gallant* last stand.
- ✦ The old man was esteemed for his *courtly* manners.
- ✦ They wrote us a *courteous* thank-you note.
- ✦ Her greeting to him was *civil* but with no sign of effection.
- ✦ The host's *complaisant* manners made everyone feel at home.
- ✦ *Chivalrous* men usually treat women with respect.

- She *cultivated* her mind by reading many books.

Antonyms

- He asked many *awkward* questions which in fact put me to shame.
- His claim of getting a high position in the IAS proved a *bluff.*
- He was nice to look at but when it came to speech his *untaught* mannerisms came into focus.
- His jokes are rather crude and *unpolished.*
- His education has not lifted him from *uncouth* mannerism.
- His advice was sound but it was rather *brusque.*
- He played the role of an *ill-bred* rustic in the new play.
- His *clownish* behaviour at the office party cost him his job.
- He is too *raw* for the job of a salesman in this emporium.
- Very often our servant becomes so *insolent* I wish to terminate his services.

POOR

Synonyms : Hard up, under-privileged, ordinary.

Antonyms : Rich, privileged, extraordinary.

Synonyms

- The depression brought down his income and made him feel *hard up.*

- The government has chalked out many schemes for the betterment of the *under-privileged.*
- Majority of the village folk in India live below the *ordinary* standard.

Antonyms

- In India the *rich* have become richer and the poor became poorer since independence.
- Mohan is a rich man and belongs to the *privileged* class.
- By topping in the university, Sohan has given evidence of being an *extraordinary* brainy chap.

POSSESS

Synonyms : Have, command, seize, own, enjoy, hold, obtain.

Antonyms : Want, forfeit, lose, need, dispossess, relinquish.

Synonyms

- We *have* a small garden which meets all our little needs of fruits and vegetables.
- I *command* complete authority over the workers of this factory.
- The police *seized* the wrongly parked car.
- Do you *own* this beautiful tennis racket ?
- We shall *enjoy* the dinner after the variety programme.
- *Hold* the rope tightly.

✦ Wherefrom did you *obtain* your tennis racket ?

Antonyms

✦ We *want* at least a two-room flat for residence.

✦ If you do not attend the function, you will *forfeit* the right to a special gift.

✦ Oh! don't worry. I will certainly reach in time. I do not wish to *lose* the privilege of the gift.

✦ I *need* all your blessings for the success of my new venture.

✦ The government can *dispossess* the owner of a property useful for public purpose on paying due compensation.

✦ The manager has *relinquished* his charge in favour of the new incumbent.

POSSIBLE

Synonyms : Likely, potential, conceivable, feasible, practicable.

Antonyms : Impossible, impracticable, unachievable, inconceivable.

Synonyms

✦ An accident is *likely* to happen at this intersection anytime due to its defective signal system.

✦ Always watch out against any possible *potential* dangers.

✦ There is no *conceivable* way to raise ten thousand rupees immediately.

- It is not *feasible* to make the trip to Allahabad and be back in one day.
- The secretary was unable to suggest any *practicable* solution to the problem.

Antonyms

- The word "*impossible*" did not find a place in the dictionary of Napoleon.
- This scheme is absolutely *impracticable* in the present circumstances.
- Some of the targets laid in the tenth plan seem *unachievable* unless the position of law and order improves.
- It is *inconceivable* that the minister was not aware of the problem.

PRAISE

Synonyms : Acclaim, flattery, approval, plaudits, cheers, cheering, compliment, applause, laudation, approbation.

Antonyms : Abuse, vituperation, slander, scorn, repudiation, obloquy, disparagement, hissing, reproof, contempt, blame, condemnation.

Synonyms

- The football team was highly *acclaimed* on its return for winning the championship.

- It is not necessary to indulge in *flattery* to win friends.
- I will not give my *approval* to any proposal in which my role is not clearly delineated.
- The play won the *plaudits* of the critics.
- Children *cheered* when the teacher announced the holding of the prize distribution ceremony.
- Mrs. Indira Gandhi was greeted by large *cheering* mobs when she addressed them.
- He was *complemented* for establishing new records in swimming.
- The audience *applauded* Lata's song. There was loud *applause*.

Antonyms

- The master *abused* his servant for buying the wrong articles.
- The meeting of the political parties was marked by personal *vituperation* and *slander*-mongering.
- The members *scorned* each other and indulged in mutual *repudiation* and *obloquy*.
- Some members were seen in *disparaging* contempt for their opponents and indulged in *hissing* sounds.

PRECIOUS

Synonyms : Costly, valuable, invaluable, prized, inestimable, treasured.

Antonyms : Cheap, worthless, despicable, valueless, useless, paltry.

Synonyms

- ✦ My father gave me a *costly* gift on my 25th birthday.
- ✦ India has made *valuable* contribution in the field of atomic energy.
- ✦ The policeman gave us *invaluable* help in finding our stolen property.
- ✦ That trophy is one of my *prized* possessions.
- ✦ The assassination of Mrs. Indira Gandhi has caused *inestimable* loss to the country.
- ✦ The boy *treasured* the teacher's good opinion above everything else.

Antonyms

- ✦ The sales-cum-exhibition at Pragati Maidan is selling some items at *cheap* prices.
- ✦ This piece of handicraft is *worthless* at this high price.
- ✦ Just imagine this *despicable* junk lying in the centre of this posh colony.
- ✦ This piece of plastic jewellery is *valueless,* not worth even a single paisa.
- ✦ Your old car has become *useless,* better dispose it off at whatever price it fetches.
- ✦ This *paltry* sum of money is not going to buy even a few vegetables and fruits, what to talk of sundry items.

PREDOMINANT

Synonyms : Over-ruling, prominent, superior, dominant, ruling, prevalent, major.

Antonyms : Minor, inferior, unimportant, junior, petty, subsidiary, subordinate.

Synonyms

- ✦ The minister *over-ruled* the advice of the secretary.
- ✦ The most *prominent* building on High Street is the new cinema hall.
- ✦ His father enjoys a *superior* position in this office.
- ✦ India has become a *dominant* power in Asia and the Far East.
- ✦ The *ruling* class everywhere exploits the poor masses.
- ✦ The custom of "Sati" is still *prevalent* in some communities of Rajasthan.

Antonyms

- ✦ There were numerous major and *minor* issues raised in the meeting of the shareholders of the company
- ✦ This pen is much *inferior* to the one I bought you last time.

- This subject is too *unimportant* to occur to the examiners.
- He is a *junior* partner in my business firm.
- Asha is a *petty* officer in the bank.
- This bank is a *subsidiary* of the State Bank of India.
- There are quite a few officers and many *subordinates* in this firm.

PREDICAMENT

Synonyms : Plight, straits, fix, puzzle, jam, perplexity, difficulty.

Antonyms : Assurance, self-satisfaction, rest, decision, ease, comfort, calmness.

Synonyms

- Mother lost her purse during the journey and was in a bad *plight*.
- She found herself in desperate financial *straits*.
- After losing all his money he was in a great *fix*.
- He has won the first prize for solving a *puzzle*.
- I am in a *jam* due to financial shortage.
- His *perplexity* increased when he reached the crossroads.
- His one *difficulty* is getting a house on reasonable rent in a good locality.

Antonyms

- I can hand over the tape-recorder to him for repairs on your *assurance*.
- He is working hard these days for *self-satisfaction* and for the satisfaction of his boss.
- The doctor has set at *rest* my doubts about the disease.
- Your *decision* in this matter is as good as mine.
- We can solve this problem with *ease*.
- My uncle lives in great *comfort* at this old age, thanks to his savings!
- Mahatma Gandhi was a picture of *calmness* in the most difficult situations.

PREDICTION

Synonyms : Announcement, prophecy, forecast, augury, foreboding, warning, fortune-telling, foresight, divination.

Antonyms : Mystery, secrecy, hiding, occult, concealment.

Synonyms

- The *announcement* of the Indian Civil Services Fxamination was published quite late this year.
- Many *prophecies* about the future of mankind are mentioned in the Bible.
- Leading newspapers publish the next day's weather *forecast* daily.

- The rainbow was an *augury* of clear weather.
- He *forebode* the mishap much earlier.
- The boss has issued him a *warning* for coming late to office so often.
- In India you can find a good number of persons engaged in *fortune-telling*.
- Mrs. Indira Gandhi was one of the few world leaders with keen *foresight*.
- The *divination* of Swami Vivekananda came to limelight after his visit to America in 1893.

Antonyms

- The fate of the deposed Ugandan president was kept a *mystery* by the army generals.
- The *secrecy* of the defence establishments was violated by a military officer.
- The accused remained in *hiding* for a few months but was then caught.
- The *occult* view of the dacoit helped the police to nab him.
- The underground leader was in due course recovered from *concealment*.

PREJUDICE

Synonyms : Presumption, unfairness, partiality, preconception, bias.

Antonyms : Certainty, reasoning, conviction, demonstration, evidence, proof, reason.

Synonyms

- Your *presumption* that he will return your loan will prove wrong.
- Although the step-daughter was so much neglected, she never complained against the *unfairness* of her parents.

- The *partiality* of the referee helped the guest team to win the match.
- Europeans had a *pre-conception* that India was a country of snake-charmers.
- His colleagues have a *bias* against him.

Antonyms

- There is no *certainty* of good rains this year.
- The finance minister has changed the financial policy of the government with enough *reasoning* and *conviction.*
- The workers held a *demonstration* outside the gates of the factory to demand increase in wages.
- The court has sought more *evidence* against the accused before admitting the prima facie case.
- There is no *proof* that he stole the pen.
- There is no *reason* to worry about this affair.

PREMATURE

Synonyms : Rash, unreasonable, previous, early, untimely, precipitate.

Antonyms : Delayed, reasonable, overdue, late, slow.

Synonyms

- It was *rash* of John to skate on the pond when the ice was too thin.
- Their demand for hike in wages is *unreasonable* and unjustified.
- Their *previous* visit to the Taj had been very pleasant.
- He leaves for work *early* in the morning.
- Fall of snow in so early a summer is *untimely*.
- The oppressive measures adopted by the government helped to *precipitate* the liberation movement.

Antonyms

- Justice *delayed* is justice denied.
- If we put a *reasonable* price for this product we can go fast on sales.
- The balance payment from his buyer is long *overdue*. Please remind him in strong language.
- Better *late* than never.
- We should go *slow* on this project.

PRETEND

Synonyms : Fabricate, sham, feign, allege, profess, counterfeit, simulate.

Antonyms : Verify, substantiate, establish, authenticate.

Synonyms

- He *fabricated* a good excuse for absenting from the class.
- We have taught our dog to lie down and *sham* being dead.
- The boy *feigned* a headache to escape school attendance.
- He *alleged* the clerk had sought bribe for doing the job, so he had to part with Rs. 50.
- He *professed* to be an expert in labour laws.
- He was arrested for supplying *counterfeit* currency.

Antonyms

- I have *verified* the facts of the statement by comparing them with official statistics.
- We can *substantiate* our claim by facts, figures and documents.
- It was with due evidence that we *established* our claim to the official premises.
- Here is an *authenticated* copy of the statement supporting our claim.

PRIVILEGE

Synonyms : Favour, grant, licence, charter, immunity, exemption, right, prerogative.

Antonyms : Inhibition, veto, interdictment, prohibition, debarment.

Synonyms

- ✦ He is always ready to do anyone a *favour.*
- ✦ The government helped small fishing villages with *grants* for building harbours for their boats.
- ✦ He has already obtained a *licence* from the government for setting up a small-scale industry in the industrial estate.
- ✦ The *charter* of demands given by our union will be considered by the cabinet today.
- ✦ Penicillin grants *immunity* against several diseases.
- ✦ Income from National Savings Certificates is *exempted* from taxation.
- ✦ The *right* of speech has been guaranteed under the Constitution of India.
- ✦ The princely states enjoyed several *prerogatives* under the patronage of British Rule in India.

Antonyms

- ✦ Modern society has given up many old social *inhibitions* that stood in the way of healthy growth of young persons.

- ✦ UN has no real power of military action against erring states as any one of the five permanent members — US, UK, USSR, France and China — can *veto* such action.
- ✦ The parliament of India has so far never issued any *interdictment* on the taking of alcoholic drinks, though some of the states have enforced *prohibition* now and then.

PROHIBIT

Synonyms : Ban, prevent, preclude, inhibit, hinder, bar, forbid, interdict, disallow.

Antonyms : Authorise, consent to, direct, suffer, tolerate, warrant, order, permit, give consent, enjoin, empower, command, allow.

Synonyms

- ✦ Smoking is *banned* in India in all public places.
- ✦ Mother fastens a strap round the baby to *prevent* him from climbing out of his pram.

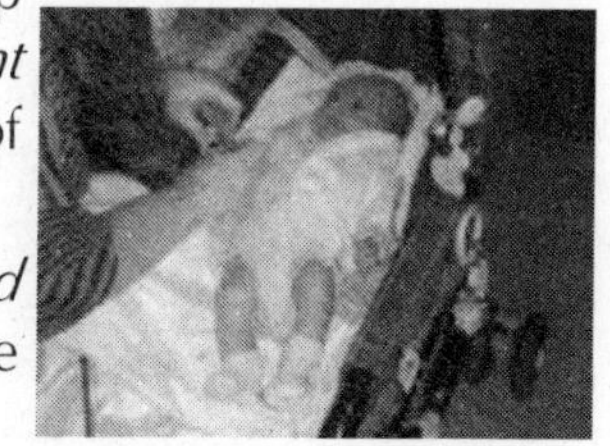

- ✦ Ill-health has *precluded* him from the list of the competitors.
- ✦ Lack of oxygen may *inhibit* brain development in the unborn child.
- ✦ Our bus was *hindered* by a large herd of cows on the road.
- ✦ He can't take the examination because the University has *barred* him for two years.

- *Forbid* him to bathe in the river till he can swim.
- His statement was *interdicted* by his own colleagues.
- The teacher *disallowed* him to attend the class as he came very late.

Antonyms

- The *authorised* capital of this company is Rs. two lakhs.
- The father of the boy did not *consent to* the matrimonial offer of the girl's father.
- I was *directed* to contact the client in the evening.
- The firm has *suffered* heavy losses due to the uncertain conditions in the state.
- I have *tolerated* his behaviour so far but will not do any longer.
- The judge issued *warrants* of arrest of the accused who was continuously absenting from the court.
- The department *ordered* the suspension of the absenting employee.

PROLONG

Synonyms : Lengthen, continue, protract, extend, stretch, sustain, accelerate, quicken.

Antonyms : Contain, lessen, shorten, diminish, abridge, decrease, contract, abbreviate, delay.

Synonyms

- Mother *lengthened* Mary's school dress to match her height.

- Inspite of difficulties, he is determined to *continue* his studies.
- He got a positive reply for recovery of money after *protracted* correspondence spread over two years.
- The garden was *extended* to include a little stream that ran beside it.
- Mary's new gloves had to be *stretched* before she could put them on.
- Their courage was *sustained* by the cheerfulness of the younger members of the party.
- The car driver had to *accelerate* before coming up the hill.
- Adoption of modern technology will *quicken* the pace of our progress.

Antonyms

- This utensil can *contain* about one kg. of milk.
- You will have to *lessen* the quantity to make use of this can.
- Your uniform is too loose; why not *shorten* it yourself.
- His influence has *diminished* with time.
- Why don't you *abridge* this good but long book and also reduce the price ?
- The value of the rupee has *decreased* in the domestic market by 33% in one year.
- Metals *contract* in winter and expand in summer.

✦ We have appropriate, *abbreviated* forms.

PROMINENT

Synonyms : Conspicuous, distinctive, celebrated, marked, notable, eminent, distinguished, leading, principal.

Antonyms : Inconspicuous, minor, junior, unimportant, petty.

Synonyms

✦ The Eiffel Tower in Paris when viewed from an aeroplane is *conspicuous* for its beauty for miles and miles.

✦ Mutual respect is a *distinctive* feature of our foreign policy.

✦ Bertrand Russell was a *celebrated* philosopher.

✦ She is a woman of *marked* intelligence.

✦ He has done *notable* work in the field of botany.

✦ Harindera is an *eminent* professor of English language.

✦ He has *distinguished* himself as an artist also.

✦ Bata is a *leading* firm of shoes in India.

✦ He is the *principal* of a very large institution.

Antonyms

- I am an *inconspicuous* guy in this small firm.
- I play a *minor* role in the production department.
- Here comes the *junior* partner of our firm. He is the son of the proprietor.
- No one of us is considered *unimportant* so long as we do our respective duties honestly.
- The salaries paid to us may be *petty* cash every month, but we get best regard and love of our boss every moment of our working.

PROMOTE

Synonyms : Advance, help, push, urge on, raise, further, exhort, assist, excite, elevate, foment, advocate, encourage, foster.

Antonyms : Allay, hinder, retard, prolong, discourage, divert, degrade.

Synonyms

- This newspaper *advances* the cause of the downtrodden.
- It *helps* the government in the promotion of new schemes of development.
- It highlights organisations which *push* the production of goods for the poor.
- It *urges* on the people to lay emphasis on better contribution to national causes.
- It *raises* issues in the public mind for assimilation of healthy ideas.

- It *furthers* the cause of the common man.
- It *exhorts* business houses to take up faster production processes.

Antonyms

- We should *allay* the fears of the public on good activities of the government.
- Some people tend to *hinder* the progress of development projects by unhealthy criticism.
- Vested interests *retard* productive activities in the country of their selfish motives.
- When people at large fall in their trap, they *prolong* the production processes of the nation.
- They *discourage* the workers by aggressive policies.
- And *divert* resources to anti-national activities and popular ideologies.

PROTECT

Synonyms : Save, cover, defend, guard, harbour, shelter, shield.

Antonyms : Expose, betray, attack, plunder.

Synonyms

- The government must equip itself militarily to *save* the country from foreign attack.
- In winter I *cover* my head with a cap and in summer with a sola hat.
- The girls in the country should be taught to *defend* their honour in emergency.

- Our armed forces *guard* our borders from foreign infiltration.
- Let us *harbour* goodwill among different communities.
- House gives us *shelter* from heat and cold.

Antonyms

- Pakistani nuclear equipments *expose* India to the danger of destruction.
- The US has *betrayed* India by providing defence and offensive equipments to Pakistan.
- There is a constant danger of *attack* on India from vested interests.
- The dacoits *plundered* the village and ran away with the booty.

PROVE

Synonyms : Justify, attest, verify, establish, show, confirm, demonstrate.

Antonyms : Refuse, negate, deny, refute, disprove.

Synonyms

- Marxists believe that ends *justify* the means.
- The candidates were required to attach the *attested* copies of their certificates with the application form.
- His bonafides were got *verified* by the police before he was granted the gun licence.

- ✦ He failed to *establish* the truth of the facts mentioned in his statement before the judge.
- ✦ He was required to *show* his identity card at the gate of the office.
- ✦ I have asked him to *confirm* the date of his arrival in New Delhi.
- ✦ The lawyer *demonstrated* how the witness was lying.

Antonyms

- ✦ I have *refused* to part with my books at any cost.
- ✦ You cannot *negate* the possibility of him having taken the money.
- ✦ I have never *denied* that my knowledge is limited.
- ✦ He may *refute* his earlier statement but he cannot disprove it.

PROVIDE

Synonyms : Supply, prepare, furnish, get, arrange, cater, procure, purvey.

Antonyms : Consume, spend, dissipate, exhaust, use.

Synonyms

- ✦ It is a statutory duty of the municipal corporation to *supply* drinking water.
- ✦ They are *preparing* themselves to launch a new project in the village.
- ✦ The court has directed the police to *furnish* full details of the case.

- Do you have time to *get* the house white-washed ?
- He can *arrange* a car for you whenever you are in need.
- The secretary tries to *cater* to the minister's every wish.
- Father has at last *procured* the kind of television set he wants.
- Our firm *purveys* freezed, dried meat in the army.

Antonyms

- We *consume* 200 kilo watts of electric power every month.
- I *spend* 20% of my salary on rent.
- A lot of money gets *dissipated* on items whose prices have risen rocket high.
- My salary gets *exhausted* on the 25th day of the month.
- I am left with nothing for *use* during the last five days.

PUBLISH

Synonyms : Proclaim, disclose, disseminate, advertise, declare, divulge, promulgate, announce, broadcast.

Antonyms : Suppress, extinguish, smother, repress, conceal, check, cloak, stifle, restrain.

Synonyms

- India *proclaimed* itself a Republic on 26th January 1950.

- The old lady would not *disclose* to anyone how she made her cherry jam. 
- Television and radio *disseminate* ideas and informations.
- Only big companies can afford to *advertise* their products through television.
- The government will *declare* its new export policy very soon.
- Mohan would not *divulge* what he has been told.
- The president has *promulgated* a new constitution for his country.
- The princess *announced* her engagement.
- The special election *broadcast* will be on the local station at eight tonight.

Antonyms

- It is wise for the government to sometimes *suppress* inflammatory news and views.
- The five fire brigade engines *extinguished* the fire in our locality.
- The child was *smothered* to death by her father.
- Dictatorial governments always try to *repress* people's feelings of freedom and liberty.
- The earthquake left a lot of broken bricks and debris with dead humans *concealed* underneath.

PUNISH

Synonyms : Afflict, chasten, subdue, humble, chastise, correct, discipline, castigate.

Antonyms : Recompense, indemnify, reward, repay, compensate, remunerate.

Synonyms

- Storm and flood still *afflict* mankind.
- He was *chastened* by the police for eve-teasing.
- The police used teargas to *subdue* the rioters.
- The king's forces were *humbled* by the peasant revolt.
- His father *chastised* Jim for not attending school regularly.
- Being his close friend you should *correct* him whenever he goes wrong.
- The teacher *disciplined* her students by holding them for one hour after the school time.
- The clerk was *castigated* for his frequent absence from office.

Antonyms

- The office *recompensed* me for my touring expenses.
- I filled the *indemnity* bond to take an advance from the bank.
- The principal *rewarded* the boy for saving his colleague from drowning.

- ✦ I have now *repaid* your loan in full.
- ✦ I will *compensate* you for interest in due course.
- ✦ What *remuneration* do you seek for this job ?

PURPOSE

Synonyms : Aim, object, plan, intention, end, meaning, intent, resolve.

Antonyms : Vague, aimless, unplanned, meaningless.

Synonyms

- ✦ Character building should be the *aim* of education.
- ✦ What was his *object* in leaving so early ?
- ✦ Does he *plan* to stay with us tonight ?
- ✦ His actions belie his *intentions*.
- ✦ All is well that *ends* well.
- ✦ Ever since his wife died, his life has had no *meaning*.
- ✦ He was charged with *intent* to kill his boss.
- ✦ John *resolved* to work hard so as to win a prize.

Antonyms

- ✦ Ram had only a *vague* idea of the place so he was lost.
- ✦ The play of the evening showed *aimlessness* of the theme and *unplanned* direction of the story.
- ✦ To me life is *meaningless* without art and recreation.

PUSH

Synonyms : Press, thrust, shove, urge, drive, propel, impel, jostle.

Antonyms : Pull, haul, drag, tow, tug.

Synonyms

- His parents are *pressing* him hard to get married.
- Harish *thrust* his hand into a hole in a tree to find out how deep it was.
- When you are standing in a queue don't *shove*.
- Mother *urged* Mohan to go to the dentist.
- Our troops *drove* away the enemy.
- My invalid *uncle* can *propel* his wheel-chair by its handles.
- Wild animals and birds are often *impelled* by hunger to come near the human beings.

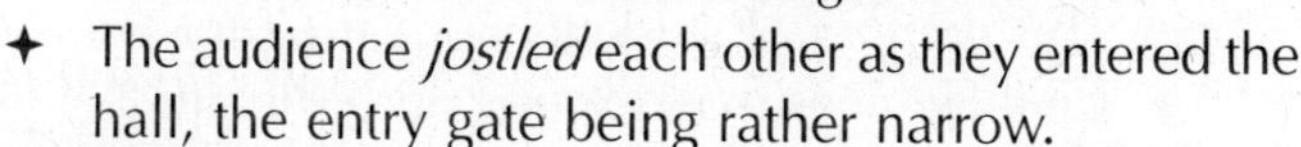

- The audience *jostled* each other as they entered the hall, the entry gate being rather narrow.

Antonyms

- The horse *pulled* the tonga with ease.
- The police *hauled* the smugglers with their drugs at the railway station.
- The policeman *dragged* the thief by the wrist.
- The gardener *towed* the lawn-mower in a zigzag manner.
- Our school played a *tug* of war game yesterday.

QUANTITY

Synonyms : Measure, amount, bulk, number, volume, aggregrate, sum total.

Antonyms : Shortage, deficiency, insufficiency, deficit.

Synonyms

- The *measure* of distance is given in kilometres.
- The government has to spend large *amounts* on armaments.
- He left the *bulk* of his estate to his wife.
- The *number* of students appearing for the Indian Civil Services may exceed our estimate this year.
- What is the *volume* of water in the tank ?

- The *aggregate* of his marks in all the papers exceeds five hundred.
- He was astonished to know the *sum total* of the value of his estate.

Antonyms

- There is no *shortage* of foodgrains in India now. thanks to better seeds, better irrigation facilities and tractors!
- You can remove the *deficiency* of blood in your body by better diet and some regular exercise.
- *Insufficiency* of electric supply stands in the way of quicker industrialisation in India.
- This year's budget is again a *deficit* budget, the *deficit* to be made up by larger borrowing and public deposits.

QUALITY

Synonyms : Excellence, property, brand, nature, trait, characteristic, attribute.

Antonyms : Ordinary, flat, commonplace, colourless.

Synonyms

- She deserves praise for her *excellence* in sports.
- The chemical *properties* of gases help us to distinguish one gas from the other.
- Which *brand* of tea do you prefer ?
- John has a very kind and friendly *nature*.
- Boldness and resolution are two of the *traits* of a good leader.
- Hot summers and heavy rains are the *characteristics* of this place.
- Generosity is one of his many fine *attributes*.

Antonyms

- A man of *ordinary* intelligence, Ramesh owes his success to hard work and determination.
- This valley has a sizable *flat* surface for agricultural development.
- As a democrat I believe in *commonplace* ways of living. I rather despise luxuries.
- Although a rich man, he is rather *colourless* in social behaviour.

QUARREL

Synonyms : Wrangle, riot, fray, contest, enmity, fight, row, strife, controversy, brawl.

Antonyms : Agreement, assent, consent, acquiesce, harmony, friendship, peace, amity, equanimity, concord.

Synonyms

- He *wrangles* with his colleagues on trivial issues.
- During *riots,* many people jump into the *fray* for no good reason.
- There was a great *contest* between them for the prize.
- They have no *enmity* for each other now.
- He was given a tough *fight* by his opponents on the playground.
- The meeting of the society turned into a *row.*

- ✦ The history of *strife* has left its marks on the tiny nation.
- ✦ There is some new *controversy* over the ownership of this piece of land.
- ✦ Most cowboy movies include a scene of a bar-room *brawl*.

Antonyms

- ✦ India and Pakistan are trying to reach an *agreement* on trade and cultural relations.
- ✦ The President has put his *assent* on the 46th Amendment of the Constitution.
- ✦ The *consent* of majority of states is necessary for amending the Constitution of India.
- ✦ The subordinate *acquiesced* to the wishes of his boss on the question of transfer from the headquarters.
- ✦ There is now perfect *harmony* between the two brothers.
- ✦ India's *friendship* with the USSR is beyond any controversy.
- ✦ The Non-aligned movement is responsible for a new desire for *peace* among nations round the world.

QUEER

Synonyms : Eccentric, abnormal, strange, odd, curious, peculiar, extraordinary, unusual, singular, fantastic.

Antonyms : Ordinary, habitual, everyday, normal, common, usual, commonplace.

Synonyms

- The old lady is becoming very *eccentric*, she loses temper on minor issues.
- He would be an *abnormal* boy if he did not want to run about and play at this carefree age.
- He told us a *strange* story.
- The giraffe is an *odd*-looking animal.
- She had a *curious* way of expressing himself.
- The tribals have *peculiar* customs of marriage.
- A snowflake seen under a microscope seems to have *extraordinary* beauty.
- A *singular* glow came from the unidentified flying object.
- Rains in January are *unusual* in northern India. 
- The story of "Sindbad, the Sailor" is a *fantastic* one.

Antonyms

- Joe has *ordinary* average habits, but he has a sterling character.
- Danny is a *habitual* drunkard.
- He drinks alcohol *everyday*.

- Joseph has a *normal* habit of going for walk every morning.
- Morning walk is a *common* feature among the old and the young in our locality.

QUESTION

Synonyms : Doubt, query, investigation, interrogation, inquisition, inquiry.

Antonyms : Reply, answer, rejoinder, respond, response.

Synonyms

- I *doubt* if he will make a good captain in the army.
- The science master put a *query* to John to check up whether he had been paying attention to his lecture.
- Scientists are now *investigating* ways of producing more and more food over the world.
- The police have found some new clues after *interrogation* of the persons detained in this case.
- He had finished his *inquisition* in this case and submitted his report.
- A commission of *inquiry* has been set up to probe into the cause of the Kanishka air crash in which 239 lives were lost.

Antonyms

- I have yet to *reply* to the queries of the income tax authorities.
- My *answers* to the queries are under preparation.

- His advocate is preparing a *rejoinder* for submission to the court in response to a charge of the complainant.
- The government has not yet *responded* to my appeal for assistance under the new scheme.
- This is in *response* to my father's desire.

QUICK

Synonyms : Fast, rapid, swift, precipitate.

Antonyms : Listless, slow, calm, calculated.

Synonyms

- It is advisable not to drive too *fast* on a crowded road.
- India has made *rapid* progress in agricultural development during the last decade.
- I walked *swiftly* to catch up with Franklin in the garden.
- The government is trying to *precipitate* the solution of the Assam problem after having settled the Punjab controversy.

Antonyms

- Jack has become *listless* in his studies and sports since his last sickness.

- I always prefer to drive *slow* in the crowded streets of the city.
- The efforts of the government in solving national problems should be *calm* and *calculated.*

QUICKEN

Synonyms : Hasten, urge, speed, further, drive, advance, accelerate, expedite, dispatch, make-haste.

Antonyms : Check, obstruct, retard, drag, hinder, impede, delay.

Synonyms

- She *hastened* to put the teapot out of the baby's reach.
- Mother *urged* Mohan to go to the dentist.
- The *speed* of an aeroplane is much greater than that of a car.
- His support *furthered* my career.
- Our troops *drove* away the enemy.
- They have *advanced* their programme for Delhi by one week.
- The car driver had to *accelerate* before climbing the hill.
- Using postal code number always *expedites* the delivery of your mail.
- This deed must be done with *dispatch.*

Antonyms

- Will you please *check* the mistakes in this paragraph ?
- The opposition party is meant to *obstruct* the taking of rash decisions by the ruling party.
- Sometimes it *retards* the progress of healthy and constructive decisions.
- The discussion on a controversial issue may *drag* on for hours in the parliament without any decision.
- It is under such circumstances that the work of the state gets *hindered* by the opposition parties.
- This *impedes* the speed of work done by the departments at various levels.
- Hence government work is said to be *delayed*.

QUICKNESS

Synonyms : Velocity, alacrity, haste, rapidity, swiftness, fleetability.

Antonyms : Slowness, sluggishness, inertia.

Synonyms

- The *velocity* of light is very great.
- He obeyed me with more *alacrity* than I expected.
- Marry in *haste* and repent at leisure.
- We were surprised to see the *rapidity* with which the child ran up the stairs.

- The ostrich runs with great *swiftness* but it can't fly.
- Antelopes escape the bigger animals because of their *fleetability*.

Antonyms

- *Slowness* of the record player has caused this unnatural phenomenon of Lata's voice sounding like that of a man.
- Anil has been rather *sluggish* since his last sickness.
- *Inertia* in physics means a property by which matter continues in its existing state or rest or motion in a straight line unless that state is changed by external force.

QUIET

Synonyms : Repose, compose, lull, mollify, sooth, allay, appease, stillness, calm, still, hush, calmness, quietude, rest.

Antonyms : Excitement, tumult, commotion, turmoil, exasperate, disturb, aggravate, disquiet, enhance.

Synonyms

- The baby is in *repose* when he is asleep.
- She remained *composed* even during the loud thunder and lightning.

- There was a *lull* before the thunderstorm.
- The angry man was *mollified* when Tom expressed he was sorry for bumping into him.
- The baby cried when he was taken out of his bath, but his mother *soothed* him with delicate powder.
- The doctor was able to *allay* the mother's anxiety.
- His hunger was soon *appeased.*

Antonyms

- Scenes of love and violence provide *excitement* to the viewers.
- The news of the lottery in favour of Jim to the value of Rs.1 lakh caused a great *tumult* in his family.
- The little controversy on an academic subject led to a *commotion* in the college.
- The news of the war caused *turmoil* round the whole world.
- The failure of his son very much *exasperated* the old man but he did not express it to the young boy.

RACE

Synonyms : Tribe, people, family, caste, nation, ethnic group.

Antonyms : Unit, individual, humanity, mankind, generation, brotherhood, global.

Synonyms

- Each *tribe* has some customs which are observed by its members compulsorily.
- Politicians generally believe that the *people* have a short memory.
- Nowadays the government is laying great emphasis on *family* welfare schemes.
- The *caste* system was very rigid in India until independence.
- A period of hundred years is not a long period in the history of a *nation.*
- In India, all *ethnic groups* enjoy constitutional rights to maintain their identity.

Antonyms

- All tribes of this region have formed a common *unit*.
- There has to be a reasonable reconciliation between the interests of the *individual* vis-a-vis his society.
- Disarmament is crucial for saving *humanity* from atomic warfare.
- *Mankind* cannot enjoy permanent peace unless the nations join together to form a world federation.
- Modern *generation* everywhere is becoming over materialistic.
- Unless the feeling of universal *brotherhood* is inculcated among all humans achievement of *global* peace is out of question.

RACY

Synonyms : Flavorous, rich, spicy, lively, poignant, spirited.

Antonyms : Cold, vapid, dull, flat, stale, prosy, insipid, tasteless, stupid.

Synonyms

- The soup is so *flavorous* that it has aroused my appetite.
- Carrot is a *rich* source of iron and vitamins.
- At lunch they serve very *spicy* dishes.
- We had a *lively* game of musical chairs at the birthday party.

- The critic wrote a *poignant* review of the movie.
- Although our team was defeated, it exhibited a very *spirited* game.

Antonyms

- My office being 50 km. from my residence I have to make do with a *cold* lunch on working days.
- This hotel serves a *vapid* breakfast.
- The *dull* atmosphere of my office repels my attendance.
- This cola is no longer fizzy, it has gone *flat*.
- *Stale* meals are served here at night.
- She tells her stories in a rather *prosy* style.
- His behaviour is *insipid* at times.
- This dish is not only stale but also *tasteless*.
- Sam often tells *stupid* stories of his colleagues.

RADICAL

Synonyms : Basic, complete, entire, essential, extreme, natural, primitive, thorough, total, perfect, positive, innate.

Antonyms : Trial, tentative, inadequate, conservative, partial, slight, superficial.

Synonyms

- The *basic* ingredient of this dish is hamburger.
- He has a *complete* set of Bertrand Russell's books.

- His *entire* home was damaged by the rioters.
- Air and water are equally *essential* for our survival.
- Political views of the communists looked rather *extreme* at that time.
- Success demands a good deal of *natural* talent and lots of hard work.
- He had a *primitive* style of painting.
- His new policies will bring about a *thorough* change in the administration.
- Mahatma Gandhi believed in *total* prohibition of alcohol.
- No man is *perfect* on this earth.
- He always had at his command very many *positive* ideas on company affairs.
- An *innate* flaw doomed the plan from the very start.

Antonyms

- Only a *trial* will convince you of the utility of this product.
- We have made a *tentative* programme for the meeting on the 11th of next month.
- In my opinion the arrangements made for the function are *inadequate* and should be reviewed.

- ✦ We have nowadays *conservative* governments in the UK and the USA.
- ✦ The USA seems *partial* to Pakistan and prejudiced against India for some reason.
- ✦ A *slight* move on your part will help me to get the job.
- ✦ His contribution to the club is rather *superficial.*

RAISE

Synonyms : Lift, hoist, elevate, uplift, promote.

Antonyms : Depress, descend, lower.

Synonyms

- ✦ The government is trying to *lift* the common people from below the poverty line.
- ✦ The Prime Minister *hoists* the national flag at the Red Fort on August 15 every year.
- ✦ The nationalised banks are supposed to *elevate* the poor farmer to a bit higher level of working and living.
- ✦ The government has floated a few ambitious projects for the *uplift* of the scheduled castes.
- ✦ Democracy is meant to *promote* the cause of the people at large.

Antonyms

- ✦ The scene of floods and the havoc caused by them *depressed* the Prime Minister.

- ✦ The bird shot by Joe with his toy gun *descended* on the ground with its injured wings.
- ✦ In order to raise the standard of living of the poor, it is necessary for the richer classes to *lower* theirs a bit.

RARE

Synonyms : Curious, odd, peculiar, scarce, unique, infrequent, remarkable, unusual, uncommon, precious, incomparable.

Antonyms : Common, usual, frequent, familiar, hackneyed, customary, trite.

Synonyms

- ✦ Children are very *curious* to know everything.
- ✦ The youth earned pocket money doing *odd* jobs.
- ✦ His attitude towards his subordinates is quite *peculiar.*
- ✦ Qualified workmen were *scarce* during the war.
- ✦ Kohinoor is one of the most *unique* diamonds.
- ✦ Fortunately, his asthma attacks are *infrequent.*
- ✦ The Congress party has achieved *remarkable* success in the recent elections.
- ✦ Appearance of a comet is an *unusual* phenomenon.
- ✦ A solar eclipse is an *uncommon* occurrence.
- ✦ He has a good collection of *precious* stones.
- ✦ Have you seen the *incomparable* beauty of the Dal Lake?

Antonyms

- The government of a country is meant to solve the *common* problems of all the citizens.
- The *usual* price of a good second hand car in India nowadays is Rs. 40,000.
- I go to this market quite *frequently*.
- I am quite *familiar* with your boss and will speak to him for your promotion if you like.
- This college has *hackneyed* methods of teaching instead of the novel methods prevalent in modern colleges elsewhere.
- It is *customary* for the father of the bridegroom to wear a red turban on the occasion of the marriage.
- This salary seems *trite* in these days of high inflation.

RASH

Synonyms : Hasty, reckless, venturesome, precipitate, indiscreet, incautious, foolhardy.

Antonyms : Careful, wary, discreet, cautious.

Synonyms

- He always repents for his *hasty* decisions.
- He has been challaned several times for his *reckless* driving.
- Rock climbing is a *venturesome* sport.

- The oppressive measures adopted by the British government in early 20th century *precipitated* our freedom movement.
- The inspector was found guilty of *indiscreet* firing on the mob.

- The bus driver indulged in *incautious* driving and ran into a car coming from the opposite direction.
- Walking a tightrope across the deep canal was a *foolhardy* venture.

Antonyms

- I am very *careful* in my driving at the turns.
- The teacher was *wary* of Dharminder's tricks in the class.
- The court is expected to take *discreet* judgement on vital matters.
- Ravinder is *cautious* in his business dealings.

RATE

Synonyms : Appraise, compute, estimate, assess, price, reckon.

Antonyms : Miscalculate, underrate, undervalue.

Synonyms

- The secretary has *appraised* the minister of the latest developments in this district.

- He *computes* the interest meticulously and charges every single paisa from his clients who buy things on instalments.
- The cost of constructing the house will very likely exceed your *estimates.*
- The tax department always *assesses* a property on the higher side.
- Eternal vigilance is the *price* of liberty.
- The government may have to *reckon* with new forces of communalism in the near future.

Antonyms

- I do not generally *miscalculate* figures as this leads to basic flaws in the pricing of products.
- I do not wish to *underrate* your talent but I wish I had the necessary outlet for its full utilisation.
- A good salesman should neither *undervalue* nor overvalue products to conduct his marketing targets.

RATION

Synonyms : Allotment quota, part, portion, share.

Antonyms : Totality, aggregate, entirety, whole, sum total.

Synonyms

- The *allotment* of houses will be made after the society gets the approval of the Registrar, Cooperative Societies.
- It is likely that the *quota* of sugar at the ration shops will be doubled soon.

- Each *part* of the body is important for its smooth functioning.
- They have lent a *portion* of their house on rent.
- Some of the members were not satisfied with the number of *shares* allotted and requested the president of the society to give them more.

Antonyms

- The computer can indicate the *totality* of a number of calculations in a few seconds.
- My *aggregate* marks are 66% although my marks in English are over 75%.
- I have described to you the situation of the problem in its *entirety*.
- A number of parts make a *whole* number.
- The *sum total* of votes cast by voters in the last elections was 32 crores.

READY

Synonyms : Quick, speedy, alert, prepared, disposed, willing, set.

Antonyms : Unwilling, slow, clumsy, unprepared, inexperienced.

Synonyms

- It is good to be *quick* but not hasty.
- Automation helps *speedy* disposal of work.
- Duties of a policeman can be performed only by an *alert* person.

- The salesman is *prepared* to visit his client at the time of the latter's convenience.
- I have *disposed* off ten cases today.
- I am *willing* to set apart some money for purchase of shares of your company.

Antonyms

- He is an *unwilling* worker and should be dismissed.
- *Slow* and steady wins the race, is an old wise saying.
- His *clumsy* look shows he must not be a smart worker.
- If you go *unprepared* for the interview, you may fumble in the midst of discussion.
- He maybe *inexperienced* but he is quite shrewd.

READINESS

Synonyms : Promptitude, willingness, eagerness, alacrity, quickness.

Antonyms : Unwillingness, reluctance, disinclination, aversion, tardiness.

Synonyms

- Rajiv Gandhi was praised by all for his *promptitude* in introducing the anti-defection bill.
- The boss will assign him a new job only after he has ascertained his *willingness*.
- He is looking forward to his new job with great *eagerness*.

- His *alacrity* to overpower the thief surprised us all.
- She answered his call for assistance with pleasurable *quickness*.

Antonyms

- Your *unwillingness* to help me at the present moment shows lack of faith.
- My *reluctance* to buy the new soap disappointed the salesgirl.
- I told her the reason of my *disinclination*, yet she clung to her salesmanship.
- I have an *aversion* for luxury products which pinch my pocket.

REAL

Synonyms : Actual, genuine, true, positive, essential, certain, demonstrable, veritable, developed.

Antonyms : Conceived, reported, visionary, untrue, imaginary, unreal, fiction, fanciful, illusory.

Synonyms

- His *actual* income far exceeds the income shown in his tax returns.
- His brother deals in *genuine* antiques.
- This picture depicts the *true* image of a typical Indian village.

- The anti-defection bill indicates the *positive* intention of the government to curb defection among politicians.
- Fundamental rights are the *essentials* of our democracy.
- Death is *certain* yet we fear it.
- This company has made no *demonstrable* progress during the last three years.
- The old professor is a *veritable* gold mine of information.
- Let's have these pictures *developed.*

Antonyms

- I have *conceived* an idea of a story for my next picture, but it will require deep thinking and imagination to give a final shape to the plot.
- The newspapers have *reported* about the extent of black money in this country.
- Jackson is a *visionary*. His stories show the moods of an angry young man.
- His basic themes are always true although in developing them he delves into *untrue imagination.*

REASONING

Synonyms : Rationale, thinking, logic, analysis, exposition, generalisation.

Antonyms : Illogicality, stupidity, nonsensical, senselessness, foolish.

Synonyms

- The *rationale* of this report is beyond my understanding.
- Man is a *thinking* animal.
- Science is based on *logic* and reasoning.
- The chemical *analysis* of the food taken by the deceased has proved that he was poisoned.
- This is not at all a true *exposition* of his views.
- His *generalisation* that most of modern youth are corrupt is wrong.

Antonyms

- The *illogicality* of his arguments sometimes irritates me beyond the point of tolerance.
- The actions of the present manager are marked by *stupidity* of the highest order.
- Only God can save the firm from bankruptcy as his decisions on finance are all *nonsensical.*
- Many of the well-wishers of the firm are becoming aware of the *senselessness* of the manager's dealings and are feeling insecure.
- Discussing among themselves, they regard the manager's decisions as *foolish.*

REBELLION

Synonyms : Sedition, mutiny, uprising, insurrection, revolt.

Antonyms : Loyalty, patriotism, devotion, faithfulness, nationalism, toadyism.

Synonyms

- In the army, the punishment for *sedition* is death.
- The first *mutiny* in the Indian army took place in 1857 at Meerut.
- Any *uprising* against this regime is suppressed ruthlessly.
- The Tamilians have been charged of *insurrection* by the government of Sri Lanka.
- Only the President can grant pardon to a person who *revolts* against the government.

Antonyms

- Anti-defection bill provides for *loyalty* by members to the party which sponsored them for election.
- Extreme form of *partriotism* is despised by right thinking people as something obstructing the growth of internationalism.
- *Devotion* to one's duty is always rewarded one way or the other.

- My *faithfulness* to my country is beyond any doubt.
- *Nationalism* is welcome only so long as it does not contradict internationalism.
- *Toadyism* stands for toeing the line of your boss blindly without regard to the merit or demerit of an action.

RECOVER

Synonyms : Heal, restore, retrieve, regain, resume, cure, recruit, repossess.

Antonyms : Die, sink, worsen, grow, fail, replace.

Synonyms

- The mother is always able to *heal* the troubles of her children.
- The famous old painting stolen from the National Museum was recovered from abroad and *restored.*
- Some of the furniture was *retrieved* from the house after the desyphoning of flood water.
- He soon *regained* his health during the holidays.
- He has *resumed* his duty after a long leave.
- This medicine will *cure* the mother's cough in a couple of days.
- A team of officers had come to our village to *recruit* soldiers.
- Our cricket team has succeeded this year by *repossessing* the trophy.

Antonyms

- The old man *died* of paralysis of the brain.
- The cargo ship *sank* in the high seas due to a severe cyclone.
- Of late the health of the old man has gone from bad to *worse*.
- I wish to *replace* my old sofa with a new one.
- We *grow* vegetables in our kitchen garden.
- Ramesh's new business project has miserably *failed*.

REFUSE

Synonyms : Veto, renounce, withhold, decline, exclude, deny, repudiate.

Antonyms : Acquiesce, agree, grant, accede, cede, admit, assent, allow.

Synonyms

- The permanent members of the Security Council can *veto* any decision taken by the General Assembly.
- He has *renounced* the world and become a sanyasi.
- His increments have been *withheld* of three years as a penalty for negligence.
- He *declined* to help his friend at the critical juncture.

- Children under ten were *excluded* from the film show.
- His mother never *denied* him anything.
- He has *repudiated* the charges of corruption levelled against him by the department.

Antonyms

- The management had to *acquiesce* to the demands of the workers to avoid a strike.
- They had to *agree* to a 20% raise on each salary.
- The workers were also *granted* a 20% annual bonus.
- The government had to intervene to make the management *accede* to the demands of the workers.

RELEASE

Synonyms : Exempt, liberate, unloose, relieve, free, disengage, disentangle, extricate, emancipate.

Antonyms : Bind, confine, restrain, enthrall.

Synonyms

- Students who attended the evening lecture were *exempted* from doing homework.
- The bonded labourers were beaten severely when they tried to *liberate* themselves from the clutches of the landlord.
- The thief *unloosed* the knots of the rope and escaped.

- ✦ The doctor *relieved* him of the headache by a single dose.
- ✦ India was *freed* from the foreign yoke after a prolonged struggle.
- ✦ The leader *disengaged* himself from the fury of the mob with great difficulty.
- ✦ He has *disentangled* himself from party politics.
- ✦ The fox tried desperately to *extricate* itself from the trap put up by the jackal but failed.
- ✦ The government has *emancipated* a large number of agricultural workers from serfdom.

Antonyms

- ✦ I can *bind* myself with your firm for five years provided you send me abroad for one year's training.
- ✦ I have *confined* myself to pure research for the next two years.
- ✦ The girl was *restrained* from going abroad due to reasons of security.

REMARKABLE

Synonyms : Extraordinary, striking, conspicuous, strange, distinguished, famous, noticeable.

Antonyms : Ordinary, commonplace, customary, normal, average, habitual, medium.

Synonyms

- ✦ India has made *extraordinary* progress in the field of space technology in the last decade and a half.

- The Eiffel Tower in Paris is a *striking* piece of beauty for miles and miles of air view.
- There is a *conspicuous* similarity between the two brothers.
- He told us a *strange* story.
- His joy knew no bounds when the *distinguished* guest welcomed him.
- His elder brother is a *famous* hockey player.

Antonyms

- This is no *ordinary* achievement — topping in the Probationary Officer's examination.
- This design has become a *commonplace* affair in cities.
- It is *customary* in Europe to remove one's hat before bowing to ladies.
- The *normal* temperature of Delhi in the summer varies from 25°C to 40°C.
- The *average* height of a Nepalese is 5′ 4″ — a little less than that of an average Indian, but the Nepalese are good soldiers.

RELUCTANT

Synonyms : Unwilling, averse, slow, opposed, indisposed, backward.

Antonyms : Desirous, inclined, willing, eager, disposed, favourable.

Synonyms

- He was *unwilling* to be transferred to Mumbai but his boss did not consider his protest.
- He is *averse* to going to bed early.
- My tenant's rent payments are always *slow*.
- Father was inclined, at first, to *oppose* the idea of Chandgi Ram's learning boxing.
- The master was *indisposed* to give him permission.
- He is a little *backward* in his studies.

Antonyms

- John is *desirous* of going to the United States for higher studies in computer programming,
- He is not *inclined* to taking up small jobs.
- He is *eager* to return to India after higher studies as a big boss.
- He has *disposed* of his guests with great difficulty.
- Her interview has been *favourable* but the result would be known after a month.

REPEAL

Synonyms : Revoke, abolish, nullify, reverse, annul, rescind.

Antonyms : Substantiate, endorse, confirm, ratify, assent.

Synonyms

- ✦ Britain passed an act of parliament in 1870 to *revoke* slavery.
- ✦ There is a campaign afoot to *abolish* current restrictions on immigration, at least from the Indian side.
- ✦ Law Commission has recommended to *nullify* a number of antiquated laws.
- ✦ You can *reverse* this table-cloth and it will still look nice.
- ✦ Both the parties have decided to *annul* the contract.
- ✦ The Supreme Court *rescinded* the High Court judgement.

Antonyms

- ✦ In order to qualify for immigration, you have to *substantiate* your claim by showing evidence of academic standing.
- ✦ The bank has *endorsed* my bill of exchange.
- ✦ This *confirms* my claim from the foreign buyer.
- ✦ The states have *ratified* the 46th Amendment Act.
- ✦ Now it will go for the President's *assent*.

REPENTANCE

Synonyms : Contrition, compunction, regret, sorrow, penitence, grief.

Antonyms : Satisfaction, complacence, pleasure, gratification.

Synonyms

- Did he not feel *contrition* for betraying his mother ?
- The businessman seemed to have no *compunctions* about cheating the consumers.
- There was great *regret* in the village at the doctor's death.
- The children felt deep *sorrow* when their cat died.
- He felt deep *penitence* for disobeying his teacher.
- His heart was filled with much *grief* when he heard of his brother's death by drowning.

Antonyms

- The tutor expressed *satisfaction* with his pupil for his excellent performance in the examination.
- India may be well prepared for defence, yet there is need to avoid any *complacence* on the part of its forces.
- I feel *pleasure* in presenting my book to the Hon'ble minister for release.
- The unscrupulous car owner offered *gratification* to the traffic policeman to evade the challan for wrong driving.

RESIGN

Synonyms : Renounce, abandon, quit, leave, surrender, abdicate, yield.

Antonyms : Hold, stay, continue, remain, maintain, retain, keep.

Synonyms

- ✦ He has *renounced* the world and become a sanyasi.
- ✦ I have *abandoned* the idea of becoming a film actor.
- ✦ He has decided to *quit* his present job.
- ✦ He has sought the permission of his boss to *leave* the station.
- ✦ After the battle, the enemy troops *surrendered.*
- ✦ King Edward VII *abdicated* in 1936 on grounds of his romance with a commoner.
- ✦ My mother *yielded* to my wish and agreed to attend the annual function of my school along with my father.

Antonyms

- ✦ Our forces *held* the ground despite heavy bombing.
- ✦ I have decided to *stay* in the hostel to *continue* my higher education in this city.
- ✦ I will *remain* in the same college.
- ✦ I will *maintain* myself by taking up a part-time job of accounts in a local firm.

✦ This will help to *retain* my self-respect in my family circle.

✦ You should *keep* to your lane while cycling on a city road.

RESPECT

Synonyms : Esteem, regard, consideration, accept.

Antonyms : Contempt, disown, disregard, ignore.

Synonyms

✦ I have great *esteem* for my teachers in the college.

✦ They also give me due *regard* for my deep interest in studies.

✦ I have due *consideration* for the ability of all my teachers.

✦ My teachers have *accepted* me as a good student.

Antonyms

✦ The Bible, or for that matter any religious book, does not advise human beings to carry *contempt* for others — not even for the enemy — as everyone of the human being is a handiwork of God.

✦ We may *disown* responsibility for wrongs done by others.

- However we humans can express our feelings for others by showing regard for the good ones and *disregard* for the bad ones.
- We should *ignore* the bad we see around but accept the good we come across.

RETAIN

Synonyms : Employ, engage, maintain, keep, hold.

Antonyms : Give up, cede, surrender, relinquish, renounce, forsake, abandon.

Synonyms

- Under this Act the contractors cannot *employ* the workers on ad-hoc basis.
- The accused was allowed to *engage* a lawyer for his defence.
- It is very difficult to *maintain* two establishments within the limited resources.
- Father allowed me to *keep* the balance.
- Mother asked the nurse to *hold* the child for another couple of hours.

Antonyms

- Sam has *given up* his studies before graduation.
- I have *ceded* a part of my property to an orphanage.
- The rebel soldiers were forced to *surrender*.
- I have not yet *relinquished* charge to my successor in the company.

- I have *renounced* my right to the anscestral property in order to help my younger brother and sisters who are not well settled as yet.
- I can *foresake* my right in your favour if it helps you in your career.
- I have *abandoned* the idea of taking up a government job.

RIDDLE

Synonyms : Mystery, puzzle, problem, paradox, enigma.

Antonyms : Answer, explanation, solution, proposition, axiom.

Synonyms

- There is a *mystery* about the habits of migrant birds in this part of the world.
- He has won several prizes for solving *puzzles*.

- Unemployment is a real *problem* for graduates now.
- It is a *paradox*, but with age she is becoming young and smart.
- Whether there is life on any other planet besides Earth is still an *enigma*.

Antonyms

- The Prime Minister *answered* to the questions of a large number of journalists at the press conference.
- His *explanation* of the domestic and foreign policies was lucidly brought out.
- His answers presented his views for the *solution* of pending problems.
- He made a *proposition* for peace in the Indian Ocean region.
- He used a few *axioms* to compare international problems between super powers.

RISK

Synonyms : Hazard, jeopardise, venture, peril, danger, endanger, stake, imperil.

Antonyms : Security, secure, save, harbour, safety, defend, shelter, shield.

Synonyms

- The ascent to the moon was a great *hazard* for the early astronauts.
- Nancy *jeopardised* her life but saved a drowning child.
- John *ventured* to skate on the ice only after it was fully frozen.
- Sailors are often in *peril* when at sea.
- He was not aware of the *danger* of touching a live wire.

- The fireman *endangered* his life to save the lives of persons trapped in the burning house.
- In international trade the *stakes* are high, but so are the profits.
- He has *imperilled* our investments by staking them on the new issues of a limited company.

Antonyms

- The bank has refused to advance me a loan without a proper *security.*
- You can *secure* 80% marks if you work hard.
- Let us *save* something every month for a rainy day.
- I have a feeling that Raison is *harbouring* evil designs in money matters.
- We ran to *safety* when bombing took place during the last war.
- India can *defend* herself from neighbours but a nuclear war is an altogether different proposition.
- Where would humans then run for *shelter* ?
- Will any place be good enough as a *shield* from nuclear effects ?

ROT

Synonyms : Decay, decompose, putrefy.

Antonyms : Flourish, bloom, grow.

Synonyms

- The matter over and under the ground *decays* in due course to become a fossil.

- The earthquake left a number of bodies under the debris which were found *decomposed* on digging.
- One could smell the stink of *putrefied* bodies months after the earthquake.

Antonyms

- During the rainy season, plants *flourish*.
- The flowers *bloom* in the spring season.
- Vegetation *grows* profusely in tropical countries.

ROUGH

Synonyms : Severe, stormy, rugged, harsh, uneven.

Antonyms : Calm, glossy, smooth, even, fine, straight.

Synonyms

- We had a very *severe* winter last year.
- The weather is rather *stormy* today with winds blowing dust and sand all around.
- The mountains keep a *rugged* atmosphere unless properly looked after.
- No use being *harsh* on children nowadays.
- The ground of this plot of land is very *uneven*.

Antonyms

- There is no wind today; the weather is hot and *calm*.

- The surface of this plastic material is *glossy* and shiny.
- The best path to a *smooth* career for a young man is appearing in a competitive examination of one's choice and trying to get selected.
- The surface of land in this region is *even,* hence there is good slope for provision of fast local transport.

RUDE

Synonyms : Discourteous, impudent, unmannerly, saucy, churlish, impertinent, impolite.

Antonyms : Civil, cultivated, polished, courteous, elegant, refined, sophisticated, genteel.

Synonyms

- We felt sorry to observe that the son was rather *discourteous* to his father's guests.
- Mrs. Laxmi complained to her friend that the errand boy had been *impudent* to her.
- These children are too *unmannerly* to be invited to a party.
- Her *saucy* remarks raised many eyebrows.
- The *churlish* brute muttered menacingly when my friend asked him to leave.
- The customers were unhappy with the *impertinent* waitress.
- It is considered *impolite* for a man to receive guests in informal night dress.

Antonyms

- He knows how to be *civil* with lady guests.
- I am trying to *cultivate* friendship with the local lawn tennis champion.
- His *polished* manners win him new friends with ease.
- His *courteous* behaviour has made him quite popular among the local elite.
- He is *elegant* enough to make high level contacts in politics.
- He is too *refined* and *sophisticated* for a rough life in the village.

SACRED

Synonyms : Holy, sanctified, consecrated, dedicated, inviolable, hallowed, divine, blessed.

Antonyms : Profane, impious, irreverent, irreligious, blasphemous, sacrilegious, temporal, worldly, lay.

Synonyms

- The Vedas contain the *holy* sayings of the Indian sages of ancient India.
- The Ramayana and the Mahabharata are *sanctified* scriptures of ancient India.
- The shrine was *consecrated* by the local philanthropist.
- A true believer does not need to have his beliefs *dedicated* by the priest.
- For Sikhs the sermons of Guru Granth Sahib are i*nviolable.*
- The church graveyard is a *hallowed* ground.

- The Quran is a *divine* scripture of the Muslims.
- *Blessed* are the meek because they will open the door of heaven.

Antonyms

- The government has taken up to check the *profane* activities of the smugglers.
- Modern pictures of violence and nudity give *impious* ideas to the youth.
- The attitude of the students towards their teacher has become *irreverent.*
- There is nothing *irreligious* in the secular policy of the government.

SAD

Synonyms : Dull, grave, dejected, depressed, downcast, melancholy.

Antonyms : Glad, gay, joyous, cheerful, excited, lively.

Synonyms

- Your college is so well-built, yet I don't know what made me smell its *dull* atmosphere.
- This is a *grave* problem for the educational authorities or universities to solve.
- I was *dejected* to note the lack of general gaiety in your college.
- The news of Jim's failure in the examination *depressed* his mother.
- Since his failure in the examination, Sunny has been looking *downcast.*

Antonyms

- I am *glad* your college has improved its all-round atmosphere by introducing co-education.
- Everything looks *gay* in your college.
- The teachers have also started looking *joyous* and *cheerful.*
- He was very *excited* to hear the news,
- The whole premises give the *lively* look of academic brilliance.

SANCTION

Synonyms : Allow, support, approve, ratify, endorse, authorise, permit, confirm.

Antonyms : Disallow, debar, veto, ban, interdict, forbid, prohibit.

Synonyms

- The teacher *allowed* the student to go home early today.
- Our aunt, who is a widow, works hard to *support* her children.
- I do not *approve* of your idea at all.
- Most nations of the world have *ratified* the UN charter.

- I am sure his boss will *endorse* his views on the issue.
- He has been *authorised* to issue letters on behalf of the principal.
- John was given a *permit* to go through the private park.
- The hotel *confirmed* our reservations by telegram.

Antonyms

- The principal has *disallowed* the use of college premises for political activities.
- The retired officers of the commerce ministry have been *debarred* from doing liaison work for private firms.
- The UN Security Council has *vetoed* the General Assembly decision to impose economic and political sanctions against South Africa.
- The government has *banned* the use of religious shrines for accumulation of weapons of any kind.
- The government has *interdicted* the publication of educational books calculated to cause communal disharmony.

SCATTER

Synonyms : Sprinkle, disperse, spread, broadcast, propagate, dissipate, disseminate, distribute.

Antonyms : Hoard, gather, husband, store, amass, pick, collect, garner, accumulate.

Synonyms

- The people who believe that man becomes pious by *sprinkling* holy water on him are great frauds and fakes.
- The class *dispersed* as soon as the bell rang.
- The news of the leader's assassination *spread* like wildfire.
- The special election *broadcast* will take place on the local station at eight every evening for 20 days before the date of election.
- The missionaries *propagated* the teachings of Christianity throughout the island by establishing shrines and educational institutions.
- The fog *dissipated* when the sun came out.
- Plato's philosophy has been well *disseminated* throughout the western world.
- The postal department *distributes* the mail by PIN Code.

Antonyms

- The blackmarketeers make money by *hoarding* scarce products and essential commodities.
- They invest their money on *gathering* stores when goods are in abundance and selling them when they are scarce.
- They *husband* their resources to store profitable goods for speculation and smuggling.
- In this way they *amass* wealth.

- The little girl *picks* flowers in the garden for making garlands.

SCANTY

Synonyms : Narrow, skimpy, pinch, slender, meagre, limited, sparing, small.

Antonyms : Profuse, abundant, lavish, unlimited, sufficient, ample, copious.

Synonyms

- The lane was so *narrow* that two cars could not pass at the same time.
- This sweater is too *skimpy* to be worn over the shirt.
- If you add a *pinch* of salt, your dish will become more tasty.

- They have grown a number of *slender* birch trees.
- The furniture in the cottage was very *meagre.*
- Father gives him *limited* pocket money per month.
- Our teacher believes in *sparing* use of the stick.
- The chartered accountants have instructions to check even the *small* details of their firms thoroughly before preparing the balance sheet.

Antonyms

- The philanthropist was quite *profuse* in his gifts to the poor.
- Tata has *abundant* resources of men, money and materials to start new projects successfully.
- He makes *lavish* expenditure on his kitchen to keep his family members healthy.
- No body has *unlimited* and absolute powers in the Indian constitution, not even the prime minister.
- There is *sufficient* provision for mutual checks and balances of the powers of the executive legislature and judiciary in the constitution.
- India has *ample* resources but limited organisational infrastructure to deserve being called a rich country.

SCOLD

Synonyms : Reprimand, censure, reprove, admonish, rebuke, chide.

Antonyms : Compliment, applaud, praise, commend.

Synonyms

- Father *reprimanded* him for over-spending.
- The clerk received a strong *censure* for his carelessness.
- When the child giggled over the remark of a visitor, her mother *reproved* her with a stern look.
- He was *admonished* for being late.

- ✦ He was harshly *rebuked* by his boss for misplacing important files.
- ✦ Our political bosses *chided* us for having lost in the international championships.

Antonyms

- ✦ The president *complemented* the Indian lawn tennis players for excellent performance at Wimbledon.
- ✦ The principal *applauded* the work of his teachers who won for the school first two top positions in the Secondary Board results.
- ✦ This film deserves high *praise* for its story and direction.
- ✦ I should *commend* the good work of our salesmen who have doubled the sale of this product in one year.

SEEK

Synonyms : Hunt, court, inquire, look for, search, solicit, ask, follow.

Antonyms : Shun, avoid, eschew, evade.

Synonyms

- ✦ It requires a great deal of courage and experience to *hunt* a tiger.
- ✦ The trade union leaders will *court* arrests today to press their demands.
- ✦ May I *inquire* who is the best singer among these girls ?

- He is *looking* for an opportunity to go abroad.
- He is in *search* of a regular job.
- The old man *solicited* help for his sick wife.
- The driver *asked* the policeman to put him on the right track.
- The detective f*ollowed* the gang to its hide-out.

Antonyms

- I always try to *shun* the company of bad characters.
- *Avoid* the use of artificial pep-ups like tea or coffee.
- The doctor advised the patient to completely *eschew* the use of cigarette or tobacco.

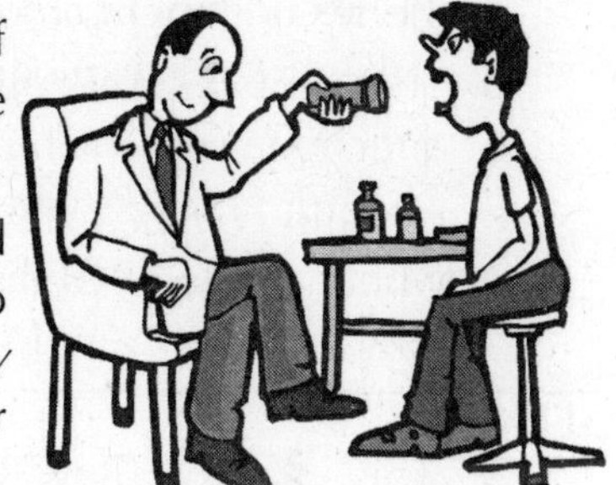

- The rich man *evaded* the payment of income tax.

SELFISH

Synonyms : Greedy, mercenary, ungenerous, illiberal, mean.

Antonyms : Generous, liberal, charitable, bountiful, lavish.

Synonyms

- No one admires a *greedy* child.

- ✦ The *mercenaries* face a tragic death when they are defeated in war.
- ✦ His boss is rather *ungenerous* in granting leave to the employees.
- ✦ *Illiberal* policies always tend to cause hardship to the people.
- ✦ Even his colleagues do not like him because he is *mean* and *selfish*.

Antonyms

- ✦ Romy is *generous* to a fault. No wonder his so called friends exploit his friendship.
- ✦ Our government has launched *liberal* policies towards businessmen for expanding their ventures.
- ✦ Some businessmen have a *charitable* attitude towards their employees and help them to live better.
- ✦ This year the rains have helped the crops to be *bountiful*.
- ✦ Modern businessmen can afford to pay *lavishly* to their sincere employees.

SENSIBLE

Synonyms : Judicious, wise, aware, conscious, intelligent, rational, observant, sagacious, cognisant, sane.

Antonyms : Unaware, senseless, idiotic, stupid, asinine, foolish, unconscious, doltish.

Synonyms

- The prime minister of a country has to be a man of *judicious* temperament.
- It was *wise* of the mother to keep the child indoors when he had a cold.
- Are we *aware* of the developments taking place in our neighbouring countries ?
- I became *conscious* that someone was moving about upstairs. I, therefore, checked but found only a cat.
- He is *intelligent* enough to understand the problem instantly.
- It is necessary to have a *rational* approach to our family budget in these days of high inflation.
- Be *observant* to this mischief of your neighbour.
- The court reached a *sagacious* decision on this complicated case.
- Is the accused *cognisant* of his rights ?

Antonyms

- Our masses are yet *unaware* of their rights and duties provided in the constitution.
- All talk of ideal and fair elections is *senseless* in the light of the role of their money.
- Anil's idiotic behaviour in the interview let him down. Highly *stupid* of him not to read a good book on interviews.
- The new teacher was rather *asinine* for the clever and mischievous students.

SEPARABLE

Synonyms : Divisible, classifiable, branched, group into.

Antonyms : Unit, indivisible, united, inseparable,

Synonyms

- Ten is *divisible* by two.
- The books in my personal library are *classifiable.*
- Just after the lake, the path *branched* out to the right.
- Class X of our school shall be *grouped into* 3 parts on the basis of merit.

Antonyms

- A *unit* is the combination of parts.
- Earlier scientists thought an atom as *indivisible* but atomic theory has disproved the old theory.
- India is a federation of states *united* by one common constitution.
- The states of India are *inseparable* parts of one country, i.e, Bharat.

SEPARATE

Synonyms : Detach, disconnect, disengage, disunite.

Antonyms : Combine, connect, consolidate, engage, unite.

Synonyms

- Some body has *detached* the battery from my car.

+ *Disconnect* the wire from the plug.
+ The receptionist told me she would connect me with her boss as soon as he is *disengaged* from a previous caller.

+ The Kapur family stands *disunited* with two of their sons migrating to the United States.

Antonyms

+ *Combine* 80% oxygen and 20% hydrogen; we will get water.
+ Please *connect* me with Mr. Kapur on extension 285.
+ The finance ministry is formulating new schemes to *consolidate* the country's developing economy.
+ I will *engage* him in talks while you can have a look into his inner office.
+ Let's *unite* and plunge into the new adventure.

SETTLE

Synonyms : Conclude, establish, fix, liquidate, finish, domicile, adjust, decide, determine, colonise.

Antonyms : Ruffle, dismantle, confuse, derange, disorder.

Synonyms

+ We will *conclude* the concert with the national anthem.

- A new post office was *established* at the far end of our village.
- They have *fixed* the next meeting of the Board at 4 pm on Saturday.
- The company has decided to *liquidate* all its assets this year.
- The meeting *finished* with the prize-giving.
- The Hindu Marriage Act applies to those Hindus only who *domicile* in India.
- He needs to *adjust* the brakes of his bicycle.
- The Nyaya Panchayats can *decide* upon petty cases only.
- The Supreme Court alone can *determine* inter-state disputes and constitutional interpretation.
- The Dutch were the first among Europeans to *colonise* new territories in Africa and Asia.

Antonyms

- The new manager has *ruffled* all the organisation of the old manager.
- The new mechanic has *dismantled* my car with a view to overhaul and cleanse each part.
- The speaker *confused* the different issues of the debated subject. No wonder he was hooted down.
- The untimely death of her son has seriously *deranged* the mother.
- When I visited the place of accident, I found everything in *disorder*.

SHALLOW

Synonyms : Trifle, superficial, slight, trivial, foolish, unintelligent, simple.

Antonyms : Wise, intelligent, shrewd, astute, discerning, deep, recondite, clever.

Synonyms

- ✦ His mother keeps telling Sam, not to cry over *trifles*.
- ✦ The new teacher seems to have a *superficial* understanding of economics.
- ✦ He is so indifferent to studies, he misses college on the *slight* pretext.
- ✦ He is so sensitive, even *trivial* things upset him.
- ✦ It was *foolish* of him to quarrel with his best friends.
- ✦ His *unintelligent* handling of the situation has implicated him in the losses of the financial deal.
- ✦ Even a child can solve this *simple* puzzle.

Antonyms

- ✦ Daly is a *wise* and witty boy.
- ✦ His *intelligent* talks have impressed his teachers and friends.
- ✦ The businessman proved too *shrewd* for the fake salesman.
- ✦ The *astute* handling of the labour problem, enabled the management to avoid the lockout.

- ✦ There is a *discerning* resemblance between the two brothers.
- ✦ Danny is a *deep* thinker. He thinks twice before speaking or acting.

SHAME

Synonyms : Disgrace, abashment, dishonour, shyness, coyness, mortification.

Antonyms : Honour, grace, courage.

Synonyms

- ✦ Smith felt *disgraced* when he spilt the ink on the boss's table.
- ✦ Jack was filled with *abashment* when he was asked by the principal to stand up on the bench.
- ✦ His collusion with the enemy brought *dishonour* to the whole family.
- ✦ His son was refused admission in the school for his *shyness.*
- ✦ She felt *coyness* when asked to recite a song.
- ✦ I forgot to preface my speech owing to stage *shyness.* What a *mortification* indeed !

Antonyms

- ✦ I felt greatly *honoured* on receiving the trophy from the sports minister.
- ✦ The principal showed due *grace* to present me to the minister.

- It needs *courage* to face a huge audience.

SHELTER

Synonyms : Guard, protect, screen, defend, shield.

Antonyms : Betray, expel, reject, surrender, refuse, expose.

Synonyms

- India has recently deployed more troops to *guard* the borders with Pakistan.
- The hen-house needs to be *protected* from the prowling foxes.
- The atmosphere *screens* the earth from infra-red rays coming from the sun.
- Tom *defended* his dog when it was attacked by a fox.
- In a hot country, men and women often wear large hats to *shield* their heads from the sun.

Antonyms

- Smugglers are the worst enemies of the country as they *betray* its interests.
- The government has decided to *expel* the foreign spies caught red-handed.
- The boss has *rejected* the demand of the employee for a raise in salary.
- The culprit *surrendered* to the police to save his life from the bullet shot.

- India has *refused* to hold parleys with Pakistan without preconditions.
- The enemy spies, on being cross-examined, have *exposed* their intention to run the terrorist movement in India.

SHOCK

Synonyms : Scare, dismay, offend, outrage, blow, collision, tremor, horrify.

Antonyms : Delight, gladden, please.

Synonyms

- She was *scared* to see a thief under her bed.
- The news of his failure in the examination *dismayed* him.
- My refusal to lend him the bicycle *offended* him.
- Cruelty to children is an *outrage* punishable under law.
- The failure of his business was a terrible *blow* to him.
- The head-on *collision* of the bus with the truck coming from the opposite side was heard for a kilometre.
- A slight earthquake *tremor* was felt in Delhi yesterday morning.
- Listening to the gruesome stories *horrifies* small children.

Antonyms

- It was a matter of great *delight* for me to shake hands with the president.
- The award of the Academy Merit Certificate *gladdened* the father of the boy.
- The visit of my friend from Shimla greatly *pleased* me.

SIGNIFY

Synonyms : Denote, intimate, mean, show, proclaim, indicate.

Antonyms : Veil, mask, dissemble, cloak, cover, hide, conceal.

Synonyms

- The hoisting of the British flag at mast *denoted* the origin of the ship.
- The headmaster *intimated* the students about the half holiday on Saturday.
- He does not *mean* to hurt you.
- His face *showed* he had taken ill of your joke.
- A public holiday was *proclaimed* in honour of the coronation.
- His high temperature *indicates* he is seriously ill.

Antonyms

- The *veiled* dress she is wearing shows she is either a nurse or a nun.
- The robbers who looted the bank were wearing *masks*.

- ✦ The motor mechanic *dissembled* my car for repairs and then reassembled it.
- ✦ Our swimming pool was *cloaked* in thick haze.
- ✦ I *covered* my head with a hankie before entering the shrine.
- ✦ The thief *hid* himself under a bed in a servant quarter.
- ✦ He kept his face expressionless to *conceal* his excitement.

SILLY

Synonyms : Absurd, senseless, foolish, unwise, nonsensical.

Antonyms : Sensible, clever, wise, sapient, intelligent.

Synonyms

- ✦ It is *absurd* to say that this textbook is useless only because some of its lessons make dull reading.
- ✦ It is *senseless* for parents to compel their wards to study the subjects which don't suit their taste and interest.
- ✦ It was *foolish* of him to openly quarrel with his boss.
- ✦ It is *unwise* to think that trade unions should be banned.
- ✦ He is fed up with listening to the *nonsensical* sermons of his boss.

Antonyms

- Rita is a *sensible* girl. I have never observed anything irrelevant in her talks.
- Johny is a *clever* boy. He could make a successful businessman.
- He remembers the *wise* sayings of all great men by heart.
- Our new economics teacher is quite a *sapient* learned man. His lectures are all very *intelligent*.

SINCERE

Synonyms : Genuine, true, frank, heart-felt, honest, open, wholehearted.

Antonyms : Affected, untrue, feigned, half-hearted, hypocritical, insincere, pretended.

Synonyms

- This book is a *genuine* research work of the first order.
- All the statements made in the book are *true* and *frank*.
- The principal spoke out his *heart-felt* views about the rash activities of some of the students which could bring dishonour to the college.
- Modern politicians arc supposed to be *honest,* at least to their party ideology.
- The prime minister has made as *open* offer to the opposition parties to keep him apprised of their viewpoint on major national issues.

- The government has decided to work *whole-heartedly* for the welfare of the poor sections of society.

Antonyms

- The disturbed law and order situation in some states has *affected* the clean thinking of many politicians in the country.
- The allegation made in some quarters about India's aggressive designs against Sri Lanka have proved *untrue.*
- He survived the massacre by *feigning* death.
- Her *half-hearted hypocritical* efforts were exposed in the end.

SKILL

Synonyms : Artistry, adroitness, finesse, mastery.

Antonyms : Clumsiness, incompetence, ineptitude.

Synonyms

- The *artistry* of India's handicraftsmen of Muradabad and Varanasi is appreciated the world over.
- The *adroitness* of the new management can save the company from bankruptcy.
- The ivory carvers of Delhi are reputed for their *finesse.*
- The carpet weavers of Jammu and Kashmir have perfect *mastery* and monopoly over their trade.

Antonyms

- ✦ The *clumsiness* of some of the engineering products of India brings a bad name to the country's craftsmanship.
- ✦ *Incompetence* and *ineptitude* of Indian management in some textile mills has brought them into the red.

SKILFUL

Synonyms : Competent, ingenious, adroit, clever, experienced.

Antonyms : Inexperienced, bungling, incompetent, clumsy, awkward.

Synonyms

- ✦ His father is a *competent* writer.
- ✦ The way the parts of a watch are put together is very *ingenious*.
- ✦ He manages the business in a very *adroit* way.
- ✦ The thief was so *clever* he left no clues.
- ✦ My uncle is an *experienced* chemical engineer.

Antonyms

- ✦ Although *inexperienced*, my assistant is proficient in accounts.
- ✦ The new treasurer has been charged of *bungling* the funds of the cooperative society.
- ✦ The manager is honest but rather *incompetent* for the high responsibility he is supposed to shoulder.

- No wonder his handling of some affairs has been rather *clumsy*.
- This has proved *awkward* for the person who recommended him.

SLANDER

Synonyms : Decry, defame, aspersion, opprobrious, accuse, malign, disparage, defamation.

Antonyms : Praise, commendation, eulogise, laud.

Synonyms

- The captain *decried* the lack of support he received from his team.
- Politicians *defame* each other to win public support.
- It's not fair to cast *aspersions* on someone you know nothing about.
- The liaison officer of the company was reprimanded for his *opprobrious* conduct.
- The servant was *accused* of stealing utensils from the kitchen.
- A fair politician debates the issues and does not *malign* his opponent.
- His father always *disparaged* his attempts to better himself.
- He sued the newspaper for *defamation* of his character.

Antonyms

- ✦ Your conduct in negotiating settlement between warring brothers deserves high *praise*.
- ✦ Self-*commendation* is no *praise*.
- ✦ The readers *eulogise* Shakespeare for his brilliance of expression and characterisation.
- ✦ The local public *lauded* the achievements of the municipal commissioner.

SLAVERY

Synonyms : Subjugation, thraldom, bondage, forced labour, submission, drudgery, servitude, captivity.

Antonyms : Freedom, emancipation, liberty, independence.

Synonyms

- ✦ *Subjugation* of poorer classes by the richer elite is a historical phenomenon which continues its sway even today in most countries in the world.
- ✦ Since money is power, the rich can always hold the poor in *thraldom*.
- ✦ One form of *slavery* in villages is *bondage* of agricultural labour by the landlord.
- ✦ The labour class is *forced* to be exploited by the landlord forever.

✦ The bonded *labour* is under *submission* to the landlord who keeps the former in very poor condition so that he may not raise his voice in rebellion or run away.

✦ All the *drudgery* of work is done by the labourers while the landlord enjoys the fruit of their labour.

✦ Thus the system of *servitude* and *captivity* has continued ever since but is being shaken off by the democratic wind blowing round the world today.

Antonyms

✦ Modern democracies are taking legal action to bring about the *freedom* of the bonded labour and the *emancipation* of the poor worker from serfdom.

✦ He is being given the *liberty* of movement from the clutches of the landlord and *independence* in the choice of work.

SMART

Synonyms : Spruce, trim, elegant, well-dressed immaculate, neat, showy.

Antonyms : Rugged, worn, shabby, untidy, unkempt, threadbare.

Synonyms

✦ In advanced countries majority of the people can maintain *spruce, trim* and *elegant* personalities on the strength of high wages earned by them.

- The common people can afford to be *well-dressed, neat* and smart.
- The economic conditions are only gradually improving and only a minority can maintain *immaculate* apparels.

Antonyms

- Most of the people in undeveloped villages or industrial townships of poor countries are seen in *rugged, worn* clothes.
- The workers employed in industries can afford only *shabby* clothes while their working conditions are *untidy*.
- His greasy, *unkempt* hair was a disgusting sight.
- His shirt too was *threadbare*.

SLIGHT

Synonyms : Ignore, disregard, neglect.

Antonyms : Attend, consider, tend, heed, prize.

Synonyms

- With the breakup of the joint family system, the older generation is *ignored* by the younger.
- There is complete *disregard* of this social phenomenon among the states in the developing countries where social welfare schemes like old-age allowance are not yet in vogue.
- The governments in poorer countries have been compelled to *neglect* the poor classes owing to financial stringencies.

Antonyms

- The prize distribution ceremony of our college was *attended* by the students, teachers and parents.
- The government is *considering* to end the system of bonded labour in India.
- Our gardener nicely *tends* the plants of our kitchen garden.
- The government must pay more *heed* to the needs of its employees.

SLOW

Synonyms : Gradual, leisurely, slack, retarded, sluggish.

Antonyms : Agile, fast, quick, rapid, speedy, lively.

Synonyms

- There is need for *gradual* automation in the electronic industry in India.
- The Indian engineers work in a rather *leisurely* fashion, otherwise our Public Works Departments and utility undertakings would be more efficient.
- The demand for TV sets has *slackened* owing to high prices and the inability of the common people to afford it.

Antonyms

- The Indian engineers are much more *agile* when working in advanced countries as they have better opportunities of showing their worth.
- India has been *fast* developing its industries since the last two decades.
- The horse runs more *quickly* in the morning.
- Some of the Indian rivers flow *rapidly* down the hills and plains.

SOCIABLE

Synonyms : Companionable, festive, affable genial, convivial.

Antonyms : Secluded, inimical, hostile, sequestered, puerilic, giddy.

Synonyms

- My uncle is such a *companionable* personality, you can never feel bored in his presence.
- The *festive* season starts in India after harvesting of the crops.
- This *affable* manners attract the young and the old.
- The retired old man has a *genial* way of amusing his visitors.

Antonyms

- Ever since his brain injury, Robin has become a *secluded* personality and I think it will take a few months before he restarts mixing with people.

- The dispute among brothers on property matters has made them *inimical.*
- Even their children are affected and are *hostile* to each other.
- Old age has made Ranjit a *sequestered* person; gone is all his old joviality and sociability.
- Although rich in money, he is a *puerilic* person, small-hearted and peevish.

SOFT

Synonyms : Plastic, flexible, pliable, yielding, malleable, supple.

Antonyms : Hard, firm, unyielding, compact, rigid, stiff.

Synonyms

- *Plastic* has become an important raw material for numerous industries, and consumer products.
- I believe in following a *flexible* approach in human relationships in view of the changing framework of society.
- Plastic is *pliable* and capable of being converted and mixed with numerous materials.
- High-*yielding* varieties of seed have greatly helped Indian agriculture to develop its productivity. 
- An actor has to be highly *malleable* and volatile his is emotional expression.

Antonyms

- ✦ The alloy of metals is very *hard* and can be used in sophisticated super-strong structures.
- ✦ It is *firm* in nature, does not bend nor melt except at a temperature of 1000°C.
- ✦ Smith is such a hard fellow to bend on principles, he is *unyielding* in temperament.
- ✦ This machine is so *compact* it can last for decades without repairs.
- ✦ India follows a *rigid* foreign policy, measured strictly by principles of non-alignment.
- ✦ The government is prepared to take *stiff* measures to maintain law and order in the country.

SOIL

Synonyms : Stain, spoil, dirty, smear, pollute, taint, contaminate, sully.

Antonyms : Clarify, clean, purge, wash, cleanse, purify.

Synonyms

- ✦ John never does anything which may *stain* his character.
- ✦ Rita is a *spoilt* child, always making mischief, never serious.
- ✦ Don't play in the mud, you will *dirty* your hands and clothes.
- ✦ I promise to do nothing which may *smear* the good name of our noble family.

- Coal-based industries tend to *pollute* the atmosphere.

Antonyms

- The principal *clarified* many controversial issues raised by the students and teachers.
- The new prime minister has promised to give a *clean* administration to the country.
- He has decided to *purge* it of inefficient and corrupt officials. 
- The washerman *washes* the dirty clothes of the people.
- In these days of good washing soaps and powders, most families prefer to *clean* their clothes themselves as an economic measure.

SOLEMN

Synonyms : Traditional, ceremonial, devotional, pious.

Antonyms : Impious, irreligious, sacrilegious, irreverent.

Synonyms

- Sonia's marriage involves performance of *traditional* ceremonies.
- The national flag will be hoisted on the Independence Day at the Red Fort in the usual *ceremonial* way.

- *Devotional* music is played at this gurudwara every morning.
- Though he is a *pious* person, he is prone to telling lies.

Antonyms

- There is nothing *impious* in performing the opening ceremony without the usual mantras.
- There is nothing *irreligious* in departing from the traditional pattern so long as the objective of a mission is noble and pure.
- The ceremony does not become *sacrilegious* so long as the spirit of the occasion is fully imbibed and enthusiasm aroused.
- If we can call agricultural and industrial projects as temples of modern age, it is not *irreverent* to compare the manager of such a temple with the pujari of the religious temple.

SOLID

Synonyms : Sound, safe, reliable, trustworthy.

Antonyms : Unreliable, undependable, unsafe.

Synonyms

- This project is based on *sound* principles of management science and technical know-how.
- Hence it can be considered as perfectly *safe* for launching at an early date.

- ✦ We must, however, ensure the selection of *reliable* supervisors and *trustworthy* financial officers for running the project.

Antonyms

- ✦ The statistics prepared by foreign sources regarding the number of people killed in pro and anti-reservation clashes in Ahmedabad are entirely *unreliable*.
- ✦ The arrangements made for the organisation of sports ciubs in every locality in the district seem *undependable*.
- ✦ The sheds constructed for use by visitors to the hot spring at Gurgaon are *unsafe*.

SOLITARY

Synonyms : Infrequented, uninhabited, secluded, lonely, isolated, sequestered, deserted.

Antonyms : Habited, popular, well-frequented, sociable.

Synonyms

- ✦ The palace, although well situated on the shore of this island, is *infrequented* as there are a few mysteries concerning its history.
- ✦ Many parts of Australia are yet *uninhabited*.
- ✦ There are many *secluded* parts even in northern Australia although it is very rich in natural resources.

- ✦ He has been feeling very *lonely* since the death of his wife.
- ✦ He has *isolated* himself from many of his old friends to keep his sorrow to himself.

Antonyms

- ✦ This city is so much *habited* and over populated that there is hardly any open space for easy breathing of fresh air.
- ✦ The prime minister has become quite *popular* since his last press conference.
- ✦ This restaurant is now *well-frequented* by military personnel.
- ✦ The president of this club is a very *sociable* person.

SOLVE

Synonyms : Decipher, decode, unravel, uncover.

Antonyms : Baffle, confuse, puzzle.

Synonyms

- ✦ Can you *decipher* this code number for the benefit of my colleagues.
- ✦ The captain has *decoded* the message received from the headquarters.
- ✦ Sherlock Holmes has *unravelled* many mysteries in his new investigation.
- ✦ The doctor *uncovered* the body of the dead patient to ascertain the cause of his death.

Antonyms

- The present political situation of Nicaragua is *baffling* for the outside world.
- Let us not *confuse* the issue by side-tracking the discussion.
- We have got to solve the numerical *puzzle* with the help of the teacher in the class today.

SOOTHE

Synonyms : Palliate, alleviate, ease, appease, solace, assuage, calm, deaden, tranquillise.

Antonyms : Irritate, nettle, inflame, agitate, animate, excite, stimulate, exasperate, enrage.

Synonyms

- The announcement of financial assistance has *palliated* the victims of the flood.
- The 20-point programme of the prime minister has *alleviated* the living condition of the poorest of the poor in many parts of the country.
- The banking institutions are helping to *ease* the financial handicaps of the farmers.
- Land reforms are designed to *appease* the more restive of the landless farmers.
- Today's rains have provided great *solace* to the drought ridden parts of the region.
- This injection will *tranquillise* him.

Antonyms

- The sultry weather today is rather *irritating*.

- The trade union has *nettled* the workers to resort to a pen down strike.
- The political leaders belonging to the opposition have been warned against *inflaming* the people against the government.
- The workers are planning to *agitate* for increased wages.
- Modern dress fashions which are marked by nudity tend to *animate* violence and crime among the youth.

SOUL

Synonyms : Mind, heart, ego, essence, vital, principle.

Antonyms : Body, matter, materialisation, embodiment.

Synonyms

- Let us devote our *mind* and body to the economic development of our country.
- Unless we put our *heart* and soul into our work, we cannot achieve success.
- *Ego* is the enemy of self-realisation among men and women.
- Discipline is the *essence* of a successful personality.
- Self-determination and strong will-power are *vital* for optimum achievement in life.

Antonyms

- A sound mind can flourish only in a sound *body*.
- *Matter* represents the outer form of living while the soul interests the spiritual side of life.
- The present mode of living is bringing about *materialisation* of the soul.
- A pure heart, conscious of the omnipresence of God, is the *embodiment* of a dynamic personality.

SPITEFUL

Synonyms : Rancorous, malignant, malicious.

Antonyms : Benign, beneficent, benignant, benevolent.

Synonyms

- A *rancorous* legal battle ensued between the two warring brothers.
- The *malignant* attitude of nations against each other can be ended only by bringing about a classless society in which the interests of individuals cease to clash but are reconciled in the framework of a peaceful united mankind.
- Nationalism and narrow patriotism are concepts which lead to the propagation of *malicious* propaganda that divides the world into conflicting groups and races.

Antonyms

- Educational systems in different countries should teach international citizenship as a compulsory subject from the early age so as to make all humans and individuals develop a *benign* attitude.

- Only a universal spirit of benignity can make everyone work for the *beneficent* functioning of a new world order of peace and mutual cooperation.
- If the world's newly attained knowledge in sciences and humanities could be applied in full force, the universal feeling of *benignance* would make the world live in peace, amity and prosperity.

SPREAD

Synonyms : Circulate, distribute, propagate.

Antonyms : Accumulate, gather.

Synonyms

- The principal has *circulated* the admission notice through the newspapers.
- The government has registered over 2 lakh fair price shops in the country to *distribute* essential commodities, including foodgrains and sugar, among the people at fixed prices.
- The government *propagates* its policies in different spheres to elicit the cooperation of the people in their implementation.

Antonyms

- ✦ The black marketeers try to *accumulate* scarce goods in their godowns to sell them at higher prices whenever there is a chance.
- ✦ In this way they *gather* lot of black profit for building more property.

SPLENDID

Synonyms : Resplendent, radiant, brilliant, beaming, shining.

Antonyms : Dull, dark, dim, tarnished, cloudy.

Synonyms

- ✦ These diamonds are so *resplendent* they can be used in only 22 carat jewellery.
- ✦ They shed their *radiance* from a distance.
- ✦ The new car is available in a variety of *brilliant* colours.
- ✦ Julie came out of her house *beaming* glamorously at her boyfriend.
- ✦ The new boot polish is *shining* reflectively on my shoes.

Antonyms

- ✦ Modest people prefer to wear clothes of *dull* colours.
- ✦ There is *dark* after sunset on moonless nights.
- ✦ He could not see her face properly in the *dim* light.

- The unearthing of smuggled goods has *tarnished* the good name of my uncle's family.
- The weather is *cloudy* today with prospects of a heavy downpour soon.

STATEMENT

Synonyms : Account, narration, declaration, avowal, assertion, announcement, utterance.

Antonyms : Refutation, disavowal, contradiction, denial, negation.

Synonyms

- The statement of *accounts* of the company shows the good progress made during the year.
- Her *narration* of the grim story of the fatal accident involving her husband brought tears to my eyes.

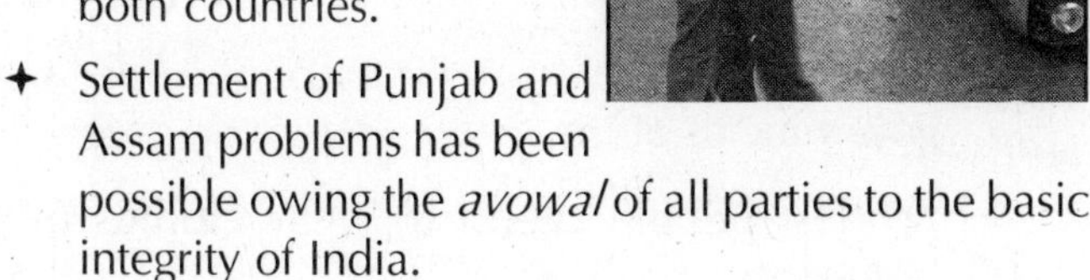

- Indo-Chinese *declaration* on future trade has been hailed by the people of both countries.
- Settlement of Punjab and Assam problems has been possible owing the *avowal* of all parties to the basic integrity of India.
- The regional parties of the two states have *asserted* their right to develop their respective languages and cultures.

- The *announcement* of the new commercial policy of India has heartened the business circles.

Antonyms

- The integrity of the country lies in the *refutation* of regional claims for autonomy.
- The Akali Party has expressed *disavowal* for violent activities of extremist elements.
- There are certain fundamental *contradictions* in the US foreign policy.

STEADY

Synonyms : Constant, undeviating, stable, regular, firm, consistent, uniform.

Antonyms : Irregular, unstable, wavering, changeable, variable, unsteady, inconsistent.

Synonyms

- Our forces keep a *constant* watch on the country's borders in the north, east and west.
- India's attachment to the non-aligned principles is *undeviating*.
- Rajiv Gandhi was trying to provide *stable* governments at the centre and in the states.
- We must expand the production of hydroelectricity if we have to assure *regular* supply of electric power to industries.
- India has a *firm* policy on non-alignment.
- It has *consistently* held to the principles of Panchsheel, since Nehru's time.

Antonyms

- ✦ Lucky has been *irregular* in his attendance in the college.
- ✦ His interest in studies has been *unstable* right from the start.
- ✦ But his option for physics as a subject of specialisation has been especially *wavering*.

- ✦ Now the subject is not *changeable* at this stage. Hence his educational progress has been *unsteady*.

STEEP

Synonyms : High, sharp, abrupt, precipitous.

Antonyms : Gradual, low level, straight, easy, gentle.

Synonyms

- ✦ Harry has reached a *high* peak in his career.
- ✦ His rise has been *sharp* during the last five years.
- ✦ This hall has an *abrupt* ending at the top.
- ✦ If one were to look down from the hill top, he will observe a *precipitous* slope on all sides.

Antonyms

- ✦ In our valley there are hills around with *gradual* ascent.

- Some hills seem descending below to the *lower levels* becoming plain-like, straight, *easy* to get down and *gentle* to walk.
- Sachin hit a *straight* drive.
- He is very soft spoken and gentle.

STILL

Synonyms : Motionless, serene, peaceful, stagnant, quiet, calm, stationary, pacific.

Antonyms : Moving, excited, flowing, disturbed, troubled, agitated, running, flustered.

Synonyms

- When I reached his room, I was shocked to find his body lying in a *motionless* state.
- I checked his pulse but it was *still*.
- His face was *serene* and *peaceful* as if he were asleep, but his half open eyes frightened me.
- When I looked at the sea beyond the window, I found the waters *stagnant* and *quiet*.
- Nothing could *calm* his anger.

Antonyms

- The train was *moving* on the plains at a terrific speed.
- I was *excited* by the scenery around and by a large river *flowing* by the side of the rail track.
- I was *disturbed* by the sheer memory of the death of my friend in the hostel.

+ My *troubled* thoughts *agitated* me in my dreams.

STIMULATE

Synonyms : Instigate, whet, purr, inflame, goad, inspire, provoked, incite.

Antonyms : Prevent, hinder, deter, dissuade.

Synonyms

+ Henry has a habit of *instigating* one student against the other and the teacher against his students.
+ Attendance of public meetings held by the Arya Samaj at the local hall has always *whetted* my thoughts about society and humanity.
+ The *purr* of our cat is highly amusing though it disturbs when I am studying.
+ The student leader *inflamed* the students against the administration by indulging in invectives and rebukes.
+ He *goaded* them to go on a week - long strike to press for demand for reduction in tuition fees and hostel rent.

Antonyms

+ Nowadays the parents cannot *prevent* children from doing what they like.
+ More freedom to children need not necessarily *hinder* their progress provided they get good educational facilities.

- Enforcement of strict discipline does not *deter* children from going wrong if their minds are not put on the right track by their own free will.
- The processes of guidance to children should not include *dissuasion* but indirect discouragement of wrong deeds.

STIMULUS

Synonyms : Spur, incitement, inducement, incentive.

Antonyms : Deterrent, dissuasion, hinderance.

Synonyms

- Modern films *spur* ideas of violence and sex among children.
- Such *incitement* does not necessarily make them bad individuals.
- Science and technology provide *inducement* to more and more products of comfort in society.
- They are a great *incentive* to the economic development of a country.

Antonyms

- Sophisticated armaments are as much a *deterrent* to wars as they are a danger to mankind.
- While science and technology help produce atomic and neutron bombs, developments in social sciences act as *dissuasion* factors against their use.

- ✦ Hence science and technology are not a *hindrance* to human progress.

STRANGE

Synonyms : Extraordinary, queer, unique, unusual, unnatural, uncommon, odd, eccentric, inexplicable.

Antonyms : Normal, everyday, usual, natural, ordinary.

Synonyms

- ✦ Sam is an *extraordinary* person with very high intelligence, but his behaviour is *queer* at times.
- ✦ One *unique* feature of this TV is the remote control with which you can set its volume or focus while sitting in your chair without having to go near the set.
- ✦ Today's cool atmosphere is quite *unusual* and *unnatural* for these days of the hot season.
- ✦ The scene of almost a vacant cinema hall is not *uncommon* these days because of competition with TV and home theatre but it is quite *odd*.
- ✦ An *eccentric* wife is never an asset in a family.

Antonyms

- ✦ Delhi had *normal* temperature yesterday.
- ✦ *Everyday* is not a hay day even for the richest man.
- ✦ This crowd represents a *usual* phenomenon of this super market's evenings.

✦ That he returns very tired in the evening after a day's hard work is quite *natural* considering his age.

STOP

Synonyms : Block, arrest, check, cease, halt, prevent, discontinue.

Antonyms : Begin, activate, continue, quicken, purr.

Synonyms

✦ The scooter was parked in the middle and *blocked* the passage to our house.

✦ The police *arrested* the smuggler for selling hashish in bulk to a scooter driver.

✦ This provision is designed to *check* the use of unhealthy drugs and their international smuggling.

✦ Mr. Lal has *ceased* to be the librarian of our college library.

Antonyms

✦ Let us *begin* the trekking of this hill from this base.

✦ We will have to *activate* our enthusiasm and will-power to reach the top of the hill.

- Let us *continue* to move at a speed of 10 km an hour.
- We can *quicken* our pace on less steep slopes.
- The car *purred* away at a steady pace.

STRONG

Synonyms : Muscular, powerful, sturdy, tough.

Antonyms : Powerless, weak, soft.

Synonyms

- It requires a *muscular* body to indulge in wrestling and boxing.
- Your punch has to be *powerful* enough to unbalance the opponent.
- *Sturdy* bodies make successful boxers.
- Their *tough* punch has to carry a strong impact.

Antonyms

- I am *powerless* in this game.
- People can make use of my *weak* points to their advantage.
- I am reputed for my *soft* yet strong character.

SUBLIME

Synonyms : Superb, grand, lofty, majestic, noble, glorious, exalted, splendid, resplendent, beautiful.

Antonyms : Mean, base, ridiculous, insignificant, little, petty.

Synonyms

- This TV is *superb.* What a performance? What colours?
- The minister was accorded a *grand* reception.
- Our principal has inculcated *lofty* ideals among the youth of his college.
- The lion is a *majestic* animal.
- Her husband has a *noble* character.
- He has a *glorious* career starting with first position in the university for his bachelor's degree.
- Mrs. Sinha is the only woman to rise to such an *exalted* position.
- Her way of dressing is *splendid.*

Antonyms

- Mrs. Sharma is *mean* to her servants, doubts their integrity, casts aspersions on their intentions, charges them of little thefts and so on.
- Her mentality is *base* as she has had no good schooling in her young days.
- Her behaviour with servants is generally *ridiculous.*
- No wonder she is socially *insignificant* in her neighbourhood.
- She talks much but of *little* and *petty* things.

SUBSTANTIAL

Synonyms : Actual, material, tangible, palpable, perceptible, corporeal, real, existing.

Antonyms : Illusive, unsubstantial, illusory, unreal, shadowy, fanciful, chimerical.

Synonyms

- Modern acting involves living the *actual* role to make it interesting.
- The *material* side of the problem is not so serious.
- There is no *tangible* picture of the business project in view yet.
- Bribing an officer to get a work done is a *palpable* offence as serious as the acceptance of bribe.

Antonyms

- The problem of poverty is *illusive* of solution due to lack of enthusiasm on the part of the administrators who run the relevant schemes.
- The reasoning furnished by you for obtaining official support for your business project is *unsubstantial.*
- You cannot win your point in a debate by giving *illusory* arguments.
- The facts presented by you in support of your case for loan are *unreal* and *shadowy.*

STUBBORN

Synonyms : Adamant, headstrong, inflexible, obstinate.

Antonyms : Adaptable, compliant, docile, flexible.

Synonyms

- ✦ Norman is *adamant* in his demands. Unless he is given what he wants, he keeps the obsession.
- ✦ The general of the regiment is *headstrong*. He moves heaven and earth to achieve what he wants.
- ✦ His objectives in military strategy are *inflexible*.
- ✦ His action is firm but not *obstinate*.

Antonyms

- ✦ The military policies of the government are *adaptable* to the demands of each situation.
- ✦ My *compliant* behaviour was appreciated by my principal.
- ✦ Our new teacher is rather *docile*, the students do not listen to her with due reverence.
- ✦ Plastic and rubber are *flexible* raw materials capable of being moulded to desired pattern.

STUPID

Synonyms : Dense, dull, slow, thick, unintelligent.

Antonyms : Bright, clever, intelligent, keen, smart.

Synonyms

- ✦ How can you be so *dense* ?
- ✦ He is very *dull*, so I have to teach him slowly.

- ✦ Samson is a *slow* learner.
- ✦ His tutor is fed up with his *thick* memory and *unintelligent* grasp of lessons.

Antonyms

- ✦ Robin is a *bright* student, always topping in his class.
- ✦ He is *clever* in his studies and *intelligent* in grasping facts and figures.
- ✦ He takes *keen* interest in general knowledge and the world around him.
- ✦ He gives a *smart* outlook.

SUITABLE

Synonyms : Appropriate, eligible, pertinent, relevant, befitting, seemly, convenient, becoming.

Antonyms : Unsuitable, inappropriate, irrelevant, unseemly, untimely, improper.

Synonyms

- ✦ Jim gave *appropriate* replies to most of the questions asked by the interviewers.
- ✦ He is *eligible* for the post applied for in every respect.
- ✦ Members of parliament asked questions of the minister pertaining to the departments under his charge and the latter gave *pertinent* replies.
- ✦ He gave *relevant* facts to prove his statements.

- The district magistrate was given a reception *befitting* his status.

Antonyms

- The dress worn by the leader on the occasion was entirely *unsuitable*.
- In his reply to the welcome address, the leader made many *inappropriate* remarks which offended the hosts.
- He made quite a few *irrelevant* statements which dampened the chances of the leader's election.
- He made an *unseemly* scene at the house of the host.

SUDDEN

Synonyms : Momentary, brief, quick, unexpected, rapid, rash, unanticipated unforeseen.

Antonyms : Awaited, gradual, anticipated, progressive.

Synonyms

- *Momentary* sentiments do not play a very deep role in human relationships. The basic factor of importance is identity of economic interests.
- The section officer prepared a *brief* of the case for submission to the deputy secretary.
- There is no sound business which may bring *quick* money without too much risk.
- The accident was so *unexpected,* its news shocked me.

✦ Every main river is served by a few *rapids* which flow in or around the valleys on sloping grounds.

Antonyms

✦ The long-*awaited* reply arrived at last but it gave us no relief.

✦ His rise in career has been *gradual* but steady.

✦ The success of this sound project can be easily *anticipated*.

✦ Rosy holds *progressive* views on politics and economics.

SUMMON

Synonyms : Call, invoke, send for.

Antonyms : Dismiss, postpone.

Synonyms

✦ The speaker of the Lok Sabha is responsible for *calling* the meetings of the house.

✦ Some members of UN General Assembly have *invoked* special emergency session to condemn the apartheid policies of the South African government.

✦ The principal has *sent for* applications by students for a few freeships.

Antonyms

- The president has *dismissed* quite a few officers on charges of corruption and negligence.
- The Lok Sabha has *postponed* consideration of an amendment bill for the setting up of a Lok Pal to overview the eradication of corrupt practices in administration.

SUPERFICIAL

Synonyms : External, shallow, slight, outward, outer.

Antonyms : Thorough, penetrating, deep, profound.

Synonyms

- *External* factors play their role in the fixation of prices within a country.
- This well is rather *shallow*; its water is, therefore, a bit saltish.
- Let us not *slight* this problem, as on its solution depends the future of the country.
- Don't go by her *outward* looks; she is the master of a golden heart and soul.
- The *outer* skin is called the epidermis.

Antonyms

- A *thorough* look at the picture shows that modern art is becoming more and more abstract.

- This book is a *penetrating* study of the problem of poverty.
- This well is very *deep*; its water is sweet, cold in summer and warm in winter.
- The leader of the opposition in a legislature is supposed to cast a *profound* influence on some of the policies of the government.

SURE

Synonyms : Certain, definite, doubtless, positive.

Antonyms : Doubtful, uncertain, unsure, wavering, improbable.

Synonyms

- I am *certain,* I can perform this job nicely.
- There is a *definite* move in the economy towards rapid progress.
- There is a *doubtless* flaw in the project at the engineering level.
- There are *positive* indications of corrupt practices in the implementation of the project.

Antonyms

- Your presumption seems *doubtful,* because I have made foolproof arrangements against corruption.
- However, I am *uncertain* about the technical flaws in the planning of the foundations.
- I am also *unsure* about the quality of engineers appointed for the project.

SURPRISING

Synonyms : Unexpected, marvellous, astonishing, amazing, startling, striking.

Antonyms : Everyday, ordinary, usual, normal, customary, habitual.

Synonyms

- ✦ This *unexpected* turn in the events has upset the original planning of the foreign inspired terrorists.
- ✦ The weather was *marvellous* in the morning but turned sultry towards evening.
- ✦ She ran 100m in an *astonishing* 10 seconds.
- ✦ It was an *amazing* performance for such a small girl.

Antonyms

- ✦ The distribution system in India provides sufficient stocks of *everyday* needs of essential commodities through fair price shops.
- ✦ There is a sea of difference in the standards of living between an *ordinary* citizen and the privileged classes.
- ✦ There is always the *usual* class struggle going on between the two categories of people.
- ✦ Only political leaders can discern this *normal* phenomenon of class struggle.
- ✦ It is *customary* for this college to hold its annual prize distribution function in August every year.
- ✦ I am a *habitual* drinker of tea and coffee.

SUPPRESS

Synonyms : Subdue, overpower, bridle, quash, restrain, quell, check, moderate, repress, impede.

Antonyms : Inflame, rouse, excite, provoke, agitate, kindle.

Synonyms

- ✦ The *subdued* feelings of the weaker sections can no longer be *suppressed*.
- ✦ If the weaker sections are not brought up in society with grace, they would *overpower* the privileged classes in due time.
- ✦ The horseman *bridled* his horse to give a pick up to his speed in the race.
- ✦ The understanding reached between the management and the workers has *quashed* the issue of bonus.
- ✦ The workers are being *restrained* with the help of the labour commissioner from going on total strike.
- ✦ I *quelled* my thirst by drinking beer.

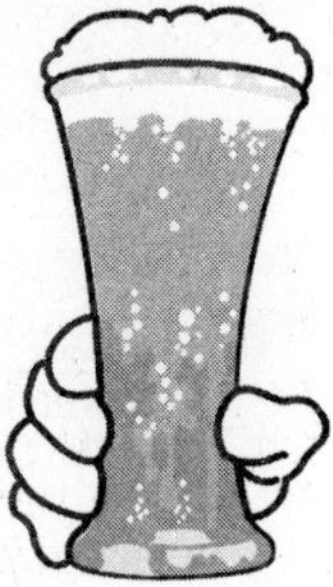

Antonyms

- ✦ The feelings of the labourers were *inflamed* by the union leaders.
- ✦ The teachers *roused* among the students enthusiasm for keen interest in studies and sports.

- ✦ Modern so-called blue films *excite* the young viewers to sex and violence.
- ✦ They *provoke* them to take to undesirable drugs.
- ✦ The labour union has decided to *agitate* for higher wages.

SUSPEND

Synonyms : Debar, stay, hinder, stop, withhold, interrupt, discontinue, fall, defer, delay.

Antonyms : Begin, keep up, urge on , protract, continue, expedite, prolong.

Synonyms

- ✦ Nelson has been *debarred* from reappearing in the examination on grounds of indiscipline.
- ✦ The tenant has obtained *stay* orders from the court against the landlord.
- ✦ Financial circumstances have *hindered* his plan of higher studies.
- ✦ I *stopped* my car at the crossing owing to the red signal.
- ✦ I am *withholding* my opinion on Kim until the result of her last examination.
- ✦ The phenomenon of occasional strike by teachers *interrupts* the coverage of the course.

Antonyms

- ✦ Sally has *begun* her studies in right earnest.
- ✦ *Keep up* the courage my boy, you will be able to fare better next time.

- I have *urged on* my younger brother to work harder.
- The accord was signed after *protracted* negotiations.
- I will *continue* playing badminton every evening to achieve my ambition of becoming Delhi champion.

SURRENDER

Synonyms : Leave, resign, yield, waive, let so, give up, give over, cede, alienate, abandon.

Antonyms : Withhold, hold, reserve, retain, detain.

Synonyms

- I have applied for 2 days' sick *leave* from today.
- I may *resign* from my present job to take more seriously the banking probationers' examination.
- The application of new machines in industry can *yield* a highly revolutionary impact on productivity.
- I would have obtained the contract for the construction of the building if the commissioner had the power to *waive* the condition of master's degree in architecture.

Antonyms

- The government should not *withhold* information about the smugglers from the newspapers.
- The government should *hold* sufficient *reserves* of foodgrains for emergency caused by drought or floods.

- The accused offered to *retain* the famous lawyer for advocating his case in the High Court.
- The police are *detaining* the culprits in their custody until the case is brought to the court.

SWELL

Synonyms : Distend, magnify, bulge, enhance, amplify, dilate.

Antonyms : Decrease, Shorten, contract, reduce, diminish, abridge, attenuate.

Synonyms

- My skin is *distending* from this boil.
- This looking glass *magnifies* one's face beyond proportion.
- Her pockets were *bulging* with sweets.
- His securing the top position in the IAS has *enhanced* his prestige.
- This transistor is meant to *amplify* the sound.

Antonyms

- The demand for record-players has greatly *decreased* with the arrival of cheap tape-recorders. 
- The habit of drinking *shortens* one's life.
- Metals *contract* in winter as they expand in summer.

- ✦ I have *reduced* the consumption of sugar in my diet as per the advice of my doctor.
- ✦ The demand for a product *diminishes* with increase in production.
- ✦ This book has been *abridged* in its new edition.

SYMPATHY

Synonyms : Kindness, love, fellow-feeling, compassion.

Antonyms : Pitilessness, cruelty, hard-heartedness, selfishness.

Synonyms

- ✦ We should show *kindness* to the poor.
- ✦ We should *love* our country and our countrymen as our brethren.
- ✦ *Fellow-feeling* for our countrymen does not mean hatred for outsiders or people of other countries.
- ✦ We should carry *compassion* for our subordinates, employees or the poor.

Antonyms

- ✦ In Germany and Italy, patriotism reached its negative climax through *pitilessness* on outsiders, non-citizens and Jews.
- ✦ Their rules were full of *cruelty* for the public.
- ✦ The Nazi Germans perpetrated untold *cruelty* on the Jews. Italians under Mussolini manifested *hard-heartedness* towards the French neighbours and African Negroes.

✦ Greed and *selfishness* are the norms of the day.

SYSTEMATIC

Synonyms : Methodical, regular, orderly.

Antonyms : Irregular, casual, fortuitous, unmethodical, occasional.

Synonyms

✦ Modern management implies *methodical* performance of business activities.

✦ I have arranged for a *regular* supply of kerosene oil in the village.

✦ Why don't you arrange for the holding of the proposed exhibition in an *orderly* fashion.

Antonyms

✦ If you become so *irregular* in attendance, in your new job, you may not be able to maintain it.

✦ Kim has taken *casual* leave for two days in order to look after his ailing mother.

✦ This source of income is *fortuitous* for him. It comes his way once a while.

✦ His functioning is so *unmethodical*. It can never bring lasting success.

✦ You should make *occasional* social calls to keep up your popularity.

TALENT

Synonyms : Ability, knack, genius, aptitude, skill.

Antonyms : Inefficiency, stupidity, unskilfulness, idleness.

Synonyms

- His *ability* to take control in emergencies of any type is admirable.
- He has a *knack* to make friends with enemies.
- He is a *genius* at the game of chess.
- Her *aptitude* in mathematics enables her to computerise every problem and solve it.
- His *skill* in designing textiles is unmatched.

Antonyms

- His all-round *inefficiency* will one day bring a crash in his business.
- His *stupidity* very often lets him down in emergencies.

- He has chosen a craft in which his *unskilfulness* makes little difference. He is a good salesman.

TACT

Synonyms : Finesse, discretion, skill, cleverness, consideration.

Antonyms : Discourtesy, frankness, roughness, bluntness, simplicity.

Synonyms

- Thomson deserves to be a diplomat; he has the needed *finesse*.
- *Discretion* is the first virtue of a great man.
- Conversational *skill* is by itself a rare qualification.
- It is only his *cleverness* that has saved him from death and destruction. Otherwise the world of the hoodlums he lives in would have wiped him out.
- My application for import licence is receiving due *consideration* in the commerce ministry.

Antonyms

- *Discourtesy* is the enemy of civilisation and culture.
- *Frankness* means being fearless and straight-forward not blunt and rude.
- He is a capable person, well-skilled in his job, but his *roughness* of a rustic devalues his achievements.
- His *bluntness* has made enemies of many friends.
- He was deprived of his legal right just because of his over *simplicity*.

TASTY

Synonyms : Appetising, luscious, delicious, palatable.

Antonyms : Nasty, sickening, nauseous, flavourless, insipid.

Synonyms

- For some people tea acts as an *appetising* agent, for others as the opposite.
- The hero looked at the *luscious* curves of the heroine and started dancing and singing.
- This is a *delicious* dish as a dessert.
- It is not only *tasty* but also *palatable.*

Antonyms

- I could never imagine such a popular restaurant will serve such a *nasty* dish.
- It is *sickening* to see a slow movie like this.
- Our kitchen is giving out a *nauseous* smell. What sort of meat is in the oven ?
- This dish is *flavourless.*
- The lecture of today's visiting professor was rather dull and *insipid.*

TEAR

Synonyms : Lanceolate, split, lacerate, rupture, sever.

Antonyms : Repair, patch, rectify, restore, mend.

Synonyms

- In the Middle Ages, the peers would play duels with swords and the women usually *lanceolated* the loser.
- Differences among brothers have led to the *split* of the land left by their father.
- The fight among the hoodlums of the neighbourhood led one to *lacerate* the other.
- The *rupture* among the partners has led to the division of the firm.
- They have *severed* business connections altogether.

Antonyms

- I have got my motor-bike duly *repaired*.
- The partners have *patched* up their differences and recombined their split firm.
- The losses suffered during the split are being gradually *rectified*.
- The profits of the old firm will get *restored* in due course.
- The partners have *mended* their ways by working out a new division of responsibilities.

TEASE

Synonyms : Irritate, chafe, provoke, vex, plague, torment, annoy.

Antonyms : Hush, compose, conciliate, appease, calm, soothe, mollify.

Synonyms

- The rash decisions of my partners in business are *irritating* me these days.
- Naturopathy recommends *chafing* of the paining part of the body.
- Jackson *provoked* his accomplice to speak out the truth.
- Continued unemployment has greatly *vexed* Hanry.
- Extremists and terrorists *plagued* some parts of the country last year with violence.
- The divorce move between their son and daughter-in-law is *tormenting* the old parents.
- The student *annoyed* his teacher by his impertinence.

Antonyms

- The corrupt officer tried to *hush* up the case of smuggling against the accused.
- I never lose my *composure* come what may.
- He has developed an attitude of *conciliation* with adverse circumstances.
- The management has adopted a policy of *appeasement* towards the agitating workers in order to keep production going.
- The manager *calmed* down the workers' representative by offering a 10% blanket increase in the salary of each worker.
- This *soothed* the resentment of the workers.

TEMPT

Synonyms : Seduce, decoy, entice, inveigle, contrive, wheedle.

Antonyms : Deter, disincline, discourage; restraint, dissuade.

Synonyms

- ✦ Some of the multinational concerns *seduce* talented young men by offering higher salaries.
- ✦ In this way they *decoy* even some of those selected by the UPSC for the IAS by offering fabulously attractive salaries and other facilities.
- ✦ The married woman, *enticed* by the charms of the strange young man, *inveigled* him into her home on a *contrived* pretext, when her husband had gone outstation.
- ✦ The young man first invited the young woman to a dinner and then *wheedled* her to his bachelor apartment.

Antonyms

- ✦ India's defence potential *deters* its enemies from taking an aggressive posture.
- ✦ India is herself *disinclined* to take any aggressive attitude unless she is first attacked.
- ✦ Rita found out the intentions of her colleague and decided to *discourage* his advances in future.
- ✦ Rita put her friend's overtures under *restraint.*

- She has not yet succeeded in *dissuading* her boy friend from meeting her.

TEMPORARY

Synonyms : Fleeting, evanescent, passing, ephemeral, momentary, transitory, transient.

Antonyms : Everlasting, immortal, invariable, permanent, persistent.

Synonyms

- A woman's youth is more *fleeting* than that of the man, as it is her body that gives shelter to the baby until his/her arrival in the world.
- The glory of a leader is *evanescent* unless he rises to the status of immortal.
- The economic depression comes to many non-socialist countries as a *passing* phase.
- Some of the insects have an *ephemeral* life, just a few moments or at the maximum, a few hours.

Antonyms

- Mrs. Gandhi has left an *everlasting* impact on India's history for many of her achievements.
- A few names in every country's history become *immortal* for their everlasting contribution to human thought.
- Certain scientific concepts are regarded as permanent and *invariable* as they will continue to be applied for the millenium.
- Please mention your *permanent* address on the form.

TENDENCY

Synonyms : Prone, trend, bias, leaning, proclivity, propensity.

Antonyms : Aversion, distaste, dislike, disinclination, antipathy, detestation.

Synonyms

- Revolutions in some countries are *prone* to cast their influence on the social, economic and scientific progress of others.
- A persistent *trend* towards materialisation of societies is discernible in the world today.
- The socialist *bias* which started with the Bolshevik Revolution in 1917 has continued to persist.
- The whole world is now *leaning* towards the concept of the welfare state.
- Modem *proclivities* of the people revolve round getting at more and more money for maximum comforts in life.

Antonyms

- I have an *aversion* for pessimists.
- He looked around the filthy room in *distaste.*
- I *dislike* being goaded into doing things; I like to be on my own.
- I can appreciate your *disinclination* to a life marked by acute materialism.
- I have an *antipathy* for pets, specially because they become a problem when they are sick.

✦ I *detest* a person who is given to mood swings.

TERSE

Synonyms : Neat, short, succinct, laconic, compact, summary, sententious, condensed.

Antonyms : Diffuse, verbose, lengthy, wordy.

Synonyms

✦ Ah! it is a *neat* and tidy typing, thanks!

✦ I telephoned Marya few minutes ago. It was a lively *short* conversation I will always remember.

✦ His questions were to the point and replies *succinct*.

✦ This description of the happenings at the airport is too *laconic*. Will you mind giving more details ?

✦ This is a *compact*, handy dictionary of synonyms and antonyms duly illustrated with the usage of words.

✦ It helps in the making a *summary* of long passages by expanding your vocabulary.

✦ The ideas contained in this book are *sententious* and *condensed*.

Antonyms

✦ This story is a *diffused* version of a little incident. It teaches the art of expanding ideas and expressions.

✦ Huxley's book is *verbose* yet interesting.

✦ Some of Thomas Hardy's stories are unnecessarily *lengthy*.

✦ It is desirable to avoid *wordy* letters. Brevity in correspondence pays.

THEORY

Synonyms : Belief, postulate, assumption, speculation, doctrine, conjecture, hypothesis, supposition.

Antonyms : Practical, realistic, actuality, happening.

Synonyms

✦ *Belief* in superstitions is still prevalent in many societies in the world.

✦ The *postulate* on which this conclusion is based has little foundation.

✦ Your *assumption* that he passes this way every Sunday morning may or may not prove true.

✦ The upwards swing in share prices is based on *speculation* trends let loose by the Stock Exchange.

✦ The *doctrine* of divine right of kings does not hold valid in this age of democracy.

Antonyms

✦ *Practical* considerations carry more weight than theoretical.

✦ Modern logic as applied to computers is based on *realistic* facts and figures of statisticians.

- ✦ The building looked as impressive in *actuality* as it did in photographs.
- ✦ The *happenings* of day-to-day life provide the base for futuristic literature.

THIN

Synonyms : Diluted, meagre, flimsy, scanty, sparse, attenuated.

Antonyms : Strong, sturdy, bountiful, wholesome.

Synonyms

- ✦ The sad realities of the poor are much more tragic than what reaches us through *diluted* versions of the news media.
- ✦ His servant is paid too *meagre* a salary for the enormous manual work he does for the company.
- ✦ The boss got rid of his impertinent subordinate on a *flimsy* charge.
- ✦ This part of India has very *scanty* rainfall.

Antonyms

- ✦ This tractor is really *strong* and solid for the heavy work it is supposed to do.
- ✦ Joe is quite *sturdy* to undertake the strenuous manual work if we pay him adequately.
- ✦ This year's kharif crop is *bountiful*, thanks to the high yielding varieties programme of the Agricultural Institute.
- ✦ This hotel serves a *wholesome* meal for its charges.

THOUGHTFUL

Synonyms : Attentive, circumspect, heedful, provident, prudent, careful, considerate, mindful.

Antonyms : Carefree, gay, remiss, reckless, negligent, neglectful, giddy.

Synonyms

- Jonathan listens to his class lectures *attentively.*
- A CIO inspector has to be extremely *circumspect* in these days of criminal proclivities of respected class of businessmen and the bureaucrats.
- An entrepreneur of consumer products has to be *heedful* of the health of the consumers.
- Housewives have been very *provident* in keeping their budgets trim.
- They have to be *prudent* in the choice of goods for consumption by the family.
- My beard is very hard. I have to be *careful* with my razor.
- Modern family life expects the husband to be *considerate* of his wife's feelings and vice versa.

Antonyms

- Sam is a *carefree* boy. He studies hard when required and then plays freely in the playground.

- He does not entertain any worries and is always *gay* and humorous in company.
- Tony, on the other hand, is often *remiss* in both studies and games.
- Mr. Pillay is a *reckless* businessman. He gambles higher stakes for his greed of money, but very often suffers losses.
- Robin is *negligent* of his games. Hence he often falls sick.
- He is *neglectful* of his bodily health.
- Alcoholic drinks make me *giddy* very soon.

TIMELY

Synonyms : Prompt, early, seasonable, opportune.

Antonyms : Tardy, unseasonable, late, inopportune.

Synonyms

- Our management deals with every enquiry *promptly*.
- I get up *early* in the morning to be in time for work.
- John Berkley is a *seasoned* politician.
- He makes use of every *opportune* moment.

Antonyms

- Rajendra's firm has a *tardy* way of functioning.
- This quality of teak seems fit for fuel to me. It looks *unseasonable* for furniture.

- ✦ Sunny reaches *late* for his first lecture every morning.
- ✦ The time is yet *inoppotune* for the inauguration of the new library in our college.

TIMID

Synonyms : Bashful, diffident, shy, chicken-hearted, timorous, submissive.

Antonyms : Audacious, daring, brave, confident, poised.

Synonyms

- ✦ He is too *bashful* to aspire to be a political leader.
- ✦ He is *diffident* of conversing with great men and to engage their attention.
- ✦ She is too *shy* to fall in love at first sight.
- ✦ He is *chicken-hearted*; not fit to face the enemy with courage.
- ✦ His *timorous* behaviour at the meeting with his girl friend's father proved disastrous for his love.
- ✦ He is too *submissive* to be a businessman.

Antonyms

- ✦ The *audacious* young man found a way with his cherished girlfriend and later with her father.
- ✦ His *daring* attitude always helps him pull through nicely.

✦ Joseph is a *brave* young man. He can take to any adventurist career.

✦ He is *confident* of what he wants and how he will have it.

✦ He remains *poised* in difficult circumstances.

TIRED

Synonyms : Exhausted, fatigued, weary, worn-out.

Antonyms : Strengthened, invigorated, refreshed, rested, relaxed.

Synonyms

✦ Poverty has *exhausted* him at the young age.

✦ The long journey has *fatigued* my nerves.

✦ His job involves a combination of physical and mental work throughout the day. Hence he wears a *weary* look.

✦ His *worn-out* suit gave him away in the eyes of his would be in-laws.

Antonyms

✦ A balanced diet and exercise *strengthens* my body and soul.

✦ The new job has *invigorated* her all-round existence.

✦ I feel quite *refreshed* by a cup of coffee after every few hours.

- These two months after illness have *rested* my tired limbs.
- My work *relaxes* me instead of tiring, as it is interesting and to my liking.

TOLERATION

Synonyms : Tolerance, temperance, endurance, laxity, forgiveness, clemency, moderation.

Antonyms : Irritation, heating up, wearing off, rigidity, overbearance, dogmatism, fanaticism.

Synonyms

- The *tolerance* capacity of this capacitor will match this radio.
- The *temperance* of this steel suits the cooking range of this pressure cooker.
- The *endurance* of this valve matches 7 ohm needed for this amplifier.
- No *laxity* will be allowed to political parties indulging in violence in this region.
- The criminals taking to violence will not be *forgiven* but punished under law.
- *Clemency* will not be shown to terrorists.
- The government expects all political parties to practice *moderation* in their election campaigns.

Antonyms

- Over-medication during my last illness has caused me *irritation*.

- The elections have *heated* up the political atmosphere in the state.
- The effect of the ennobling speeches of the prime minister is *wearing off.*
- There is *rigidity* in iron-based alloys.
- The democratic wind is manifesting some *over-bearance* in India's political atmosphere.
- The socialists have loosened their old *dogmatism* and fanaticism.

TOPICAL

Synonyms : Indicative, symbolical, regular, illustrative, normal.

Antonyms : Abnormal, singular, divergent, peculiar.

Synonyms

- A mixed economy is a system which is *indicative* of the existence of the public and private sectors side by side.
- It is a universal phenomenon *symbolical* of the co-existence of the rich and the poor.
- There is a *regular* competition among the private entrepreneurs on the one side and a regulated coordination between the public and private sectors on the other.
- They system is *illustrative* of the logical pattern that runs the economy of all (including socialist) countries today.
- It provides *normal* thinking to humans in their mutual relationships in economic life.

Antonyms

- In the Middle Ages, the relationship among humans was *abnormal.* There were feudals and serfs, aristocrats and the common.
- There was emphasis on the *singular* interest of the feudals, the kings and the nobles.
- The philosophers had *divergent* views on how humanity should organise itself.
- Some of the *peculiar* philosophies held sway. The philosophy of divine right of kings and subdivine right of the nobles were started as destined by God!

TORTURE

Synonyms : Anguish, pain, agony, torment, distress, persecute.

Antonyms : Allay, soothe, relief, comfort, palliate, ease, deaden, lessen.

Synonyms

- There is *anguish* in world circles over the lack of concrete agreement among superpowers on disarmament. 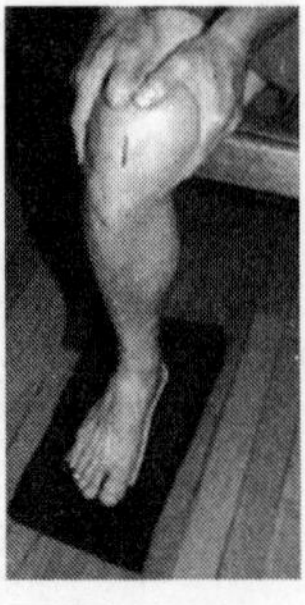
- I have developed a severe *pain* in my legs since the last accident.
- An atmosphere of *agony* prevailed in the family over the untimely death of a member.

- It has caused particular *torment* in the heart of the old mother.
- I am *distressed* over my failure in the IAS examination.
- The government of Iran has *persecuted* a number of Shias in the country.

Antonyms

- She did her best to *allay* his fears but failed.
- Government assistance to the poorest of the poor in tribal areas has *soothed* the feelings of the tribal communities.
- The government is providing *relief* to the drought-hit farmers in Bihar.
- Modern scientific inventions have given quite a number of *comforts* to the people of the world.
- The feelings of the poor can be *palliated* by floating new schemes for their upliftment.
- I felt at *ease* on knowing the favourable result of my interview for a job in the bank.

TRAGEDY

Synonyms : Misfortune, disaster, affliction, calamity, catastrophe, adversity.

Antonyms : Farce, comedy, humour, drama.

Synonyms

- It was a great *misfortune* for India to lose Mrs. Indira Gandhi on October 31, 1984.
- It was treated by the people as a national *disaster*.

✦ The country was *afflicted* by a wave of violence for a few days.

✦ It seemed some great *calamity* had befallen the country.

✦ The leader's assassination proved to be a great *catastrophe*.

Antonyms

✦ The dialogue between India and Pakistan for the resumption of trade proved to be a *farce*.

✦ This feature film depicts a *comedy* of errors.

✦ It is marked by *humour* and *dramatic* overtones.

TRANSPARENT

Synonyms : Clear, lucid, limpid, crystalline.

Antonyms : Foggy, obscure, vague.

Synonyms

✦ This picture depicts its theme in a *clear* way.

✦ This piece of literature has a *lucid* style of narration.

✦ The girl's *limpid* eyes bewitched the on lookers.

✦ Some springs have water of *crystalline* purity.

Antonyms

✦ As the weather is *foggy* this morning, it is better to avoid driving the scooter.

- This essay is very *obscure*. It does not bring out the subject matter clearly.
- The ideas expressed are *vague* and do not show any logical sequence.

TRANSIENT

Synonyms : Brief, fleeting, fugitive, short, flying, transitory, momentary, passing, evanescent, temporary.

Antonyms : Long-lasting, detailed; permanent, persistent.

Synonyms

- His stay in our college hostel was very *brief* but memorable.
- The *fleeting* moments spent with him are fresh in our memory.
- Mr. Singh stayed with us in 1942 as a *fugitive* from law — a freedom fighter during the Quit India Movement.
- He joined the army on a *short* commission.
- The aeroplane went *flying* past the post.

Antonyms

- Rita was looking for a *long-lasting* relationship but Sohan was not interested.
- *Detailed* instructions ensured that he reached the venue in time.
- They are now living together on a *permanent* basis.

TREACHEROUS

Synonyms : Disloyal, unfaithful, unreliable, untrustworthy, perfidious.

Antonyms : Faithful, loyal, trusted, devoted, reliable, trustworthy.

Synonyms

- Citizens who prove *disloyal* to their country are prone to punishment under law.
- It is immoral to be *unfaithful* to a friend.
- This brand of the motorbike part is *unreliable* for durability and accuracy.
- Some of the employees in my firm are *untrustworthy.*
- Some of the terrorists have been arrested by the government for their *perfidious* activities.

Antonyms

- I am a *faithful* citizen of India.
- I am a *loyal* devotee of the Congress ideology.
- He is one of the *trusted* employees of this institution.
- I am *devoted* to the cause of education.
- He is a *reliable* member of the managing committee of this college.
- Mr. Robinson is a *trustworthy* businessman, always seeking and rendering honest dealings.

TREMBLE

Synonyms : Vibrate, shudder, oscillate, quiver.

Antonyms : Stiffen, petrify, steady.

Synonyms

- Everytime time a train went past, the windows *vibrated.*
- I *shudder* at the thought of losing my beloved.
- The pendulum of the clock *oscillates* consistently.
- The earth *quivers* whenever there is an earthquake.

Antonyms

- I *stiffened* when the policemen gave a whistle seeing my riding double on a bicycle with my friend.
- The suddenness of accident on the opposite pavement *petrified* me with horror.
- I *steadied* my cycle to witness the tragic scene.

TRICK

Synonyms : Wile, skill, ruse, gull, imposture, cunning.

Antonyms : Innocence, frankness, guilelessness, truth, sincerity.

Synonyms

- The *wiles* of the monkey greatly amused the onlookers.
- This mechanic has the *skill* of rectifying a blocked engine.
- The *ruse* of the horse-rider in the circus amused the children.

- The salesman *gulled* us into buying a carton of imitation soap at exhoribitant price.
- In fact it was his *imposture* holding the forged card of a salesman of a reputed company.

Antonyms

- The *innocence* of the visitor impressed us into giving him a good hearing.
- *Frankness* is a virtue of the bold.
- *Guileless* persons never beguile anybody. They are frank and fair.
- *Truth* and *sincerity* are the most welcome traits of good humans.

TRUST

Synonyms : Reliance, confidence, keeping credit, office, duty, expectation, hope, credence, belief.

Antonyms : Distrust, faithlessness, breaking of pledge, deception.

Synonyms

- My *reliance* on the parents for further studies is not in keeping with my values in life.
- I have *confidence* in my own ability to earn and learn at the same time.
- My parents *keep* the *credit* for affording my early education.
- To build an *office* you have to work hard.
- Alongwith rights a citizen also has to perform certain *duties* towards the country.

Antonyms

- There is no question of *distrust* in my parents but it is one of self-respect and self-determination.
- I am not accusing myself of *faithlessness* for my parents.
- I am simply trying to fulfil my own ambition of becoming self-reliant. I am not causing any *deception* to myself or *breaking any pledge* to others.

TRY

Synonyms : Strive, endeavour, attempt.

Antonyms : Leave, drop, quit.

Synonyms

- We must *strive* to do the best in life — to ourselves and to others as far as possible.
- We must *endeavour* to serve the motherland to the best of our ability.
- We must *attempt* to develop maximum capability to do so.

Antonyms

- We must *leave* no stone unturned to achieve greatness.
- We must *drop* the selfish elements from our existence in order to be useful to others.
- I will *quit* the present job if it does not help to fulfil my ambition of serving well my motherland.

TYRANNY

Synonyms : Totalitarianism, autocracy, oppression, despotism, rigour, harshness.

Antonyms : Pity, love, compassion, sympathy, softness.

Synonyms

- ✦ *Totalitarianism* is a political concept which thrived during first part of the 20th century up to Second World War in Germany and Italy.

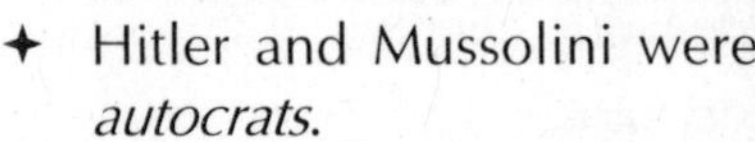

- ✦ Hitler and Mussolini were *autocrats*.
- ✦ Hitler and Mussolini let loose *oppression* of the people and made them to obey the government in their wrongful activities.
- ✦ They were *despots* of the harshest variety.
- ✦ They ruled with all the *rigour* and *harshness* at their command.

Antonyms

- ✦ Opposite to the tyranny of the dictators is the government of the democracies in which *pity* and *love* are the key policies for the people at large.
- ✦ The rich should have a *compassion* for the poor.
- ✦ In a country where the rich show sincere *sympathy* for the poor, the government adopts a policy of *softness* for the rich.

UGLY

Synonyms : Homely, plain, unattractive, unsightly.

Antonyms : Attractive, beautiful, charming.

Synonyms

- Rita is healthy but a *homely* type of beauty.
- She has *plain* features, not so beautiful.
- Ameeta is rather *unattractive*. She has odd features, no good figure, emaciated cheeks.
- Some people call her *unsightly*; she repels charming boys.

Antonyms

- Sophia is a very *attractive* young lady.
- She has a *beautiful* face, knows manners, has sharp features, a stub nose, a resounding voice.
- She can be called a real *charming* person, with all the virtues of an ideal lady.

UNANIMITY

Synonyms : Harmony, unison, agreement, accord, concord.

Antonyms : Disagreement, contention, difference, variance, disharmony.

Synonyms

- ✦ There is scope for greater *harmony* among the people of India — businessmen, servicemen, employees of firms, workers of factories, farmers, landlords and others.
- ✦ The choir sang the tune in *unison.*
- ✦ Rajiv Gandhi had been able to achieve quite a few *agreements* with dissidents.
- ✦ The *accord* in Assam solved the six-year old dispute over foreigners who migrate to the state from Bangladesh.
- ✦ It has brought *concord* among the people of the state.

Antonyms

- ✦ Recent accords have considerably reduced areas of *disagreement* on vital issues of autonomy and reconciliation of economic interests of different regions in the country.
- ✦ Numerous bones of *contention* have been removed by peaceful negotiation.
- ✦ *Differences* among political groups have been removed by logical discussion.

- Points of *variance* among politicians have been clarified to mutual satisfaction.
- Causes of *disharmony* among groups have been successfully removed.

UNCERTAIN

Synonyms : Fluctuating, inconstant, fitful, irregular, unreliable, changeable, precarious.

Antonyms : Reliable, stable, trustworthy, unchangeable, regular, steady, permanent.

Synonyms

- The world economic situation keeps *fluctuating* from one period to another.
- The circumstances of the world are generally *inconstant*.
- The economies of different countries are often *fitful*, depending on various national and international factors.
- The curves of prosperity and depression in a free economy are always *irregular* owing to ups and downs in trade and commerce.
- The factors of production and consumption are *unreliable* in an unplanned economy.

Antonyms

- There is need to introduce a *reliable* system for the working of demand and supply conditions in a regulated manner.

- Such a system provides for *stable* mechanisms in different sectors of an economy.
- A controlled economy, however, succeeds only if the country has at its disposal a *trustworthy* team of efficient economists.

UNCONCERNED

Synonyms : Nonchalant, apathetic, cool, disinterested, indifferent.

Antonyms : Solicitous, interested, concerned, anxious.

Synonyms

- He is a person of such a cool mind, he remains *nonchalant* under the most provoking circumstances.
- He has an *apathetic* nature.
- He has a *cool* temperament, hence he can take unbiased and impartial decisions like he does.
- A judge has to take a *disinterested* view and measure the facts of both sides in terms of law.
- In modern societies, judges have to interpret the law but they need not remain *indifferent* to the basic tenets of the constitution whenever a point comes up for their discretion.

Antonyms

- The *solicitous* enquiries paid a personal visit to the scene of rail accident to know the fate of the victims.

- *Interested* parties responded to the advertisement by the Central Housing Board for allotment of new flats in the major cities in the country.
- I felt deep *concern* over the death of such a prominent leader.
- I was *anxious* to know the cause of his death.

UNCONQUERABLE

Synonyms : Insuperable, invincible, indomitable, insurmountable

Antonyms : Weak, powerless, feeble, conquerable.

Synonyms

- Mount Everest remained *insuperable* until 1953 when it was first conquered by Edmund Hillary and sherpa Tensing.
- Man has reached the moon but other planets remain *invincible*. 
- Indian army has shown *indomitable* courage during all the wars with Pakistan.
- The problems created by the new management are becoming *insurmountable* day by day.

Antonyms

- Recent illness has left him too *weak*.
- Man is still *powerless* before the vagaries of nature.

- The power of man is *feeble* compared to that of nature despite recent achievements in science.
- The common diseases that perpetrated death on men have been conquered or made *conquerable.*

UNDERTAKING

Synonyms : Contract, endeavour, trade, enterprise, engagement, venture, promise.

Antonyms : Irresponsibility, refusal, truancy, escapade, avoidance.

Synonyms

- M/s. A B & Co. have secured the *contract* for the construction of roads in this city.
- They have *endeavoured* to provide good services in the past in the neighbouring villages.
- They have been in the *trade* for over two decades and their financial standing and technical know-how are quite sound.
- They are an old *enterprise* with a good record and a promising future.
- They have a sister concern *engaged* in the manufacture of road-making equipment.
- I wish them success in their new *venture.*

Antonyms

- Sense of *irresponsibility* can make a fool of even an intelligent businessman.
- Your *refusal* to entertain your boss is going to cost you your job.

- Your *truancy* without information to the boss is likely to spoil your impression.
- You cannot always find *escapade* as a protection from routine.
- *Avoidance* of duty is a crime — social and religious.

UNFAIR

Synonyms : Unjust, inequitable, partial, dishonest, wrongful.

Antonyms : Fair, just, honest, unprejudiced, neutral, impartial, equitable.

Synonyms

- The social order in India is and will remain *unjust* unless there are legally fixed upper and lower limits on incomes of citizens.
- The social order will remain *inequitable* so long as an upper limit on the property owned by an individual is not fixed.
- The fixation of minimum wages is only a *partial* step towards the goal of social equality.
- The country has a large number of *dishonest* officials in the government.
- There are still many *wrongful* laws coming down from the pre-independence days.

Antonyms

- *Fair* deal must be meted out to the poor.
- The administration should be *just* and *honest* in its objectives.
- We must take *unprejudiced* view of things in our decisions.
- The judges must be *neutral* and *impartial* in their judgements, not ignoring the spirit of the constitution.
- The constitution needs to be amended to provide for more *equitable* social order.

UNITE

Synonyms : Combine, coalesce, blend, join, knit, merge.

Antonyms : Scatter, disjoin, unconnect.

Synonyms

- It is now a fashion for the workers to *combine* into unions and the businessmen into chambers of industry and commerce.
- A number of political parties have *coalesced* to form a united opposition in the parliament.
- The mixture is a new formula — a *blend* of chemicals and plants.
- Let us *join* our forces *knit* into a common organisation with common objectives.
- The two firms should *merge* immediately to save themselves from unhealthy competition.

Antonyms

- The rays tend to *scatter* on all sides as the distance from the source of light increases.
- *Disjoin* these wires and then test their respective electrical strength.
- The two *unconnected* elements have a different capacity from those duly connected.

UNIVERSAL

Synonyms : All-embracing, international, complete, whole, general, comprehensive, entire.

Antonyms : Parochial, sectarian, partisan, sectional, factional.

Synonyms

- God is almighty and *all-embracing.*
- Educational institutions of higher level should provide for the teaching of *international* citizenship.
- Any atomic war between the US and USSR can cause *complete* annihilation of mankind.
- It will put the *whole* world in a *general* blackhole.
- Our college provides *comprehensive* training in business management.

Antonyms

- The growth of *parochial* tendencies in the nation should be checked from the very beginning.
- *Sectarian* politics in some states is raising its ugly head.

- A judge is never expected to take a *partisan* view in his judgements.
- *Sectional* heads of this department are supposed to supervise their sections as effectively as possible.
- This is an all-country party. There is no place for discussion of *factional* problems.

UNUSUAL

Synonyms : Extraordinary, remarkable, peculiar, uncommon, exceptional, singular, rare.

Antonyms : Usual, common, commonplace, hackneyed, habitual.

Synonyms

- This is an *extraordinary* temple. There are many carved walls and ceilings.
- He is a *remarkable* personality. He becomes the centre of conversation whereever he goes.
- His *peculiar* stories enchant everyone.
- He has an *uncommon* gait which attracts every onlooker.
- Dr. Laren is an *exceptional* medical man. There is no disease he cannot cure.
- His medical excellence is *singularly rare.*

Antonyms

- The *usual* procedure as laid down in the election rules will be followed in the elections of the states.

- ✦ The *common* man is regarded as a VIP during elections.
- ✦ There is nothing *commonplace* about Ramesh who has sophisticated tastes in every walk of life.
- ✦ The textile mills in India follow the *hackneyed* technology. Hence some of them do not flourish the way they should.
- ✦ I am a *habitual* coffee drinker.

UPHOLD

Synonyms : Champion, back, support, maintain, defend.

Antonyms : Betray, drop, destroy.

Synonyms

- ✦ India has always *championed* the cause of the poor countries at all international forums.
- ✦ The Congress Party sponsors and *backs* such candidates in elections who stand for the upliftment of the poor.
- ✦ I *supported* the view of my colleague at the meeting of the managing committee.
- ✦ The Supreme Court *maintained* the judgement of the High Court on the issue of property rights of individuals in the country.
- ✦ The prime minister claims India can *defend* itself adequately against any foreign attack.

Antonyms

- ✦ Never *betray* your friend for a temporary benefit.
- ✦ *Drop* bad objectives in your day-to-day life.

✦ It is good to *destroy* evil thoughts from your mind.

UPSET

Synonyms : Disturb, disconcert, disrupt.

Antonyms : Soothe, calm, relieve, relax.

Synonyms

✦ My present arrangements are too good to be *disturbed*.

✦ The withdrawal of your support can *disconcert* all your political friends.

✦ The earthquake *disrupted* the life of the city for decades.

Antonyms

✦ Indian classical music greatly *soothes* my tired nerves.

✦ The daily prayer every morning helps to *calm* our day-to-day life.

✦ The new drug *relieved* me of my pain.

✦ A brief nap in the afternoon *relaxes* me for hours.

URGENT

Synonyms : Critical, pressing, important, insistent, imperative.

Antonyms : Minor, inconsiderable, unimportant, trifling, petty, insignificant, trivial.

Synonyms

✦ His sickness has reached a *critical* stage and needs best possible medical attention.

- ✦ His *pressing* need is finance which he cannot raise.
- ✦ It is *important* for all of us to cooperate with the government in constructive programmes of development.
- ✦ The need of funds to initiate more public undertakings is *insistent* and *imperative.*

Antonyms

- ✦ I have no spare time to attend to *minor* problems.
- ✦ I am too busy to deal with matters of *inconsiderable* importance.
- ✦ This matter is too *unimportant* and *trifling* to receive my attention.
- ✦ The clerk should keep the record of *petty* cash.

USUAL

Synonyms : Common, accustomed, regular, customary, ordinary.

Antonyms : Occasional, specific, unusual, unparalleled.

Synonyms

- ✦ TV has become an object of *common* use by the middle classes in India.
- ✦ People have become *accustomed* to some kind of recreation after their day's work.
- ✦ He has *regular* habits of study and exercise.
- ✦ It is *customary* to go for the morning walk among the old people.

- Smith is no *ordinary* boy as he always tops in his class.

Antonyms

- I do pay an *occasional* visit to relatives living in my city.
- There is no *specific* purpose for which I have come to you. I was just passing by and thought to wish you good health.
- My visit is *unusual* yet I hope I am not unwelcome.
- This leader is *unparalleled* for his certain virtues — literature and sports.

UTILITY

Synonyms : Service, use, advantage, profit, benefit, policy, avail, usefulness, serviceableness.

Antonyms : Disadvantageous, worthless, useless.

Synonyms

- It is the responsibility of the local government to provide utility *services* like drinking water, sanitation, health centres and electric supply.
- These services are of immense *use* to the public.
- It is through these that humans enjoy the *advantages* of modern science.
- These services help businessmen run businesses to make *profit,* although these are provided on the principle of no-profit no-loss.

- In this way organised societies enjoy the *benefits* of civilisation.

Antonyms

- My high caste has proved *disadvantageous* to me because the job I was to get has been reserved for a scheduled caste.
- Very soon, solar energy will be so well developed it may make petroleum *worthless*.
- This medicine is entirely *useless* as a painkiller.

VACANT

Synonyms : Unoccupied, waste, vacuous, unfilled, empty, unemployed, untenanted, leisure, blank, devoid.

Antonyms : Occupied, jammed, replete, packed, brimming, filled, full, brimmed, brimful, busy, crammed, gorged.

Synonyms

- ✦ This palatial house has remained *unoccupied* for six months.
- ✦ It means a national *waste* of Rs. 30,000, even if you rate it at Rs. 5000 a month.
- ✦ He is so made he can keep his expression *vacuous* under any circumstances.
- ✦ This tank has remained *unfilled* for lack of sufficient pressure.
- ✦ *Empty* vessels make lots of noise.
- ✦ A huge percentage of the youth are still *unemployed.*

Antonyms

- I may not be able to attend today's meeting as I am fully *occupied* in the afternoon.
- A small accident *jammed* the whole stream of traffic in Connaught Place.
- The theatre was *fully* packed.
- After the result Ryan was *brimming* with confidence.

VAGUE

Synonyms : Haze, dim, obscure, indistinct, indefinite.

Antonyms : Clear, defined, plain, sensible.

Synonyms

- His speeches have put a *haze* on the political objectives of the party. .
- There are *dim* prospects of his success at the polls.
- This leader has *obscured* the basic economic issues on which controversies have raged in recent decades.
- His views on putting limitations on individual property have remained *indistinct*.
- The workers of the factory have gone on strike for an *indefinite* period.

Antonyms

- The prime minister has given a *clear* indication of his future policies.
- He has *defined* precisely the aims of his administration.

- He has had negotiations with opposition leaders in *plain* and *sensible* words.

VALID

Synonyms : Binding, defensible, powerful, efficacious, cogent, logical.

Antonyms : Invalid, unconvincing, unsound, lame, feeble, weak, illogical.

Synonyms

- An agreement usually has clauses *binding* the parties signing it.
- An agreement arrived at between any two or more parties within the framework of law of the country is *defensible* in a court of law if and when violated by any of the parties.
- Trade and labour unions have become *powerful* institutions in modern societies.
- They are *efficacious* in bringing about harmony among managements and their workers at different levels.
- They provide *cogent* parameters to trade and industry.

Antonyms

- The Supreme Court has the power to declare as *invalid* any law passed by a legislative body outside the framework of the constitution.
- The stand taken by the opposition on this controversial issue is *unconvincing.*
- The project seems *unsound* in its practicability.

- Sam made a *lame* excuse for absenting himself from the class.

VARIOUS

Synonyms : Different, multitudinous, numerous, variegated, sundry, manifold, many, several, multiform.

Antonyms : Identical, few, exceptional.

Synonyms

- There are *different* solutions to this problem; each solution has *multitudinous* dimensions.
- Our country is facing *numerous* problems in political and economic spheres.
- Mr. Henry is a *variegated* personality. He is a writer, speaker, manager, singer, actor and sportsman combined into one.
- They have to take into account the *sundry* expenses.
- Once invested your money is bound to increase *manifold*.

Antonyms

- These twins have such an *identical* face it becomes difficult to identify them from their looks.
- There are only a *few* instances of such twins in the world.
- It is one of the *exceptional* cases in human history.

VEHEMENT

Synonyms : Eager, earnest, passionate.

Antonyms : Feeble, mild, affected.

Synonyms

- I am *eager* to join your club but you must accept my subscription in instalments.
- I *earnestly* request you to accept my application for membership of the club.
- I am *passionately* in love with the billiards game practiced in your club.

Antonyms

- My desire to join your club is *feeble*.
- His application is, therefore, framed in *mild* language.
- Your club has now a reputation which is adversely *affected* by the haughty behaviour of the richer members.

VICTORY

Synonyms : Triumph, supremacy, success, achievement, conquest, mastery.

Antonyms : Defeat, subservience, failure, frustration, descent, fall.

Synonyms

- The Punjab accord implies the *triumph* of forces of national integrity and communal harmony.
- It proves *supremacy* of good over evil.

- It means *success* of the efforts of sane thinking people and failure of those who stood for secession and breakup of the country.
- It is a commendable *achievement.*
- The *conquest* of Mount Everest by Edmund Hillary and Tensing Norgey shows their *mastery* of the art and science of mountaineering.

Antonyms

- Brave people do not accept *defeat* come what may.
- The weak are *subservient* to the brave.
- They accept *failure* easily as their power of resistance is low.
- A few failures cause *frustration* in a man by gradual degrees of descent.

VIOLATION

Synonyms : Trespass, infraction, infringement, transgression.

Antonyms : Compliance, adherence, concurrence, observance, acquiescence.

Synonyms

- Since this is a military area and our going through this road may mean *trespass,* we will have to take the longer route to reach our destination.
- *Infraction* of law brings one due punishment.
- *Infringement* of rights of others has its adverse impact on one's own rights.
- There is a distribution of functions among different departments of administration so that there is no *transgression* or overlapping of responsibilities.

Antonyms

- *Compliance* of our duties is as important as the enjoyment of our rights.
- As citizens we are expected to *adhere* to the obligation laid down in the constitution of our country.
- To pass a law the Lok Sabha must obtain the *concurrence* of the Rajya Sabha and vice versa.

VOID

Synonyms : Abolish, negate, nullify, cancel, revoke, repeal.

Antonyms : Establish, endorse, legalise, permit, renew, uphold, validate.

Synonyms

- The system of 'Sati' was *abolished* in the 19th century with the efforts of Raja Ram Mohan Roy.
- The role of money in elections more or less *negates* the functioning of democracy in India.
- Corruption in bureaucracy also *nullifies* some of the good points of democracy as it fails to *cancel* the creation of black money by businessmen.
- You will have to submit an application to the authority to *revoke* your licence.

Antonyms

- The public sector was first *established* on an ambitious scale in the second plan.
- The president has *endorsed* the anti-defection bill and it has since become law.

- ✦ Many of the new economic reforms are designed to *legalise* black money by the more clever of the income tax evaders.
- ✦ I have obtained an all-India *permit* for my new deluxe tourist bus.
- ✦ I have *renewed* the licence for my old car.

VOLUNTARY

Synonyms : Gratuitous, discretional, willing, unconstrained, optional.

Antonyms : Enforced, imperative, compulsory.

Synonyms

- ✦ Some of the businessmen make *gratuitous* contributions to memorial hospitals to divert some of their black money.
- ✦ In some cases the judges have to make *discretional* judgements with a view to interpret the law in the light of each case involved.
- ✦ I am *willing* to join the picnic party provided you also come.
- ✦ In a free country you can take up *unconstrained* activities without fear of infringement of law.
- ✦ The third question of the exercise is *optional*.

Antonyms

- ✦ The membership of the party is *enforced* on all government servants in communist states.

- It is *imperative* that the government of India took up the enforcement of land reforms more vigorously.
- Education upto the 8th grade has been made *compulsory* in India.

VULGAR

Synonyms : Coarse, crude, gross, obscene.

Antonyms : Exquisite, polite, refined, polished.

Synonyms

- This is very *coarse* khadi. I want a softer one.
- His *crude* behaviour compelled me to slap him on the face.
- My *gross* income exceeds the net income by over 25%.
- This film has a few *obscene* shots.

Antonyms

- This is an *exquisite* design suiting my taste.
- He is a *polite* salesman. Let us give him some business.
- I want *refined* coconut oil, not the uncleaned crude lot like this.
- Wilson has *polished* manners. No wonder he makes friends in no time.

WAGES

Synonyms : Payment, hire, compensation, remuneration, salary, reward.

Antonyms : Rewardless, unproductivity, fruitless, waste.

Synonyms

- I have not yet made the *payment* for the last insurance premium.
- I have *hired* the new house for two years to start with.
- The government has decided to pay *compensation* for the acquired building.
- I have asked for a *remuneration* of $100 per day for my services.
- My monthly *salary* is $1500.
- A *reward* was announced for the arrest of the killers of the prime minister.

Antonyms

- ✦ This job can be called *rewardless* for the little money paid for too much laborious work involved.
- ✦ This firm has introduced a new machine to end its *unproductivity*.
- ✦ This effort will prove *fruitless* unless better management techniques are employed.

WANT

Synonyms : Indigence, penury, poverty, privation.
Antonyms : Affluence, plenty, prosperity, wealth.

Synonyms

- ✦ The magnitude of *indigence* is rising year by year in India despite so much economic development owing to inability of the administration to run the welfare activities efficiently.
- ✦ The common man in India makes a mockery of the socio-economic system by living in *penury*.
- ✦ The government has yet to eradicate *poverty* in India though a number of programmes have been undertaken.
- ✦ Sunil had to undergo a lot of *privation* due to loosing his job.

Antonyms

- ✦ *Affluence* of the elite is in sharp contrast with the poverty of the lower classes.
- ✦ Despite a situation of *plenty* of foodstuffs in the country, the poor cannot enjoy two wholesome meals.

✦ India can enjoy its *prosperity* only if a more equitable distribution of the country's national wealth could be established.

✦ The trader had amassed a great *wealth*.

WASTEFUL

Synonyms : Prodigal, spendthrift, lavish, improvident, imprudent, reckless, unthrifty.

Antonyms : Sparing, economical, prudent, frugal, miserly, provident.

Synonyms

✦ Those who possess black money tend to be *prodigal*.

✦ The ladies of black-marketeers easily develop *spendthrift* habits.

✦ They spend *lavish* sums on dresses and jewellery.

✦ They forget the existence of God and become *improvident*.

✦ They have so much money they become *imprudent* and *reckless* in expenses.

Antonyms

✦ Rahul gave it a *sparing* thought.

✦ Those who become prosperous by dint of hard work or organising capability have *economical* habits as they value the hard earned money.

✦ Such people are *prudent* in their budget and *thrifty* in expenditure on luxuries.

- ✦ Of *frugal* temperament, they spare some money for their poorer brethren.
- ✦ They may be *miserly* on avoidable luxuries, they do save some money regularly for the rainy day.

WAVERING

Synonyms : Oscillating, unsteady, fluctuating, undecided, undertermined, inconstant, vacillating, faltering, quivering.

Antonyms : Steady, unwavering, determined, firm, resolute, unhesitating, steadfast.

Synonyms

- ✦ In this computer the *oscillating* disk completes a full circle and returns to its original position at the end.
- ✦ Rafi's position in politics is *unsteady*. He is too poor to float his ideas through the media with speed.
- ✦ He keeps *fluctuating* from socialism to communism and again from communism back to socialism.
- ✦ He is *undecided* about the future course of action.
- ✦ At this juncture he was *undetermined* whether to back or oppose the proposal.

Antonyms

- ✦ He is *steady* like a rock in his ideology.
- ✦ There are newspapers which welcome this ideology and they give him *unwavering* publicity.

- ✦ They are *determined* to push him up to political power.
- ✦ This manager is *firm* in his determination to translate his ideas into reality.
- ✦ He pursues it *resolutely* through the media.

WEAK

Synonyms : Decrepit, feeble, frail, infirm.

Antonyms : Energetic, hardy, healthy, strong, stout, sturdy, tough.

Synonyms

- ✦ Rajiv's mother is now a *decrepit* old woman who has to lean on other members of the family even for going to the bath room.
- ✦ This transistor has a *feeble* sound, perhaps its battery has exhausted.
- ✦ My grandfather has become *frail* and *infirm* after crossing the age of 80.
- ✦ Being *infirm* has always cost him a lot.

Antonyms

- ✦ In his young days my grandfather was known to be a very *energetic* and *hardy* man.
- ✦ He was *healthy* and *strong* although his profession was teaching.

- My father is *stout* and *sturdy* but occasional illnesses have made him anaemic.
- He is not as *tough* as my grandfather was at his age.

WEAKEN

Synonyms : Attenuate, enfeeble, sap, impair, debilitate.

Antonyms : Strengthen, fortify, brace, harden.

Synonyms

- Daily prayer *attenuates* the errors and opinions of day-to-day life.
- The angry remarks of the teacher *enfeebled* the weaker students instead of encouraging them.
- The hot sun *sapped* our energy.
- The principal advised the teacher to deal with children sweetly and not *impair* their originality by harsh handling.
- The fever has *debilitated* Shishir.

Antonyms

- The aim of education is to *strengthen* the character of the students.
- The sweetness of the teacher should *fortify* the intellect of the learners instead of debilitating them.
- The extra-curricular activities are designed to *brace* the young children and create in them courage.
- Activities like hiking *harden* the power of resistance of children.

WEALTH

Synonyms : Abundance, substance, riches, profusion, money, property, plenty, prosperity, possessions, pelf.

Antonyms : Poverty, destitution, privations, distress, want, impecunity, insufficiency.

Synonyms

- ✦ Developed countries possess *abundance* of wealth and can afford old-age pensions to even non-government citizens.
- ✦ There is enough *substance* in your argument that abundant wealth is necessary to launch more and more welfare schemes.
- ✦ We should not feel unhappy over the *riches* of the rich but over the poverty of the poor.
- ✦ Flowers bloom in *profusion* at Mughal Gardens.
- ✦ *Money* dominates every walk of social life today.
- ✦ Harry does not own any *property* but he has *plenty* of mental ability and intelligence.

Antonyms

- ✦ *Poverty* has sapped the energy and opportunity for development of the teeming millions.
- ✦ The government has launched a few schemes for the care of the *destitute* but these are only a drop in the ocean.

- The poor people continue to suffer from *privations* of day-to-day life.
- The scene of poverty *distresses* all balanced people bestowed with patriotism and fellow-feeling.

WET

Synonyms : Drenched, damp, humid, rainy, showery, moist, soak.

Antonyms : Dry, arid, parched, dehydrate, parch.

Synonyms

- I was suddenly caught by the downpour which *drenched* my clothes.
- The monsoon makes the atmosphere *damp.*
- Towns along the sea coast generally have a *humid* climate all the year round.
- The *rainy* season generally precedes the autumn.
- Rain clouds bring *showery* weather in their trail.
- Water the plants regularly to keep the soil *moist.*

Antonyms

- In the plains, the weather is *dry* and cold during the winter.
- The deserts have on *arid* climate all the year round.
- Dry surface when burnt by sun rays gets *parched* and cracked.

- ✦ New technology is being developed to *dehydrate* the over moist regions so as to provide for smoother agricultural growth.

WICKED

Synonyms : Iniquitous, criminal, vile, villainous, corrupt, evil, immoral, bad, heinous, sinful.

Antonyms : Virtuous, incorrupt, moral, upright, chaste.

Synonyms

- ✦ Socio-economic system in India countinues to be *iniquitous* as even as there is no linking of maximum and minimum incomes and wealth by a just ratio.
- ✦ The *criminal* activities of the rich go unspotted owing to corruption at high levels.
- ✦ The *vile* deeds of the black-marketers are keeping the poor people half-starved.
- ✦ The bureaucrats are playing their *villainous* role in keeping the social order as unjust.
- ✦ He was suspended for his *corrupt* practices.
- ✦ Mephestophilis was also an *evil* character in the play.

Antonyms

- ✦ The *virtuous* deeds of the brave inspire the young.
- ✦ However *incorrupt* the political leadership, it has so far not succeeded in *chastening* the bureaucrats to any *moral* or *upright* ideals.

WIDE

Synonyms : Expansive, spacious, large, broad, extensive.

Antonyms : Narrow, cramped, confined, circumscribed, close, limited, small.

Synonyms

- The stream is *expansive* for the water carried. Hence it is not deep.
- This *spacious* bungalow belongs to the state government and is used as a guest house.
- A *large* crowd gathered at the Boat Club lawns to listen to the esteemed opposition leader.
- This article gives a *broad* outline of the agreement reached between India and the USSR.
- The agreement provides for *extensive* cooperation between the two countries in science, trade and economic fields.

Antonyms

- A *narrow* lane connects the two main roads in the city.
- The houses built in this colony are *cramped* and unventilated.
- The development here is *confined* to the provision of drinking water and electricity; there are no good roads, streets or sanitation.
- This lake is *circumscribed* by a wide pucca road on all sides.
- Her *closed* mind has hampered her progress in life.
- I have only a *limited* use for my truck. Shall I hire it to farmers?

✦ Mine is a very *small* house — a bed-cum-drawing room; a kitchen and a bathroom.

WILD

Synonyms : Ferocious, fierce, savage.

Antonyms : Gentle, timid, harmless, domesticated.

Synonyms

✦ The tiger is a *ferocious* animal.

✦ There was a *fierce* battle at Panipat between the Muslim invaders and the Rajputs in the beginning of the 11th century AD.

✦ The *savage* activities of the dacoits have frightened the villages of the region.

Antonyms

✦ Cow is the *gentlest* animal in the world.

✦ The *timid* behaviour of the policeman encouraged the robbers to slip away.

✦ The camel is a *harmless* animal. It has been tamed to be useful in deserts.

✦ Marc and Suzie have had an unhappy married life as Suzie has proved too *domesticated* for Ramesh's ideals of a married woman.

WISDOM

Synonyms : Knowledge, intelligence, discretion, sense, learning, erudition, discernment, sagacity, prudence.

Antonyms : Stupidity, ignorance, silly.

Synonyms

- My *knowledge* of biology is quite limited.
- The UPSC nowadays tests the *intelligence* of candidates to various competitive examinations by putting multiple-choice questions.
- Wise people use *discretion* in their vocabulary while speaking to men of culture.
- My *sense* of hearing has been weakened by the noisy atmosphere in my factory.
- I am *learning* to write commercial letters.
- The judge uses *erudition* and *discernment* while delivering his judgement.
- The official used his power with *sagacity and prudence*. Hence, he earned the reputation of an ideal civil servant.

Antonyms

- *Stupidity* is an innate trait of a person, it is not based on lack of knowledge of languages or academics.
- *Ignorance* of law is no excuse for committing a crime.
- Marx's ideas were initially regarded as *silly* by most intellectuals but in due course they were supported by an ever-increasing number of political thinkers of the times.

WORTHLESS

Synonyms : Cheap, base, degraded, valueless, despicable, paltry, contemptible.

Antonyms : Excellent, good, transcendent, estimable, costly, valuable, admirable.

Synonyms

- ✦ This is no *cheap* invention. We have to test its applicability in modern industry.
- ✦ This is a *base* coin. It won't circulate.
- ✦ Don't feel *degraded* simply because you have missed the first class by a few marks.
- ✦ This is a *valueless* invention. It can't be practised economically for many decades.
- ✦ Rohit is a *despicable* character.
- ✦ They were fighty for a *paltry* sum of money.

Antonyms

- ✦ Your suggestions are *excellent*, but we have to determine their practicability before giving them a trial.
- ✦ The wise man is one who can discriminate between *good* and bad.
- ✦ Buddha performed his *transcendental* meditation for a number of years until he achieved 'Nirvana'. 
- ✦ His achievements are too many to be *estimable*.
- ✦ This is too *costly* a saree for my pocket.
- ✦ The principal gave me a *valuâble* gift for topping the examination.

XANTHOUS

Synonyms : Light-skinned, golden-haired, yellow-haired, fair-haired, blonde, fair.

Antonyms : Brown, black, wheatish, thick skinned.

Synonyms

- The Europeans are a *light-skinned* race.
- She is a *golden-haired* blonde from Switzerland.
- Some of the females in Australia and New Zealand are *yellow haired*. This is again a physical phenomenon.

Antonyms

- Mary has matching *brown* eyes and hair.
- The original residents of Africa have a *black* skin.
- Most Indians have a *wheatish* complexion.
- Some people are *thick-skinned*. They do not react to the indignities perpetrated on them.

YAWN

Synonyms : Gape, open, wide, part, split.

Antonyms : Close, shut, abride, shorten peephole.

Synonyms

- I *gaped* at the way the monkey carried out his trickeries at the circus.
- I *opened* my mouth *wide* to yawn.
- I could hardly *part* with my beloved when the bell rang.
- I *split* the coins into two parts and gave an option to my wife to choose one.

Antonyms

- I *closed* the door after me.
- Never *shut* your eyes on duty.
- The journalist *abridged* the speech of the politicians.
- The Suez canal has *shortened* the distance between Europe and Africa by over 500 miles.
- I have affixed a *peephole* at my entrance.

YEOMAN

Synonyms : Commandeer, volunteer, petty officer, selfless.

Antonyms : Lord, governor, officer, landlord. boss.

Synonyms

- The great leader *commandeered* the freedom movement with zest and courage.
- He was able to obtain numberless *volunteers* to support his movement.
- A *petty officer,* he did great sacrifices for the cause.
- He rendered *selfless* service to the cause of the down trodden.

Antonyms

- Anil Chopra considers himself a big *lord.* Is he the *governor* of this large estate ?
- Who gave him the authority as the *officer* of these forests ?
- He behaves like a mean *landlord.* He despises his tenants.
- He thinks he is a big *boss.*

YIELD

Synonyms : Give way, submit, accede, surrender, renounce, abandon, forgo, crop, produce, waive.

Antonyms : Resist, withstand, refuse, keep back, withhold, reserve, restrain, oppose, assail, contend, confront.

Synonyms

- The bridge was defective and *gave way as* soon as the train passed over it.
- He has *submitted* the requisite documents to the college.
- His mother *acceded* to his demand for a holiday tour.
- The enemy could not resist our forces and had to *surrender*.
- He has decided to *renounce* the world and become a sanyasi.
- I have *abandoned* the idea of becoming a singer.
- Mary was willing to *forgo* the pleasure of the trip and let Julie go instead.
- The *crop* of barley was very good this year.
- The farmer has sold this year's *produce* in the market for a good profit.

Antonyms

- I could not *resist* the temptation of cold coffee and accepted his kind offer.

- I could not *withstand* the heat of the summer and proceeded to Shimla for relief.
- I could not *refuse* the kind offer of a lucrative job in my friend's firm.
- I am *keeping back* some savings for the rainy day.
- The judge *withheld* his decision to the next sitting.
- The government has built sufficient *reserves* of food stock for an emergency.

YOKE

Synonyms : Link, couple, string.

Antonyms : Release, divorce, abandon.

Synonyms

- India has broken the *link* of imperialism with Britain, though she continues its link with the Commonwealth as a full-fledged member.
- The two parts of this machine come into operation when *coupled*.
- There is no *string* attached to the foreign aid coming to India.

Antonyms

- The government *released* all political prisoners after attaining independence.
- The question of political system prevailing in a country cannot be *divorced* from foreign relations.
- I have *abandoned* the idea of marriage for the time being.

YOUNG

Synonyms : Youthful, boyish, new, fresh, childish, recent.

Antonyms : Mature, elderly, ripe, aged, late, full.

Synonyms

- ✦ He is old but has *youthful* habits which everyone can appreciate.
- ✦ He is above forty but still has a *boyish* look.
- ✦ He makes *new* friends in no time with his sociable outlook.
- ✦ We drank *fresh* lemon in the forenoon.
- ✦ Maria behaves in a *childish* manner sometimes and offends her boss.
- ✦ This is a *recent* publication on today's society.

Antonyms

- ✦ His *mature* ideas have benefitted the company in a big way.
- ✦ Though he is an *elderly* person, he is active and energetic like a young man.
- ✦ Separate the *ripe* mangoes from the raw ones.
- ✦ The *aged* lady could not see the car coming and met with an accident.
- ✦ Amir always arrives *late* in the meetings.

ZEAL

Synonyms : Zest, dedication, eagerness, earnestness, devotion, warmth, energy.

Antonyms : Coolness, weakness, laziness, carelessness, apathy.

Synonyms

- Hope is the *zest* of life.
- His *dedication* to work has earned him a very good reputation.
- His *eagerness* to make friends was exploited by the other boys.
- His *earnestness* to bring an improvement in the system is clear from the actions taken by him.
- The parents were gratified to see the *devotion* of the nurse to the care of their child.
- The mother welcomed her son with great *warmth*.

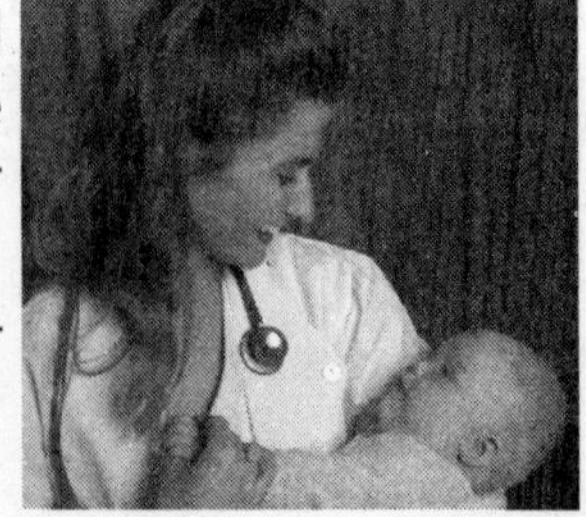

- The small boy was exhausted and had no *energy* left to carry the big box.

Antonyms

- His *coolness* often dwindles to the level of indifference.
- His calm face has often been exploited as his *weakness*.
- His *laziness* will cost him his job some day.
- His *carelessness* is now a matter of habit. But his other virtues keep him safe in his job.
- He has an *apathy* for serious reading.

NOTES

NOTES

NOTES

NOTES

NOTES